D-DAY

THOSE WHO WERE THERE

THE D-DAY ASSAULT

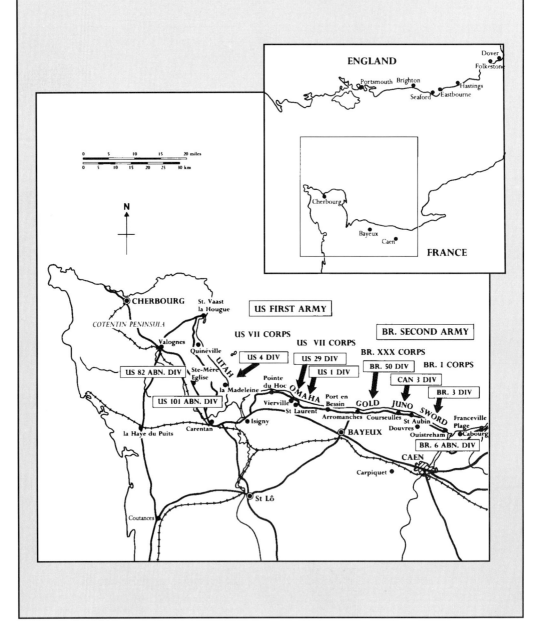

Juliet Gardiner

D-DAY

THOSE WHO WERE THERE

BCA

LONDON   NEW YORK   SYDNEY   TORONTO

This edition published 1994 by BCA by arrangement with
Collins & Brown Limited

CN 8636

Conceived with the help of Peter Williams of Studio Z Limited and based
on a Studio Z production for Meridian Broadcasting and Westcountry
Television

Managing Editor : Colin Ziegler
Editor : Gabrielle Townsend

Art Director : Roger Bristow
Designer : Claire Graham

Reproduction by Typongraph, Italy
Printed in Great Britain by The Bath Press

CONTENTS

FOREWORD

D-DAY, 6 JUNE 1944, is one of those landmarks in history rather like the day on which President John F. Kennedy was assassinated. If you were alive at the time, you remember precisely where you were. Nor do you have to have the significance of that day spelled out to you. Quite simply, it was the day on which the Nazi occupation of the continent of Europe, sealed four years earlier at Dunkirk, began to be rolled back; the day when we all started to believe that the Germans could be defeated and that, at long last, the world could return to an approximation of normality.

But there are generations, now, who have no first-hand sharing of that experience, no recollection of that explosion of exultation and relief. For them the memories are second-hand or celluloid, sanitized by Hollywood and romanticized by fiction. Yet the facts are extraordinary enough.

Hundreds of thousands of troops and a mountain of equipment and stores crossed the English Channel and were moved over the beaches in appalling weather, and, to make it all possible, an artificial harbour was built in England and towed to France.

The television series on which this book is based was three years in the making. Juliet Gardiner has drawn upon the hundreds of conversations and interviews carried out by the Studio Z team who made the programmes, and has skilfully added her own context and narrative.

For myself, as producer of the series, the chance to share the experiences of these men and women who spearheaded OVERLORD, the greatest invasion in history, was an enormous privilege. Not so much in the recollections of the moment - though that was both graphic and harrowing - but more because so many chose to share the impact that day had had upon their lives in the years since 1944. Quite simply, for so many of them, life was never quite the same again.

For some, it was a physical wound; for most it was psychological. A padre said: 'I will never forget what happened that day. Never. It has gone too deep...' And he spoke of the men who had died in his arms. A Gordon Highlander saw his best friend blown to pieces and spoke of the fanaticism of the German troops: 'They were fearsome. They were fanatical. I had the feeling that they really wanted to kill you; that they wanted, above all, to be good soldiers; that they were passionately anxious to win the war. Me? I was passionately anxious to survive the war. I'd have negotiated a pact with the devil to make sure I got home!'

The commander of a flamethrower tank knew all about death as he had seen so many of his friends die. 'Dying was the most common, but not the only, fear we had. No-one wanted to be crippled, for instance. But the fear of dying was with you constantly - in the morning, in the night, during the day when you were preparing for the attack.'

But war is about both dying and killing. It was on a verandah of a bungalow on the New Jersey coast that a US Ranger admitted: 'I know the Commandment says: "Thou shalt not kill", and that's the only thing I'm having trouble with. I *know* I'm going to have to answer for the lives I've taken.' He paused, and then went on: 'In fact, there have been times when I haven't pulled the trigger; sparing lives, I guess, as a way of atoning for the lives that I've ended.'

The overriding impression that emerges from becoming immersed in these varied lives is the comradeship that developed in the stress of the moment. Men and women 'grew up'. They 'learned a lot' from those around them. They 'looked continually but vainly' in the years that followed 'to find the kind of closeness we had there in Normandy. The fact is that it was never to be achieved again.'

The reunions we attended were emotional and salutary. A lieutenant in the Armoured Division said: 'On the quite rare occasions that I find myself brought together with the people beside whom I was so close, I look at them, and they look at me, and we embrace one another, and it's great to see one another again - but...I'm still looking at them as they were fifty years ago, and they're looking at me as I was fifty years ago. And the truth is that we are different people...'

In the towns of the south of England, we talked to the civilians who experienced the friendly 'occupation' by the Allied forces as they prepared for D-Day, and in the villages of mainland Europe we spoke to the men and women, French and German, who had waited for the invasion to fall upon them. As we tried to understand and record the world-shaping events of that summer fifty years ago, one comment applied to all to whom we spoke. It was a Canadian who said it, a Canadian who learned in the week before D-Day that he had lost his brother, killed in the Italian campaign. 'You have to walk in a man's footsteps to begin to understand what a soldier goes through in the front line...'

This is a book that tries to help us understand that. A book about people who risked their lives without a thought for the morrow - which, for so many, never came.

Peter Williams

INTRODUCTION

'THE HISTORY OF WAR does not show any such undertaking so broad in concept, so grandiose in scale, so masterly in execution' telegraphed Josef Stalin to Winston Churchill of D-Day.

There were many D-Days during the Second World War as in any war, days targeted for action. Today we remember only one by that name: 6 June 1944, when British, American, Canadian and Free French troops crossed the English Channel by air and sea, invaded the fortified beaches of Normandy and gained a foothold in Occupied Europe from which they would advance in bitter combat towards Germany and victory.

Fifty years later the significance of D-Day is as important to us as it was in 1944. It is a story both in its scope and in its detail that has caught the imagination for half a century. Many books have been written about D-Day: memoirs of men who fought on the beaches, explanations and recollections of the planners and commanders of the massive 'Operation OVERLORD', official histories, regimental records and narratives of drama and incident like the most famous book - and film - of D-Day, Cornelius Ryan's *The Longest Day*.

The genesis of D-Day lay in the outbreak of war in September 1939. Hitler would have to be defeated on the continent of Europe: the Allied retreat from Dunkirk after the fall of France in the summer of 1940 strengthened this resolve whilst making its implementation far in the distance.

D-Day has been labelled the start of a 'crusade in Europe', a 'prelude to victory' yet it is in no way to diminish its importance to locate it, as we do today, as part too of the total war fought across the globe between 1939 and 1945, a war that swept civilian populations into the battle.

The four years of planning, preparation and waiting for D-Day were part of the lives of all the people of the Allied nations in various and different ways. *D-Day: Those Who Were There* tells the story of the people's D-Day: soldiers and civilians, men who trained and fought, and the men and women who were involved in the planning and the success of D-Day - and in its tragedies.

I am particularly grateful to Peter Williams of Studio Z who made available to me the transcripts of the interviews he conducted for the Meridian television series he directed, and gave me help and advice in addition. I am greatly indebted to those interviewees who have allowed me to quote them at length, and to all the other men and women who replied to my various requests for their recollections of D-Day.

I would like to express my thanks to the staff of the Imperial War Museum, particularly Terry Charman, Roderick Suddaby and Christopher Dowling. I am most grateful to readers of the *Sunday Express* for permission to quote from their letters about their memories of D-Day for a competition in that newspaper in 1974; to the Mass-Observation archive at the University of Sussex for permission to quote from their archives: to Richard Collier for his great generosity: to Michael Conway of the 1940 Association and to Henry Horwitz.

CHAPTER ONE

'WE WILL GO BACK'

'THEY WERE SHOUTING OUT for volunteers. I went and signed on at the local customs offices in Whitstable - and so did a good many others. They sent us off to Lowestoft and Lowestoft sent us back to Newhaven but by the time we got back here it was too late to do anything about it, the boys were disappearing off the quays,' remembers William Sponder who had joined the Royal Naval Volunteer Reserve at the outbreak of the Second World War when he was nineteen.

All along the south coast of England from 27 May to 4 June 1940 men with boats - fishing boats, pleasure boats, ferries, anything seaworthy - were volunteering too, eager to join the flotilla of small boats making for the French coast at Dunkirk to snatch the remnants of the British Expeditionary Force from the conquering German tanks advancing across France.

A London woman recalls her intention to take her eighty-year-old mother and eight-year-old son for a treat - a trip by river boat from Westminster to Greenwich. But when they arrived at Westminster, she was told reprovingly by the pier-master that 'There'll be no boats on the river this month. They're all needed on the beaches of France.'

The reassuring Yorkshire voice of J. B. Priestley talked about the boats, too, in one of his regular *Postscripts* on the radio on the evening of 5 June 1940. 'We've known and laughed at them all our lives,' he said of the 'bath-tub flotilla' that had managed to ferry a total of 338,226 exhausted and defeated troops - of whom 225,000 were British - home across the Channel. The *Gracie Fields*, one of the Isle of Wight's ferries, had been lost along with hundreds of other small craft, but Priestley was resolute: Dunkirk should be seen not as a defeat but as prelude to victory: '...Our great-grandchildren, when they learn how we began this war by snatching glory out of defeat, and then swept on to victory, may also learn how the little holiday steamers made an excursion to hell and came back glorious.'

The headline in the *Daily Mirror* read 'Bloody Marvellous', but the feeling of relief was short-lived. Ruth Buchanan, who lived at Rottingdean near Brighton, recalls the men coming back after Dunkirk: 'They seemed defeated. They talked defeated. That's how it seemed to me.'

'They were in a pitiful state,' thought a Dorset woman as she watched trainloads of Dunkirk veterans arriving to recuperate; 'they tumbled out of the train so weary and tired that they hardly knew what they were doing. Their uniforms were torn and dirty...their boots cracked and worn out. A few were in stockinged feet.'

Bill Holden was a boat builder in Newhaven doing repair work when the troops started to arrive back from Dunkirk:

> There was a stream of hospital ships came to Newhaven. First they brought off the wounded and after that they'd wheel off the dead…and then we'd see a pile of boots and clothes all thrown on the quayside. What they'd taken off the wounded I suppose, and we'd go aboard the boats and do what repairs we could. Most of the boats had lost their gangplanks at Dunkirk and their timber supplies were very depleted so we had to load a truck up and push it down to the quay and put the planks of timber on to the hospital ships, so that when they got over to Dunkirk again, they could put them on the quayside and get more of the wounded aboard. But they never brought any back because once they got their load of men, they just pulled away as fast as they could, and the wood fell into the water.

Bill Holden's brother was the skipper of a local tug that had gone to Dunkirk to bring some soldiers back and when he was there he heard

> a helluva bang, and he went searching and came across a destroyer that had been in collision with another ship, and he managed to get hold of her with his tug and he towed her stern first back across the Channel. He was fifty hours at the wheel getting back. And when he did get back he wasn't in a very good shape so I took him home, and his wife wasn't in, so I put him to bed, and when I peeled his socks off his feet were completely covered in blisters where he'd been standing for so long. But he was only home for a couple of days and then he was off out there again to bring more men back.

In the House of Commons the Prime Minister, Winston Churchill, bluntly told the nation that Dunkirk was a 'colossal military disaster'. Mass-Observation, the organization of largely volunteer observers that monitored British public opinion on various aspects of the war and compiled reports about morale, reported what people were saying in June 1940. 'There is no doubt that we shall be exterminated. We fight alone now, they've all deserted us…but they haven't won yet'; 'If France and England can't do it together, I don't see what we can do alone…'; 'It looks as if all we can do is give up. It's no use throwing away lives when there's no hope…'

Mollie Panter-Downes, a writer who was filing despatches from London to *The New Yorker* noted that 'London was as quiet as a village' when news of the Fall of France was announced:

> For once the cheerful Cockney comeback of the average Londoner simply wasn't there…the public seemed to react to the staggering news like people in a dream, who go through the most fantastic actions without a sound. There was little discussion of events, because they were too bad for that.

'We are at bay in our tight little island,' Priestley broadcast and John of Gaunt's image of Britain as a moated island was a powerful one in the days after Dunkirk. The Channel seemed Britain's best defence. 'A very good anti-tank obstacle,' the defeated French Commander-in-Chief General Weygand called it ruefully, after he had watched the

The beaches of France 1940: lines of British and American
troops await evacuation from Dunkirk.

German panzers outflank France's defensive Maginot Line and crash though the 'impossible, impenetrable' Ardennes.

But in June 1940 the Channel seemed to many to be no more than that: an obstacle that the mighty German war machine would soon overcome, not a barrier that guaranteed Britain's safety. Harold Nicolson, who as Parliamentary Secretary to the Ministry of Information was charged with boosting British morale, had privately made his own assessment of the situation, and his own way of dealing with it: 'I know that I shall kill myself and Vita will kill herself if the worst comes,' he wrote in his diary on 15 June 1940.

> Thus comes a point where Hitler will cease to trouble either of us...my reason tells me that that it will now be almost impossible to beat the Germans, and that the probability is that France will surrender and that we shall be bombed and invaded. I am quite lucidly aware that in three weeks from now Sissinghurst may be a waste and Vita and I both dead. Yet these probabilities do not fill me with despair. I seem to be impervious both to pleasure and pain. For the moment we are anaesthetised.

The threat of invasion was grave. Hitler recognized that moving a large military force across the Channel would be a formidable task: initially he expected Britain to recognize the hopelessness of her position after the Fall of France and capitulate. But Churchill made it clear that despite 'the colossal military disaster', Britain would 'never surrender':

> We shall go on to the end...we shall fight on the seas and oceans, we shall fight with growing confidence and growing strength in the air, we shall defend our

island whatever the cost may be. We shall fight on the beaches, we shall fight on the landing grounds, we shall fight in the fields and in the streets, we shall fight in the hills, we shall never surrender...

'That was worth a thousand guns,' thought the Labour MP, Josiah Wedgwood, but even this stirring speech envisaged the threat of invasion, sketching a scenario of hand-to-hand fighting in Britain. On 16 July Hitler had decreed in Directive No. 16: 'Since England, in spite of her hopeless military position, shows no sign of coming to terms, I have decided to prepare a landing operation against England and, if necessary, carry it out.' The 'average Englishman' might, according to Mollie Panter-Downes, be 'singularly unimpressed by the fact that there is now nothing between him and the undivided attention of a war machine such as the world has never seen before' but the military authorities were fully aware both of the danger of invasion and of the inadequacy of the resources to combat that threat. 'We wouldn't have stood much of a chance against a well-organized invasion,' reflected Sir Brian Horrocks whose brigade had only 3,000 men to defend a ten-mile stretch of the Sussex coast. William Sponder, who had been denied the chance to participate in the Dunkirk evacuation, was immediately put to work manning one of the pleasure boats used by the Naval Auxiliary patrol to scour the Channel for signs of an impending invasion.

> We were looking for E-boats or for anything at all. We had no guns, no armaments, no nothing. The first patrol that went out had just three paraffin lamps to signal with, one painted red, one painted white and one painted blue, just ordinary paraffin lamps, that's all we had. Our first weapons after that, believe it or not, were cutlasses, but then they gave us a Very pistol, the sort that fires flares. We were told that if we challenged a boat using our paraffin lamps holding them up one over the other and the other boat didn't answer in the right order, we were to get as close in as possible and fire the Very pistol over the boat so that the shore batteries could see what to fire at. Though I don't know what that would have done because there were three hundred soldiers stationed there on the shore and they had just six rifles between the whole three hundred of them. Of course we wondered what would happen to us if they started firing...

As a carpenter, Bill Holden was involved in converting boats for military purposes.

> These boats that were patrolling the Channel to see that we weren't going to be invaded had no wireless on, so we had to fix sky rockets on them. We'd screw racks alongside the wheelhouse and drop a rocket on to a five- or six-foot stick - I presume that this was our communication with the shore in case anything happened. And we also had to fix guns to the decks; every time a fresh gun came along, there were more alterations, the guns got heavier and stronger all the time, and after a while we fitted them with mines, too. We had to devise a way of fitting these on to the patrol boats. We made wooden boxes to take three mines. The boxes were then fitted on to the ships at an angle with a little slipway we made out of wood too, and we greased the slipway and pushed it in the hole we'd made in the box, and then we set the mine in there with three wedges round them and a

Welcome home flags strung over the runner-bean supports of an English garden salute the trains carrying the British Expeditionary Force soldiers on their return from Dunkirk in June 1940.

pin to hold them in. There was a coil of grass rope, so if the Germans came near the shore, these mines would be dropped into the sea, and the grass rope would float, and if Jerry saw it, he'd pick it up and pull it into the bow of his boat, and it'd pull the mines round and hit the side, but I don't think that anyone ever dared to try them out.

The mines used to be sent to Newhaven in boxes - they weren't very big mines - and then they were stored in an air raid shelter which was below where the Air and Sea Rescue people were billeted and they didn't think much of the idea of having mines stored underneath where they were living. So we took them out and hung them along the breakwaters at Newhaven. Of course along came a storm and washed them all over the side, and they drifted all up the coast, as far as Seaford, under the Seven Sisters. So all the old sailors were called out and some of the crews of the patrol boats, and they were sent off all along the coast looking for these mines. They weren't primed of course, they wouldn't have gone off. I was told by one of the men in a patrol boat that they had to go as far as Eastbourne picking them up, and they stored them on the pier there, and while they were on the pier they decided to requisition the grand piano that was there, so they

"*I was saying just before you came in, Mr. Titmouse, that in the event of an invasion the defence of these islands would in the main devolve on us. Find yourself a pew and make yourself comfortable.*"

screwed off its legs and bought it back to Newhaven on a lorry and set it up on HMS Forward which was a club for sailors at the time. It was the spoils of war.

Bill Holden remembers the boats that went out to patrol from Newhaven:

The first boats had real problems getting alongside the quay. We threw ropes to them, but they just couldn't manage to bring the boats in. But it wasn't long before they got really good at handling the boat…there were farmers, and butchers and bakers and all sorts, but there were some good lads there and they soon got expert in those boats.

He was also a lifeboatman during the war, and he remembers that when the invasion scare was at its height, they were all issued with notices to the effect that if the invasion came they were either to use the lifeboats to get away in, or they were to destroy them. 'I'd have set light to it, I expect.' The lifeboat crew were kitted out with gas masks, a tin helmet, a pair of rubber boots and given a piece of gas piping with a bayonet stuck in the end to deal with the enemy if he came. But even this strained supplies and after a fortnight the tin helmet and rubber boots were taken away to be deployed elsewhere and the defenders were left with just their heavy-duty gas masks.

There was a great shortage of fighting matériel in 1940. The Dunkirk evacuation, Operation DYNAMO, had miraculously saved thousands of men but their equipment had been abandoned on the beaches of France. When Churchill had delivered his rousing speech about fighting the invasion to the last man, he was supposed to have muttered an aside: 'and beat the buggers about the head with bottles: that's all we've got.'

On 23 June, hours after France had signed the document of surrender to Germany, a lightning raid on Boulogne was mounted in defiance by men who would become the core of the Commando force. They had managed to kill two German soldiers, armed only with twenty tommy guns - all the British Army could spare from its total reserve of forty. George Orwell noted that his Local Defence Volunteers' platoon had one rifle for six men and no weapons other than incendiary bombs.

It was some time before William Sponder and his fellow members of the Naval Auxiliary Patrol prowling the shore line were equipped with anything that could inflict any damage *had* they encountered the enemy. Finally each man was issued with an old-style Lee Enfield long-barrelled rifle - but only five rounds of ammunition per boat went with the rifles. Eventually these weapons of war were replaced by Hodgkiss machine guns - First World War vintage.

The huge influx of men into the forces - by 1 July 1940 the services had taken more than half the British males aged between twenty and twenty-five and more than one-fifth of the entire male population between sixteen and forty - exacerbated the problems of training and supply.

Training sometimes had to be done with broom handles and table legs and when rifles were issued they were objects of fascination to men who had never seen such a thing before but had been drilled to the knowledge that the defence of their country might any day now depend on their expertise in handling these untried weapons. Britain might be 'in the biggest mess since the Battle of Hastings', as an MP opined, but that had been 900 years ago, and A. P. Herbert scornfully addressed Hitler:

> Napoleon tried. The Dutch were on their way,
> A Norman did it and a Dane or two,
> Some sailor-king may follow one fine day
> But not, I think, a lowland rat like you.

The Queen was being 'instructed every morning how to fire a revolver' and was determined not to 'go down like the others' (her Continental cousins and counterparts who had fled into exile); the ringing of church bells was forbidden except to warn of approaching invaders; Lord Beaverbrook's *Daily Express* sponsored a campaign for 'a hand-grenade dump by every village pump', and postmen slipped official pamphlets in with the mail, 'telling householders what to do if Britain is invaded.'

The official advice was to stay at home unless told by the proper authorities to leave, 'because, if you run away, you will be machine-gunned from the air, as were civilians in Holland and Belgium' - and it might have added, clog the roads as the fleeing French did, fatally hampering army movement.

People were reassured that should German parachutists

> come down near your home, they will not be feeling at all brave. They will not know where they are, they will have no food. Do not give any German anything. Do not tell him anything. Hide your food and your bicycles. Hide your maps. See that the enemy gets no petrol...If you keep your head you can tell whether a military officer is British or only pretending to be.

Hitler's prediction of a German cross-Channel invasion rested on a crucial assumption: it would be successful, he recognized, 'provided that air superiority can be attained and certain other necessary conditions fulfilled.' It was this superiority in the air that Churchill was determined to deny to the German Luftwaffe during the desperate summer of 1940. Goering, Commander of the German Air Force, targeted British shipping - already depleted as a result of Dunkirk and raids on Narvik in Norway - to cut supply lines and turn the country's privileged island status into one of dangerous isolation. On 1 August 1940 Hitler issued another directive ordering the Luftwaffe to 'overpower the English Air Force with all its forces in the shortest possible time' by wiping out aircraft production factories and the RAF in the air and on the ground. The aim was to enable the invasion of Britain, code-named Operation SEA LION, to be launched on 15 September 1940.

On 7 September 1940 Britain was put on immediate alert: airfields across the Channel were observed to be packed with massed bomber and fighter planes; barges and small boats were assembling in French and Belgian ports and that afternoon wave after wave of German bombers swept across south-eastern England in the heaviest raid yet on the London docks. At 8 o'clock that evening the Home Front HQ issued the codeword 'CROMWELL' - invasion imminent - and for twelve days the Army and the Home Guard stood ready at action stations along the beaches of England, Wales and as far north as the Hebrides. There were rumoured to be plans to pour hundreds of thousands of gallons of precious oil stored all along the south coast on the sea and set it alight as the German assault approached.

Britain expected Hitler to fulfil the threat he had made in a rousing speech given at the Berlin Palace of Sport on 4 September when he had whipped a rally of nurses and social workers to a frenzy with his peroration warning the British 'He is coming! He is coming!'

But the invasion never happened. On 17 September 1940 Hitler postponed Operation SEA LION indefinitely. The invasion force of 168 transports, 1,910 barges, 419 tugs and 1,600 motor boats was dispersed. The German Army moved inland again. At a terrible cost of men and machines, the Battle of Britain had denied the Luftwaffe mastery of the skies and the Blitz had failed to bring the British people to their knees.

The German war effort swung to a campaign of attrition against British war production and civilian morale. Relief at an invasion averted was soon to be tempered by the relentless hardship at home caused by rationing and the need for increased productivity to turn the country into an arsenal that could counter the seemingly unstoppable British losses. British forces were locked in battle in the Middle East against the Italian armies (Mussolini had declared war on Britain and France in June 1940) and Rommel's Afrika Korps in February 1941; Greece fell to the Axis powers in May 1941; the British were ignominiously thrown out of Crete with heavy losses exacerbated by disastrous naval reverses; the British Empire was threatened by Japanese aggression in the Far East, with Hong Kong and Singapore under immediate threat. On 8 December 1941 Churchill wrote to the US President, Franklin Roosevelt, 'The form which this war has taken and seems likely to hold does not enable us to match the immense armies of Germany in any theatre where their man-power can be brought to bear. We can, however, by the use of sea-power and air-power meet the German armies in regions where only comparatively small forces can be brought to action.'

*This moated isle. Members of the Local Defence Volunteers (soon to be renamed
the Home Guard) mobilized to protect Britain from invasion after the fall of
France in June 1940, mount guard scanning the Channel from behind
coils of defensive barbed wire.*

Although Mass-Observation was able to report that never less than a majority of seventy-five per cent of the British people believed in ultimate victory it seemed in the bleak months of 1940-41 that this was a triumph of hope over reason.

At 4 a.m. on on 22 June 1941 Hitler attacked Russia, his erstwhile partner in the Nazi-Soviet pact, on a 500-mile front. Operation BARBAROSSA changed the terms of the war. Russian losses were to be devastating and Churchill, whose anti-Bolshevism had sometimes seemed to match his opposition to Fascism, responded unequivocally to the changed situation. Britain must find common cause with the Soviet Union. 'If Hitler invaded hell, I would at least make some favourable reference to the devil in the House of Commons,' he said and went on to broadcast to the nation, urging 'We have but one aim and one irrevocable purpose. We are resolved to destroy Hitler and every vestige of the Nazi regime.' He reminded his BBC audience how vital this was since Hitler 'wishes to destroy the Russian power because he hopes that if he succeeds in this he will be able to bring back the main strength of his army and air force from the east and hurl it upon this island, which he knows he must conquer or suffer the penalty for his crimes. His invasion of Russia is no more than a prelude to an invasion of the British Isles.'

The response to his message that Churchill received eighteen days later made it clear how Stalin saw the new Allied partnership working:

> It seems to me...that the military situation of the Soviet Union as well as of Great Britain would be considerably improved if there could be established a front against Hitler in the west - northern France - and in the north - the Arctic. A front in northern France could not only divert Hitler's forces from the east but at the same time would make it impossible for Hitler to invade Great Britain. The

establishment of the front just mentioned would be popular with the British Army as well as with the whole population of southern England.

Churchill had no doubt about the necessity for a 'Second Front': he was resolute that the British would one day storm Hitler's 'Fortress Europe' - somewhere. In the dark days after Dunkirk he had pledged, 'Britain will fight on...If necessary for years...If necessary alone...' and he had added 'We shall go back...' In the weeks after the fall of France when the invasion threat was at its height Churchill had been able to draw some comfort from the recognition that the 'invasion of England in the summer and autumn of 1940 required from Germany local naval superiority and immense special fleets and landing craft.' Now, a year later, the terms of success for a British invasion were the same. The Battle of Britain in the air, the land and sea warfare in the Mediterranean, the naval losses in the Far East, the battles in the Western Desert and the deadly success of the U-boats in sinking Atlantic supplies, had all served to reinforce the conviction of the Prime Minister and his military Chiefs of Staff that the German war machine was immensely powerful and that British resources were woefully inadequate and overstretched. Churchill, mindful, too, of the disaster at Gallipoli in which he had been so implicated during the First World War, replied to Stalin on 20 July 1941:

> The Chiefs of Staff do not see any way of doing anything on a scale likely to be of the slightest use to you...The Germans have forty divisions in France alone and the whole coast...bristles with cannons, wire, pill boxes and beach mines...To attempt a landing in force would be to encounter a bloody repulse, and petty raids would only lead to fiascos doing far more harm than good to both of us...

Later he was to write:

> The Russians never understood in the smallest degree the nature of the amphibi-ous operation necessary to disembark and maintain a great invasion army upon a well-defended, hostile coast. Even the Americans were at this time largely unaware of the difficulties. Not only sea but air superiority was indispensable. Moreover, there was a third vital factor. A vast armada of specially constructed landing craft, above all tank-landing craft in numerous varieties, was the founda-tion of any successful heavily opposed landing.

This armada was almost non-existent in the autumn of 1941. For Churchill there could be no possible thought of a cross-Channel invasion until mighty resources of men and matériel were not just leased from United States but fully integrated into the Allied war effort.

In this the sober assessment of the War Cabinet was at one with the department most intimately involved in the planning of amphibious warfare, the Inter-Services Training Department, which in examining 'the scope of future operations which will be necessary to secure the ultimate defeat of Germany' was entirely basing its planning on 'the assump-tion that the US is a belligerent'.

In the early morning of Sunday 7 December 1941 Japanese aircraft attacked the huge US base at Pearl Harbor in the Pacific. Winston Churchill was dining with the American Ambassador at the Prime Minister's official country house, Chequers, when the news of Pearl Harbor came through. He wrote later:

No American will think it wrong of me if I proclaim that to have the United States at our side was the greatest joy. I could not foretell the course of events. I do not pretend to have measured accurately the martial might of Japan but now at this very moment I knew the United States was in the war, up to the neck and in to the death...So we had won...Britain would live...We should not be wiped out. Our history would not come to an end.

The Prime Minister resolved to go to America at once. Writing to the King, George VI, Churchill explained, 'I have formed the conviction that it is my duty to visit Washington without delay. The whole Anglo-American defence and attack plan has to be concerted in the light of reality. We have to be careful that our share of munitions and other aid does not suffer more than is, I feel, inevitable...' Churchill was setting off across the Atlantic to ensure that the US would stick to its agreed 'Europe first' strategy, a commitment he feared could be jeopardized by the Japanese attack. Influential strategists in Washington contended that the best interest of the US lay in defeating the Japanese who were a direct threat to American interests, rather than embroiling their nation for the second time in little more than twenty years in the conflict in Europe. It was a view certainly held by Admiral Ernest J. King, Chief of Staff of the US Navy, who fumed, 'I fought under the Goddamn British in the First World War, and if I can help it no ship of mine will fight under them again.'

The British strategy, articulated at the Washington meeting in December 1941, was unequivocal:

> The war cannot be ended by driving Japan back to her own bounds and defeating her overseas forces. The war can only be ended through the defeat in Europe of the German armies, or through the internal convulsions in Germany produced by the unfavourable course of the war.

The Washington Conference finally endorsed this analysis and agreed that 'the two powers would maintain only such positions in the Eastern Theatre as will safeguard vital interests and deny to Japan access to raw materials vital to her continuous war effort while we are concentrating on the defeat of Germany.'

Churchill was jubilant. The first US troops arrived in Northern Ireland on 26 January 1942, as part of Operation BOLERO, the code name given to the build-up of American troops in the UK which, like the dance which gave the operation its name, would build up to a huge climax - in this instance a force of over one and a half million GIs stationed 'over here' to launch a cross-Channel attack on Hitler's Europe.

The plan was that a noose should be drawn tight around Germany by Allied domination of the Mediterranean and the liberation of North Africa, while the objective of making preparations 'for the liberation of the captive countries of western and southern Europe by the landing at suitable points successively or simultaneously of British and American armies strong enough to enable the conquered populations to revolt' was pencilled in tentatively for 1943.

Initial jubilation at the US entry into the war was muted by the disastrous winter of 1941-2: in the Far East the important British possessions of Hong Kong and Singapore fell to the Japanese; Malta was under siege; Rommel's forces were advancing on Egypt and

'The object is to confuse the enemy'. Under the threat of invasion, signposts removed from crossroads in southern England are stacked away 'for the duration'.

British and US shipping and supplies were threatened by the success of the German U-boats which scuppered 1,500,000 tons in the first three months of the year. And on the 'First Front' Hitler's Operation BARBAROSSA seemed unstoppable with German claims that their former Russian partners had lost 2,500,000 men, 1,400 aircraft and 180,000 tanks since June 1941.

The Russian plight immediately captured the British imagination. The British Communist party, long opposed to the 'capitalist war of aggression', swung wholeheartedly behind the war effort: in June 1941 Beaverbrook lobbied for support for Russia both within the War Cabinet and also in the pages of his *Daily Express*, soon joined by *The Times*, to claim that 'We cannot afford to neglect anything that which may help Russia.' Industrial production soared when the product was destined for the Eastern front and Winston Churchill found it politic to extend the hand of friendship to the 'Trade Unions of Russia'. Mrs Churchill launched an appeal for aid to Russia which eventually raised £8 million; even the Athenaeum Club caught the mood and elected the Russian Ambassador, Maisky, a member. But the BBC declined to play the 'Internationale' along with the anthems of other Allied nations (albeit defeated) before the nine o'clock news on Sundays - the excuse being that by August 1941, there were just too many Allies.

The call for a 'Second Front now' became more insistent during the spring; the tentative chalked appeals replaced by painted slogans: there seemed a very real danger that the Red Army would be defeated if pressure wasn't taken off. In the US Roosevelt was facing

Congressional elections that autumn, heckled by resentful voices claiming that US troops were in Britain waiting whilst all the British government seemed concerned to do was to prop up her Empire rather than taking on the enemy across the Channel. In March the US President wrote to Churchill that 'he was becoming more and more interested in the establishment of a new front this summer on the European continent.' On 8 April 1942 Harry Hopkins, the President's right-hand man, and General Marshall arrived in London with firm American proposals for a Second Front drawn up by General Eisenhower. Plans should be made for an invasion of France by forty-eight divisons of which eighteen would be British: the invasion would be supported by 5,800 combat aircraft of which Britain would supply a little less than half: 7,000 landing craft would be needed for the assault which would take place on the Normandy coast between Boulogne and Le Havre. 100,000 men a week would be needed to reinforce the initial invasion and fight across France. 'Speed is the essence of the problem,' the planners maintained. And it was urgent - everything must be ready by 1 April 1943, if not sooner, for, as Marshall added, 'A plan must be prepared and kept up to date for immediate action by such forces as may be available from time to time. This may have to be put into effect as an emergency measure, (a) to take advantage of a sudden German disintegration or (b) as a sacrifice to avert an imminent collapse of Russian resistance.'

In May that year a rally in Trafalgar Square calling for the opening of a Second Front attracted an estimated crowd of 50,000 people. Molotov, the Soviet Foreign Minister, was in London in May on his way to see Roosevelt and announced that his country was desperate: Stalin was insisting on the immediate opening of a Second Front to divert at least forty Wehrmacht divisions from their relentless pounding on the Eastern Front. On his way back to Moscow Molotov again visited London and he and Anthony Eden, the Foreign Secretary, signed a 'Twenty-Year Pact' between Britian and Russia; Eden intimated that full agreement had been reached 'with regard to the urgent tasks of creating a second front in Europe in 1942'.

The pressure seemed to be irresistible. Mollie Panter-Downes noted the popular mood in her dispatch on 19 July 1942:

> Londoners who have recently been dropping in at the Soviet Exhibition in Piccadilly to see the handsome saddle brought for Marshal Timoshenko with British subscriptions were hoping last week that the sympathy of this country with the Marshal's present struggle would soon be expressed in a more acceptable form of leatherwork - the planting of British and American boots on Russian soil...whatever Whitehall thinks and knows about the possibility of an Allied landing in force during this critical summer, there's no mistaking how the bulk of the population feels. Maybe this is one of the times when the powerful uninformed instinct of a nation is as valid as the informed caution of its military leaders. What instinct seems to be telling the Englishmen right now, to judge by what they are saying over the nice cup of tea in the canteen and half of bitter in the pub, is that next year would certainly be better but it would almost certainly be too late. For at the bottom of English teacups...even people with no clairvoyant gift for reading the leaves but with just ordinary ability to read a map could make out the shape of ominous things to come if the German thrust to the Volga should succeed in

eliminating Russia as a striking force. Though the difficulties of getting a foothold across the water are apparent even to civilians who would have trouble in getting a platoon across the road, it may also be plain that the undertaking looks healthier now, in many ways, however it may appear in a sober staff report, than it would after the release of the crack panzer divisons currently tied up near the Don.

Not everyone agreed. In one of his doggerel verses A. P. Herbert chided

> *Let's have less nonsense from the friends of Josef*
> *We laud - we love him, but this nonsense: NO.*
> *In 1940 when we bore the brunt*
> *We could have done, boys, with a Second Front.*

And the 'undertaking' didn't look any healthier to Churchill. Harold Nicolson summarized the dilemma:

> The Government are in a difficult position. If they create a Second Front as a forlorn hope, we shall have another Dunkirk. If they do not do so, they will be accused of letting down the Russians. But if they explain why they cannot do so, people will feel that there is no chance of our beginning to fight this war before 1945.

The Prime Minister had handed Molotov a note as he left London: 'It is impossible to say in advance whether the situation will be such as to make this operation feasible when the time comes. We can therefore give no promise in the matter...' In a memorandum to Roosevelt on 8 July he reiterated that 'No responsible British General, Admiral or Air Marshal is prepared to recommend SLEDGEHAMMER [the code name for an Allied cross-Channel invasion] as a practical operation in 1942.'

Churchill's plan was for a Second Front not across the English Channel to France, but a North African landing which would attack the 'soft underbelly' of the Axis powers. To many US planners this was simply a diversion, a 'Mediterranean adventure', on Britain's behalf. To Churchill it was a way of simultaneously 'tightening the noose' round Nazi Germany and keeping the US forces engaged in a British theatre of operations. On 25 July 1942, in the face of British intransigence and domestic political concerns and to demonstrate that the US could be associated with action and victory, Roosevelt agreed to Operation TORCH. There would be no full-scale cross-Channel invasion of Europe in 1942. But there would be an invasion.

But it wasn't only the Americans who wanted action by the summer of 1942. The Canadian 2nd Division had been stationed in Britain since December 1939 but had seen no active service. Eddie Chaze, who had come to Britain with the Cameron Highlanders of Canada and was billeted on the Sussex coast, recalls: 'It was kinda boring after a bit, but every so often they'd put us on manoeuvres and schemes...we moved around, stayed in different places, Newhaven, Seaford, all along the coast'. Alex Graham, another Cameron Highlander from Winnipeg, was billeted at Mount Pleasant just outside Newhaven and remembers having quite a peaceful war in those first years:

> An awful lot of us were of British extraction and so we sort of knew what to expect and most of us had relatives in the British Isles. I thought that Newhaven

"Now I want you to imagine that the Alert has sounded . . ."

was a lovely place. The people were nice...and we had all kinds of comforts and good food brought from Canada. It was very extensive compared to what the British people had. Our mess was in a Nissen hut and we used to fill our mess tins with things that were left over, chickpeas and Cheddar cheese [the British had been rationed to, on average, one to two ounces of cheese a week and a little over the equivalent of half an egg a week, for example] and fruit, we knew what the children liked, and every night there they were waiting outside the mess hall. They were glad to get it - and we were glad to give it. There were a few raids in Newhaven, but nothing to speak of, and there were a few scares when the *Scharnhorst* [a German battleship that was eventually sunk off Norway] was running up and down the Channel when we were on 24-hour duty, on what the British called coastal alert.

Twenty-four days before the outbreak of war in September 1939 children and mothers with infants had been evacuated from the cities considered to be in danger of aerial attack to the country, including the seaside, and many south coast families took London children into their homes. But after the Fall of France in 1940, the danger of invasion had made the coast seem as perilous as the cities and not only were evacuated families moved elsewhere, but local women and children were encouraged to pack up and move inland to different parts of the country as the coastline of south and west England became a barbed wire wasteland.

Bill Holden's wife, who had just returned from Stratford-upon-Avon where she had been sent to have their second child, was immediately evacuated again with a toddler and the new baby, this time to Bedford. Vacated homes and deserted hotels and boarding houses were requisitioned for troops and Bill Packham, a policeman who had been posted from East Grinstead to Newhaven, found a place 'more or less denuded of people...I should think that half the town was evacuated by September 1940', fill up with Canadian troops who 'made a lot of extra work'.

They made a lot of extra fun, too, for the young women left in the Sussex towns and villages. There were dances in local church halls - often three a week - but at first the Canadians were treated with suspicion by the local townspeople - particularly with regard to girls. 'My dad sat us down, my older sister and I, and he told us "You must stay away from them [the Canadian soldiers], they're a bad lot," ' recalls Ruth Buchanan:

> I was seventeen at the time and we'd be walking through the village and you'd hear these footsteps coming behind you and then these Canadian troops and they'd just be trying to talk to you, and we'd almost be running home because we were so scared. Anyway I never met anyone who caused any problems. After a bit we used to have a lot of them come to the house for tea.

Indeed Ruth married a Canadian soldier in March 1942 after meeting him at a dance the year before.

Mary Marks (later Pilote) married a Canadian soldier, too, despite assuring the sister at the Church Army Canteen, where she'd volunteered to help serve the soldiers after her day's work as a piano teacher, that she certainly wouldn't be 'running after Canadians...you needn't worry about me, I've got a good home and mother and father, I wouldn't want to go to Canada.' But within months of his arrival Mary had met a French-Canadian soldier who was delighted to find that she spoke French since his English was so halting, and they had fallen in love.

It wasn't so much relations with the girls that gave some of the Canadians a bad name with the local forces, though there were some altercations with local boyfriends and brothers. In the eyes of a local policeman it was the pubs that were the cause of the trouble: 'The Canadians were paid once a fortnight, and they - and the Americans, too - were getting at least double the amount that our troops were getting,' recalls Bill Packham.

> And then, of course, for about three days and three nights, all you had was drunken soldiers about the town. After they'd spent all their money, they used to be quiet, it wasn't too bad then. Of course they had their own military police on patrol in the town, especially evenings, and when there was any trouble, they were always around. One day a young Canadian, about twenty-one, fine build, he was billeted on Mount Pleasant and he disarmed the sentry at the bottom of the hill and he was going to shoot the colonel. And he got into the billet where the colonel was, and one of the military police came out at the top of the stairs, and the soldier shot him instead, killed him outright, so we had to go out hunting for

'The invader should be apprehended'. Respectable citizens of St Austell in Cornwall oblige as 'Nazi' prisoners in a Home Guard exercise in 1940.

this chap. We didn't know whether he was still armed or not, but fortunately the Canadians picked him up. And then one Saturday evening there was a row in one of the Newhaven pubs, and the Canadian soldiers set on the sailors, there were only a few of them. So on the Sunday evening the navy came out in force. And there was a real dingdong. They were all fighting each other...swinging fists and everything. The High Street was chock-a-block - I don't think they knew who they were hitting...there must have been at least five hundred or more out there fighting. The naval police were there and the army police, so I wanted to join in. But I was off duty, I wasn't in uniform, so the wife said 'No, you come home'. So I had to go home and read about it in the morning.

But on the whole, PC Packham thought the Canadian troops were

very good...they used to have scuffles...I had my haversack stolen one night by one of them, but I got it back the next morning. They were six or seven thousand miles from home, they didn't care all that much what happened during the war, they didn't know whether they were going to get back, whether they were going to survive or not.

The perception that their troops were sitting around with nothing much to do but chase girls and get drunk posed problems back home in Canada. It reflected on the military recruitment programme. Who wanted to enlist if it meant sitting around on your back-side in some god-forsaken camp in the rain-sodden English countryside? 'Our army of noble idlers' was becoming a political embarrassment to the Canadian Prime Minister MacKenzie King who pressed Churchill to use his men in a military operation: 'I don't know how long I can go on leading my country while our troops remain inactive.'

The raid on Boulogne on 23 June 1940, when a handful of men from what would become the Commando forces had mounted the first of a number of 'pinprick' raids along the 3,000 miles of enemy coastline, had been designed both to train men and to experiment with amphibious craft and weaponry.

These raids were to come under the Combined Operations Staff established by Churchill in the summer of 1940 with men from all three services. Their task was to plan and execute commando raids into Occupied Europe immediately, and, as a longer-term objective, to formulate a military strategy for a cross-Channel assault and begin to devel-op and test amphibious vehicles and equipment capable of such an enterprise. In the autumn of 1941, a young naval officer, Lord Louis Mountbatten, was appointed to replace Admiral Sir Roger Keyes as the head of Combined Operations. Churchill told him:

> You are to prepare for an invasion of Europe, for unless we can go and land and fight Hitler and beat his forces on land, we shall never win this war. You must devise and design the appliances, the landing craft and the technique to enable us to effect a landing against opposition and to maintain ourselves there. You must take the most brilliant officers from the Navy, Army and Air Force to help as our planners to plan this great operation. You must take bases to use as training estab-lishments where you can train the Navy, Army and Air Force to work as a single entity. The whole of the south coast of England is a bastion of defence against the invasion of Hitler: you've got to turn it into a springboard for attack.

The first tentative steps to test the possibilities of this springboard were mounted in August 1942. The venture was to involve Canadian, British and some Free French troops. The French port of Dieppe was targeted for a Combined Operations landing to over-whelm the fortifications and seize the harbour by a landing with amphibious vehicles.

CHAPTER TWO

DRESS REHEARSAL FOR DISASTER

DIEPPE WAS KNOWN AS 'poor man's Monte Carlo' before the war, its casino a draw to holidaymakers who liked a flutter and to gamblers with more serious purpose as they rolled dice in the building that looked like a wedding cake. Every summer cross-Channel ferries plied the sixty-seven-mile stretch of water from Newhaven in Sussex to the Normandy port and back again. It was this established route that had been chosen for a 'reconnaissance of force', a small-scale Allied assault on occupied Europe.

The object was for the troops, under cover of Allied fighter support, to storm ashore along a ten-mile stretch of coast accompanied by the newly-designed Churchill tanks, scale the cliffs that edged the beach, overpower and disable the German gun batteries ranged to repel any such invasion, capture the port, destroy the aerodrome at St Aubin and recce the radar installation at Pourville - all in a nine-hour raid which allowed five hours ashore to accomplish these objectives and four to withdraw.

The Dieppe force was to consist of the 2nd Canadian Division, two British Army Commandos units, Nos. 3 and 4, and the Royal Marine Commando 'A', plus a detachment of fifty American Rangers and two dozen Free French soldiers.

The raid, originally code-named Operation RUTTER, had been scheduled for 3 July 1942 but the 1st Airborne Division insisted that the wind factor was too high for a successful parachute landing. It was scrapped to be resurrected a few days later with a new and more upbeat name, Operation JUBILEE, but without the participation of the 1st Airborne. Lord Lovat, the Lieutenant-Colonel in charge of No. 4 Commando, recalls how he was put in the picture in late July 1942:

> A big raid was on. [The Brigadier] did not say where. Two Commandos were needed to replace parachute battalions chosen to knock out coastal batteries covering the sea approaches to a certain town...'Can you climb cliffs?' Yes, [we] had sixty men who could climb anything with a reasonable surface, provided there was no overhang. The word 'chalk' was not mentioned - the worst stuff to negotiate.

Lovat still felt confidence in his men's ability and tough training - and in the planning of the raid.

> Usually a battle is fought at short notice, with little or no plan of action. Here the data had been sorted out and sifted like a jigsaw puzzle. We had an admirable model prepared to scale by RAF Intelligence. We knew the range and distance to

Evacuation. Boys from King's School, Canterbury, arrive by train at St Austell where the school had been evacuated in the summer of 1940. Cornwall seemed a safer place for them than Canterbury which was on the Luftwaffe's bombing run.

be covered and learnt every fold and feature set out on the ground. The demolition squad could blow gun breeches in their sleep. Wireless communications were tested and counter-tested. Every weapon was fired over measured marks…we practised crossing wire, throwing rolled rabbit netting over the defensive aprons. We fired Bangalore torpedoes to blast a way through barbed entanglements. We laid smoke to cover withdrawal to sea. Correct seating in each boat was worked out with meticulous detail. Junior officers changed places with their supposedly wounded superiors. Landing craft were sunk in theory for instant improvisations, carried out with no delay.

On a raid it can be more unpleasant coming back than going in, specially in daylight. Final withdrawal was practised first as a drill, then with stretcher cases, then with fierce opposition, and finally under cover of smoke. All officers and senior NCOs inspected the layout of coastal defence systems. The men were splendid and I was well pleased. If we put down on time in the right place, eventualities seemed well covered. It was interesting to speculate what might go wrong!

Wally Russell, a small arms instructor, had been at sea with the Royal Marines when he heard of the call for volunteers for 'hazardous duties - only the 100% fit need apply'. All the Commandos were hand-picked volunteers: 'One volunteer is worth ten pressed

*Essential war work. The Chaplain of King's School, Canterbury, turns his hand
to giving pupils a short back and sides when the school was evacuated
to wartime quarters in Cornwall.*

men', the Commander of No. 4 Commando, Lord Lovat, used to say. 'I asked all men to remember that we came from an island race...that Britain's best performances had been at sea. We sought the sea, lived on the coast and took to the new life like ducks to water.' Training was tough and discipline tougher. 'One slip and you were out was the rule - and there were always others queueing up to take your place.'

Russell 'was a young bloke and wanting to get cracking, so I volunteered and they selected 400 officers, NCOs and men from the whole of the Corps.' After extensive interviews he was selected for Commando training and sent to the training school at Achnacarry in Scotland. In July 1942 the Commandos who had been selected for the raid came south to hone their training for Dieppe.

> We were very fit, and we were very highly trained. We were practising unarmed combat and we were abseiling in Portsmouth dockyards going from the jetty on to the boats and then back from the boats to the jetty, climbing rope ladders, scaling the sides of ships, all this in addition to our general training which was pretty tough, long marches and so forth.

The Canadian 2nd Division had been training for two months at Freshwater on the Isle of Wight. Bud Buchanan, who had married a Newhaven girl in March that year and was drafted as a Quartermaster with the Cameron Highlanders remembers that it was 'pretty rigorous training scaling the steep cliffs and traversing the rocky coastline of the island. We had a pretty good idea that we were training for a raid...'

Those people who were still living in the seaside towns along the Sussex coast realized that something big was happening when entry was barred to the harbours and the surrounding roads. The landing craft that had arrived at Newhaven were concealed under a huge canvas screen, but the interest of the German Luftwaffe was clearly aroused and it flew as many as twelve sorties a day photographing the impressive assembly of shipping assembled at Newhaven. Sylvia Watts (*née* Packham), who worked as an ambulance attendant alongside her regular job on the haberdashery counter of Ballister's department store in the town recalls:

> I lived quite close to the harbour and though you couldn't go anywhere near it, you could see some boats going back and forth all the time and on the other side of the river there were tanks were lined up ready to be loaded. There was definitely a feeling of tenseness in the air, as if something was going to happen...

Eddie Chaze had already prepared for Dieppe once: he had been aboard a ship that had been detailed for Operation RUTTER back in July when it was decided that the tides weren't right and that conditions made a paratroop landing dangerous. 'We'd waited too long, we were sent back to the mainland and given leave...we were told that Dieppe had been cancelled.' But on 18 August he was again told that he and his fellow Cameron Highlanders were

> going on a scheme...we kinda suspected that something was up because they gave us all the ammunition we wanted, all the bandoliers we wanted, all the grenades we wanted, all live stuff. And when we got to Newhaven and got out of our trucks people were standing on the pavement waving us off, wishing us good luck so we knew there was something going on. If the civilians knew we were going somewhere, I guess we soldiers might know that soon too...

Lieutenant-Colonel John Durnford-Slater, and his No. 3 Commando had to queue in the street outside the Newhaven docks on the morning of 18 August because there 'were so many Canadian troops embarking'. By this time the watching crowd had fallen 'dead silent' as they emptied out of their houses to watch this first attempt to return to France.

As the 'pea shooter' armada of infantry landing ships, 'Hunt' class destroyers and tank landing craft slipped out of port at Newhaven, Shoreham and Hastings at 11.30 p.m. and headed towards the Channel which had been swept of mines, the chaplain to the Canadian Fusiliers Mont-Royal of Quebec marvelled at the morale of his men: 'Such enthusiasm as I had never witnessed before, and never will again.'

Durnford-Slater had noticed that the Canadian forces 'were full of confidence' when he had visited their Divisional Headquarters to talk them about the troops about what the Commandos had learnt on their raid on Vaagso in Norway at the end of December 1941. 'But I was afraid that they were in for a very tough time, owing to the strength of the defence on the beaches they were due to attack.'

In the event the 'tough time' started even before the flotilla had reached the French beaches. The night of 18-19 August 1942 was moonlit, calm and balmy and the flotilla slipped effortlessly - and remarkably silently, given its size - across the Channel. Four miles east of the main harbour, at 3.47 a.m. on 19 August 1942, German E-boats on routine escort duty sighted the landing barges and opened fire. Tracer shells exploded and made 'night into day.' Within minutes the bridge of Durnford-Slater's ship was 'piled with the dead and wounded like a collapsed rugger scrum'. A landing craft approached carrying the tall Charlie Head. A veterinary surgeon in civilian life, Head was put to work tending the wounded who were reassured that he was a doctor and gratefully accepted his attentions - and a large measure of rum.

Intelligence sources had indicated that Dieppe was 'only lightly defended'. In fact it was riddled with a web of machine-guns and anti-tank guns sunk into the cliff. But these were only the routine defences along the Atlantic Wall since the German Commander-in-Chief, von Rundstedt, considered that 'Dieppe is a most unsuitable place for a landing.' He was to be proved right.

In fact whilst many of the fragile wooden landing craft had been lost in the action, a few had got through and landed on the beaches. Major Peter Young managed to lead a contingent of Commandos up a narrow gully in the cliffs towards the Berneval battery that had powerful 150mm guns with a twelve-mile range, while 'Shimi' Lovat led his Commandos to scale the 400-foot cliffs and overpower the Varengeville six-gun battery nearly a mile inland - the only completely successful action of the entire raid.

Wally Russell had crossed the Channel in the company of the Free French soldiers and the American Rangers. On the way over the French skipper had invited the Marine Commandos' Platoon Commander to toast the venture. The troops had brandy poured into their coffee mugs and raised them to the cry 'Vive la France'. Their job was to make straight for the harbour but the ship was strafed by German planes, Messerschmitts and Stukas, so the troops transferred to landing craft and made for the shore.

> Then we saw the beaches. It was terrible. I've done a lot of landings since then, Sicily and Italy and so on, but never anything like that. It was hell, that's the best description. There were bodies floating everywhere, there were tanks high and dry on the beaches, there were what looked like hundreds of Canadians lying on the beaches dead and injured...the beach was being raked with gunfire, planes were firing, everything...Colonel Phillips could see it was hopeless. He put on a pair of white gloves and stood up in the bows to cancel the operation and he was shot and killed, and the Adjutant was killed and the Coxswain was killed, and we were drifting near to the beach and there weren't many of us left, and I said, 'Every man for himself, abandon ship,' and we jumped over the side into the sea fully booted and spurred. I remember saying to my young skipper, Lieutenant Over, before we jumped, 'Well, cheerio Derek, see you in Pompey and whoever gets there first puts up the pints,' and he was killed as we jumped over. When I turned round to look, I couldn't see much of him, I think his head was pretty well gone...I was only ashore for a little while. I dashed up the beach with the Platoon Commander's batman behind one of these Churchill tanks. They were hopeless, they just got stuck on the beach and couldn't move and the Canadian crews were all dead, they were lying on the beach, some of them were under the cliffs, they'd just been pinned down on the beaches, they couldn't do a thing, the beaches had

Training for invasion. Royal Marines negotiating barbed wire barriers during invasion exercises in August 1942.

just been raked with gunfire. So we ran back to the shore and I was in the water for three or four hours and I saw the boats starting to go back, and they couldn't see me because of the swell, but eventually I was picked up by a tank landing craft...I went down below and there was a young surgeon there and...he was amputating as fast as he could go...a Canadian was lying there, just the torso, he'd taken off his legs and arms and he'd been shot through the nose, and this young surgeon was crying...it was shocking, I've never seen anything like it...it lives with me today...we sat there and all we had were blankets and then some marines on board dug out some trousers and gave us a tot of rum and tea and a Commando, I think he was a First Lieutenant, came down and said 'Who's the senior one down here?' They'd captured a German pilot who'd ditched in the sea, and all my blokes said 'It's Sergeant Russell,' so the Lieutenant said to me 'I want him in one piece when we arrive at Newhaven, if anything happens to him that's a Court Martial for you.' I thought, 'What the hell am I going to do with him?' And my blokes were saying, 'Go on, shove off Sarge, we'll look after him,' and without a doubt they'd have cut him up and fed him to the fishes - the Germans had been machine-gunning us whilst we were in the water. So I went on the upper deck and asked the Chief Petty Officer what I should do with the German and he suggested the chain locker. But that was no good, it was too open where they'd kicked the anchor chains in, and I'd have had to stay with him, so we looked around and found the paint locker which is about three feet square, and he was saying

'Comrade, comrade.' I'm sure he thought that I was going to shoot him, so I said, 'Down there' and shoved him in this cupboard full of all these tins of paint. And when we arrived at Newhaven he came out all red, white and blue and every other colour. I took him up to the bridge and said, 'There he is in one piece.' And the skipper said, 'My God, where's he been?' And I said, 'Well, he's in one piece.' And that was it.

Bud Buchanan had been looking after his platoon's stores as the Cameron Highlanders trained for Dieppe.

The morning they got ready to go, I wasn't on the roster at all, and the one of the boys went sick, and they came and told me to get my gear on, I was going. It didn't particularly bother me, they told us it was just another manoeuvre, although we knew perfectly well that it was more than a manoeuvre the way they were loading us down with ammunition.

In fact the Buchanan family was well represented in the Dieppe landings: nine cousins made the crossing.

When Bud arrived on the French coast

it was very early in the morning, and it was as if the whole place was on fire. You could see tracer bullets landing in the sea in front of you, skimming the water and shells were going off, and the planes were overhead and they were doing a lot of damage too...a Saskatchewan regiment went in ahead of our unit, and they stirred things up, and so by the time we got on to the beaches it was pretty hot, in fact it was damned hot. We were put out of the boats about fifty feet out to sea and we had to make our way ashore. We lost a lot of men right there on the beach, we lost our company Commander and some of our NCOs...it was a mess. Once you lose your leaders you just do for yourself, you just do the best you can.

At 10.22 a.m. Captain John Hughes-Hallett who was Lord Mountbatten's observer aboard HMS *Calpe* signalled 'Vanquish': Operation JUBILEE was pulled.

1,000 Canadian troops hadn't even gone ashore, hundreds of troops - Canadian, British, and French - lay dead or wounded; the first American soldier to lose his life in the European Theater of Operations, Lieutenant Edwin V. Loustalot was slain by a bullet and hundreds of the luckless invaders had been taken prisoner. Of the 6,100 troops that took part over 3,500 were killed, missing or taken prisoner and 105 Allied aircraft were shot down whilst much valuable equipment, including the thirty new Churchill tanks, were once again left on the beaches of France. 'This is the first time', Hitler was to mock, 'that the British have had the courtesy to cross the sea to offer the enemy a complete sample of their weapons.'

Bud Buchanan remembers the evacuation:

They laid a smoke screen and we got to the beaches under the cover of the smoke and the Germans followed us on to the beaches and we were being shelled too...I got on to a boat, but it was overloaded so I swam across to another one and I got on to that and my cousin Jackie Hunter was on it, and he got hit...he wasn't killed immediately, but he was wounded so badly - he was partially cut in half - that he said that there was no hope for him, so he went overboard, he threw himself into the water.

Of the nine members of Bud Buchanan's family that went to Dieppe three were killed, three were taken prisoner and only three returned.

Bud's wife, Ruth, whom he had married only five months before, didn't know that her husband had been sent to Dieppe at the last moment.

We didn't know anything about the raid until I think it was six or seven o'clock in the morning when the milkman came and said we'd invaded France and then we turned the radio on and it was Dieppe and the sky was black with planes, and we could hear the gunfire...Bud wasn't supposed to go on the raid...he wasn't trained for it...when I realised he'd gone, it was just panic stations till I heard from him. He came home as soon as they released him when he got back to Newhaven, and he was limping on one leg, he'd hurt his ankle, but apart from that he was safe and that was the main thing. But he was very young, it affected him quite badly...he lost so many of his friends, so many of the boys were killed...or taken prisoner...he couldn't stay, he wanted to get out of it so he went before the Army Service Board and ended up in Italy!

Mary Marks did know that her French Canadian boyfriend, Marc Pilote, was one of those on the Dieppe raid:

He wrote to me from his camp at Wisborough Geen and said, 'If you happen to hear that a landing has been made by the 2nd Canadian Division on the French coast, say a prayer for me'...and I thought, well, that's strange, he hadn't been trained for the raid, because a lot of his regiment went to the Isle of Wight for about six weeks' training for a landing, but Marc hadn't been chosen because he was helping in the office at the time so he didn't have to go to the Isle of Wight, so I couldn't understand why he said 'say a prayer for me...' then I heard on the radio that the landing had been made by the 2nd Canadian Division and, oh dear, I knew he was on it. And when the soldiers started coming back, I went out and stood at the end of the road watching the ambulances take the wounded up the Brighton Road to see if I could see him, but I never saw sign of him. The raid took place on Wednesday and so on the Monday I went right up to the camp at Wisborough Green to see if there was any news of him. They looked down the list and they said, 'Well, he's missing believed dead,' but as I was leaving someone said, 'There's so many wounded, some of the injured have been taken to Scotland. Your boyfriend might be in a hospital somewhere.' But I thought he was dead. Though I used to hope and pray I never got any news for two months and then on my birthday which was on 19 October two months after the raid, I thought, 'Oh, wouldn't it be wonderful to have some news today,' and when the postman came, I picked up the letters and one was a peculiar-looking envelope, and when I opened it it was a letter telling me that he was in a prisoner of war camp, and asking me if I would wait for him till the end of the war...My parents said that it

Home from Dieppe: 'their uniforms were very tattered and torn and wet through, a lot of them had been in the sea for a long time before they were picked up'.

wasn't very sensible to wait for him because after the end of the war, he'd probably go straight back to Canada, but he didn't. I was the first one he contacted when he got back to England and we got married in July 1945.

When he did come back he told me all about it. He'd had to go on the raid because there were so many absent without leave, they took anyone they could find to make up the numbers, even if they hadn't been trained, even if they'd been in the office like he was. When he got to Dieppe the gunfire was so bad that he hid behind a tank for a long time, and then he got some shrapnel in his lip and it was painful, but he'd managed to get into a boat and was heading back to Newhaven when a bomb fell near the boat and they were all thrown out into the sea, and he managed to get his heavy army boots off but they were a long way out from the shore and he was exhausted swimming and he was taken prisoner. They were marched a long way barefooted and his feet were bleeding. He was a prisoner for nearly three years…and he hated the Germans because he said they ill-treated the prisoners and kept them short of food and they were handcuffed with ropes tied round their wrists. They had those handcuffs on for thirteen months, from the time they woke up in the morning until they went to bed at night, and they had to eat with the handcuffs on and my husband told me that he used to write letters to me with the handcuffs on, and as a souvenir he had the handcuffs tatooed on his arm and Stalag 8B [the POW camp] on his forearm. It was a terrible thing. The Germans did it as a reprisal for what they had done to their men…

Alex Graham of the Cameron Highlanders of Canada was taken prisoner at Dieppe, too. He was the Regimental Piper and his job was to pipe the company ashore.

We were about four or five hundred yards from the shore and the motor of the boat we were in stalled, so the naval officer asked me to play because the men were trying to fix the motor and we were under a lot of heavy fire…tracer bullets coming our way, and he said it might give the men something to think about…so I played 'Gibraltar' and after a while they couldn't get the motor started and a mine-laying craft came in and threw us a rope which they tied on and headed for shore at a very fast clip, and then they cut the rope and we coasted in…at the time I was playing 'The Hundred Pipers' which is our company march past. You're in a pretty exposed position as a company piper…I was under heavy fire when I was playing on the boat, I thought maybe I was just lucky…I had to do something to summon the soldiers who were just waiting to go ashore…at least I felt I was doing something…in the old days, if there was a charge or something then the officer usually asked the piper to play and away they went…but this was a little bit different…I understand that there were no other Canadian pipers allowed to play men into action after Dieppe because they thought that they were losing too many…most of our band were casualties of one kind or another…but once he's played, a company piper is just another soldier…the other bandsmen are usually on duty at the first aid post, something like that, so we're just another fighting person.

When Alex Graham started up the beach 'it was terrible. There was an awful lot of dead men around…and the machine-gun fire was just like rain dropping on the road, the pebbles were bouncing off the beach with machine-gun fire'. But he managed to get across the beach and got up to the sea wall: 'And they couldn't get at you there…and eventually the Company Commander stood on the Sergeant Major's shoulders and got over the wall…and the Sergeant Major pulled us up…and we were inland.'

After the battle was over, sometime around noon, Alex Graham was making his way back across the beach trying to get the wounded to safety when he was set upon by a

whole platoon of Germans…we couldn't very well fight them off. We were outnumbered and we knew that we weren't going to get home because the battle was over and there were no more boats coming in…and we knew that our chances of getting out were pretty bad because we knew what it was like coming in…so I became a POW…the Germans took my bagpipes off me. They take everything that they can take off you…including your watch and everything else…I imagine the pipes became one of the fortunes of war and are probably now somewhere in a museum in Germany. They put us in box cars with 'Britain Second Front' written on the outside…and we ended up in Silesia…then after we'd been there for a few weeks they decided to rope us. We were tied with our hands behind our backs at first, and when when we couldn't breathe properly, they tied us with our hands in front…so after a while the rope burns caused a skin disease all over and then they took the ropes off and we were handcuffed with a chain, and that went on for about thirteen months…they tied us up because we tied up some of their prisoners at Dieppe…I think the Germans misconstrued it. The idea was that just one man could be put in charge of German prisoners and our own walking wounded…so in order to make the prisoners a little bit more defenceless they tied their thumbs together…but I think that during the raid some of them were killed by their own aircraft strafing the beaches and it was said that the prisoners were thrown into the sea tied up but…I don't think they were thrown into the sea. I think they were trying to get on the boats and these became overloaded and they drowned…we lost a lot of our men that way too…There's this terrible confusion in war.

Eddie Chaze was one of the Canadian soldiers who did eventually manage to get off the beach at Dieppe:

I got on to a destroyer and there were a lot of wounded men on it…and our clothes were all soaking wet, so the sailors took the men's clothes and gave them dry ones, but by the time I got on board the fatigues had gone, so all I got was a blanket. I staggered ashore at Portsmouth and all I was wearing was a grey army blanket and my tin helmet.

Sylvia Watts was waiting on the quayside at Newhaven with her fellow ambulance attendants when the boats which were bringing the survivors and the wounded from Dieppe began to dock.

Some of the men who came off the boats were pretty badly injured and all of them were dishevelled. We'd seen them go out…it was amazing to see so many of them gathering to go, but they didn't come back like that at all…their uniforms were very tattered and torn and wet through, a lot of them had been in the sea for a long time before they were eventually picked up. And to be honest, they looked as if they really didn't want to live another day, they were absolutely, completely worn out. They brought back the ones that could walk first and we just gave them mugs of cocoa…nothing was organized really, we didn't know the truth of what had happened over there. Then they started bringing in the injured, and they were put in ambulances and directed to hospitals, and some of us went in the Canadian ambulance to navigate because there weren't any road signs because they'd all been taken down and the Canadian drivers didn't know where they were going, Brighton might have been a million miles away.

Audrey Ashdown, another ambulance attendant waiting on the quayside remembers:

It was so sad to see them, some of them were so very young, a lot of the Commandos seemed shell-shocked, they were shaking and one man had a knife and he just didn't seem to know where he was, he was just going berserk. And then they'd brought some German prisoners back, and they were blindfolded and they were standing shaking, not knowing where they were, what was going to happen to them.

If they weren't too badly wounded the men were seen by the Army or the Navy medics first, and they tied a label on them, saying 'right leg wound' or whatever, and they were put in our ambulances. We tried to talk to them, to comfort them, and give them a drink of water if they didn't have a 'nil by mouth' sign pinned on them. And they kept repeating what a shambles it had been, that everything was just a shambles, but most of them just couldn't talk about it, they didn't want to talk about Dieppe. Some of them had horrific wounds, serious head wounds, they were all shot up...the Germans had machine-gunned the crafts as they were bringing the soldiers off the beaches...there was one naval commando who was just lying there, he was flat on his back, badly shocked, and one of his boots was OK, but the other was all shattered, and the doctor came along and removed his boot, which fell to pieces, and then he removed the man's toes, right there in the ambulance, without any anaesthetic or anything. The fella didn't flinch, and the doctor said to me, 'Talk to him', so I held up this copy of *Picture Post* that was in the ambulance and just said, 'Have you seen one of these before?' and the doctor put a tourniquet on his foot and we made for Hellingly Hospital which was a mental hospital at the time, but they'd cleared a ward for casualties, and we couldn't go to Brighton General Hospital or Sussex County because they were queueing up there, lying on stretchers waiting for beds. It all happened so quickly, there were so many injured, all the hospitals in the area were working at full stretch, the nurses could hardly cope.

There was one minor casualty of the Dieppe raid that brought a little light relief to that grim day, 19 August 1942. Gwen Chadwick was a Wren stationed at Newhaven and working as the Naval Paymaster's assistant. When her cat had kittens one was adopted by the nearby naval base and used to enjoy the freedom of their craft. On the morning of the raid, the cat, Sooty, was sleeping undetected and made the crossing in a landing craft. He was missing for two days and two nights, but finally returned on the same craft, with a torn ear, and deaf from the gunfire but apparently otherwise unharmed. When Gwen Chadwick took the cat to the vet, he pronounced the animal fit - but female 'the only "she" to go over...so the boys at the base made a little "VC" to hang round her neck and her photograph appeared in the local paper.'

Those men who weren't injured were shepherded into marquees and given 'a tot of rum', Wally Russell remembers, and 'we were interviewed by British and Canadian officers, who seemed mainly to want to know what acts of bravery we'd seen.'

'Close-quarter fighting is a messy business, leaving the survivors drained and mentally exhausted...so we returned to England - each to his thoughts, wrapped in a dream', wrote Lord Lovat. Shocked but alive, survivors of the Dieppe raid light up.

Captain (later Colonel) Patrick Porteous, who landed at Quiberville, four miles west of Dieppe was one of the men whose act of bravery was noticed and acknowledged by the award of the Victoria Cross, as was that of a Canadian officer, thirty-three-year-old Lieutenant-Colonel Merritt of the South Saskatchewan Regiment, and a Canadian Chaplain, John Foote, who tended the injured under fire on the shingle, carried them to the boats, but refused to leave, allowing himself to be taken prisoner and continue to help the wounded in captivity.

A bullet went through Patrick Porteous's thigh, but failed to puncture the femoral artery. He found himself in a military hospital with a number of Canadian casualties. It was there that he recalls a Canadian Red Cross helper calling over to him, 'Hey, Limey, do you smoke?' 'No,' he replied, but a pack of 200 cigarettes landed on his bed anyway, so he became a smoker. He remembers that a Canadian battalion was stationed nearby and he was surprised to see soldiers come to visit their injured friends wearing heavy greatcoats despite the fact that it was high summer, until he realized that these were excellent cover for the bottles of whisky they were bringing in. But Porteous also recalls the bitterness of the Canadians:

> They'd lost a hell of a lot of chaps. There's a monument today in Dieppe saying 'Two Canadian soldiers died here', but those were the only people who managed to get into the town, the rest didn't get off the beaches, they were gunned down there, and those that didn't die on the shingle - of those that landed on Puys beach, east of Dieppe, a little narrow beach with large pill box at each end and a battery of defences - only one man actually got over the sea wall, and out of the whole battalion, only twelve got back to England. It was chaos, total chaos, and one of the brigadiers commanding the central front took his operation orders with him and he was taken prisoner. So then the Germans had the whole operation in front of them, they knew exactly what we were trying to do.

'It was to be a sea parallel to the Charge of the Light Brigade,' recalled the commander of the assault boats of the Free French Chasseurs who were 'coming home' - temporarily - for the first time in over two years. The tanks failed to breach the fortifications and enter the town: more than 3,500 of the Canadian, British and Free French troops taking part were killed, wounded or taken prisoner.

Major Brian McCool of the Royal Regiment of Canada who had been the Principal Military Landing Officer was one of those taken prisoner by the Germans. 'What was it?' his interrogator asked him; 'It was too big for a raid and too small for an invasion.' McCool had no answer.

The Dieppe raid had been regarded by many with great scepticism before it set off. The First Sea Lord, Admiral Sir Dudley Pound, had refused to risk a battleship in the Channel narrows. Air Vice-Marshal Arthur Harris had refused to provide the 300 bombers requested. So there was no pre-assault bombardment which Lord Mountbatten, Head of Combined Operations, and his Naval adviser Captain John Hughes-Hallett and General Montgomery, who had overseen the early stages of the planning, had insisted were essential. 'The troops will be pinned down on the beaches at the very beginning,' prophesied Air Vice-Marshal Leigh Mallory; 'They'll never get going again.'

*Lieutenant-Colonel the Lord Lovat talks to his fellow Commandos
on their return from Dieppe, 19 August 1942.*

To Patrick Porteous Dieppe was

> the biggest disaster that ever happened and the people that planned it should be
> shot. It was impossible for it to have succeeded, the Intelligence wasn't good
> enough. The plan depended entirely on total surprise, the slightest variation on
> that and the whole thing collapsed. It was only mounted to raise morale in Russia,
> and in England too when we'd been forced back in the Western desert, and to
> give the Canadians something to do, they'd been hanging around so long getting
> bored.

However Lord Mountbatten considered that it was 'one of the most vital operations of the
Second World War. It gave the Allies the priceless secret of victory...If I had the same
decisions to make again I would do as I did before'. Porteous agrees that 'certain lessons
were learned, but most of those lessons could have been learnt on the beach at Weymouth
or anywhere else in England.'

'Was Dieppe a worthwhile effort?' Lord Lovat of No. 4 Commando, asked himself.

> It is difficult to think so. There were no military objectives to justify a landing in
> France...our losses in the air, on land and at sea were in inverse proportion to the
> enemy's, and that is an understatement. These sorry figures are not the stuff of

which victories are made. Of 4,963 Canadians who sailed from Southampton, only 2,210 returned next day. A total of 466 naval and commando personnel were killed, captured or reported missing. One destroyer and thirty-three landing craft were lost at sea. The RAF had 105 fighter planes shot down, something they could ill afford owing to severe shortage...I hold that the raid...was a disaster...

Politicians and military planners had to agree. At a tragically high cost Dieppe had driven home the realities of a cross-Channel assault: the need for accurate Intelligence, advance saturation bombing, tanks to support the first wave of assault troops, the near impossibility of taking a fortified port by direct assault. 'The next time we bring our harbour with us,' vowed Hughes-Hallett. In 1942 such resources were unavailable. There could be no Second Front with a half-realistic chance of success for many months to come.

Whilst Goebbels's propaganda machine boosted German morale by portraying the Dieppe Raid as 'a full-scale invasion that failed' Hitler was to warn the Wehrmacht commanders: 'We must realise that we are not alone in learning a lesson from Dieppe. The British have also learned. We must reckon with a totally different mode of attack and at a quite different place.'

CHAPTER THREE

THE YANKS ARE COMING

'O VER THERE,' ENTHUSED George L. Cohen's song from the First World War,

> Send the word, send the word over there,
> The Yanks are coming, the Yanks are coming...
> Send the word the Yanks are coming, so prepare, say a prayer,
> Send the word to say beware, the Yanks are coming.

and, the words continued in a convoluted but determined fashion,

> We won't come back over here till it's over over there.

The first Yanks who would fight in the Second World War had arrived in Britain on 26 January 1942, within weeks of Churchill's and Roosevelt's agreement in Washington on New Year's Day 1942.

The US troops had come to Britain as evidence of America's commitment to a 'Germany First' policy and to give logistical reality to that policy. Over the next two and a half years changes in policy and strategy would result in a stop-start build-up of American troops and equipment in readiness for a cross-Channel assault on Europe.

Before the attack on Pearl Harbor on 7 December 1941 America's policy of isolationism, a reluctance to intervene once again in little more than twenty years in what many American's regarded as a 'European civil war' had kept the United States maintaining a policy of non-belligerence. However when at the end of December 1940, the US President, Roosevelt, had received an urgent request from Britain for war matériel - heavy bombers in particular on which the country 'depend[ed] to shatter the foundation of German military power', Roosevelt had responded in a way that Churchill was to call 'one of the most generous and unsordid acts of history'. On 29 December 1940 Roosevelt had announced America's new policy of aid to Britain which was to become known as Lend-Lease. The production of ships, tanks and other war supplies was to be rapidly increased and no longer be sold to Britain, but lent - for an unspecified time and without an invoice date. The President explained his reasons starkly:

> If Britain should go down, all of us Americans would be living at the point of a gun, a gun loaded with explosive bullets, economic as well as military...We must produce arms and ships with every energy and resource we can command...We must be the great arsenal of democracy.

From the end of January 1942, with America now in the war, this 'great arsenal' started to be transferred across the Atlantic and

> *Dear old England's not the same,*
> *The dread invasion, well it came,*
> *But no it's not the beastly Hun,*
> *The Goddamn Yankee army's come…*

Pathé News showed these GIs (GI meant Government Issue and stood for guns, blankets, boots, soap, toilet paper as well as the soldier himself) arriving in Britain. 'The US troops are well aware why they have crossed the Atlantic,' the commentary explained, 'they have come to stamp out Hitler and all his works,' and as if to emphasize the point, the troops were shown disembarking across 'Welcome mats' emblazoned with a familar caricature of the Führer's face.

Few of them in those early days knew how long it would be before they got anywhere near the Führer, but, around the time of the Dieppe raid in the summer of 1942, when there were only some 1,000 American troops in Britain, Mollie Panter-Downes noticed their impatience:

> To the general atmosphere of watchful waiting has been added the impatience of the American troops now in London, most of whom talk as though they were somewhat doubtful of being able to give the town a quick once-over before leaving to keep a date with von Rundstedt [the German Commander-in-Chief in the west], which they seem to imagine will be around Thursday week at the latest. Any Canadians who happen to be present when this little jaunt is outlined usually smile with the same weary irony of men who thought much the same thing two years and several hundred pints of beer ago.'

By the time the GIs did have their 'date with von Rundstedt' two and a half years later, there were 1,500,000 American combat and service troops, 500,000 Canadians, and thousands of troops from Occupied Europe stationed 'over here' in an island with a population of 48,000,000, that, as the Americans were fond of pointing out, was smaller than the State of Oregon.

At the outbreak of war the US army comprised 185,000 men as compared to the 6,000,000-8,000,000 in the German army. None of its units had a full complement of men. No infantry division approached its combat strength. There was not a single armoured division: the total number of men in scattered in tank units was less than 1,500 while the entire embryonic Army Air Corps consisted of 1,175 planes designed for combat and 17,000 men to service, maintain and fly them. As General Dwight D. Eisenhower, who was to become Supreme Commander of the Allied Forces in Europe, and would be in charge of the D-Day landings pointed out, 'When the nation began in 1939 [the] first steps towards strengthening its military establishment, it started from a position as close to zero as a great nation could conceivably allow itself to sink.'

In the face of considerable opposition, Congress passed a Selected Service Act in September 1940, three months after the Fall of France. Of the nearly 8,500,000 men in the US Army at its peak strength in 1945, over 7,000,000 men had been drafted, or

The GIs go marching in. A US Army brass band parades through a Cornish village in 1942.

'selected' as the Army preferred to call it. The GI army that came to Britain was a mixture of draftees, regular servicemen and members of the National Guard - but most of them had been drafted into the army as civilians and turned out as soldiers wearing two dog tags round their necks giving their name and service number.

The recruits were sent to training camps scattered around the country where they found a situation not dissimilar to that of the British troops after Dunkirk: shortage of equipment. Much of the military hardware in the early days was strictly First World War stuff, including ancient tanks - though there were so few tanks available for training purposes that not infrequently soldiers trained using trucks hung with a cardboard sign saying TANK, whilst saplings hacked from around the training ground were used to represent guns when there weren't enough to go round. Thomas Todd who trained at Camp Reynolds in Pennsylvania had to go through exactly the same assault course as an infantryman even though he had been selected for a desk job as a German interpreter:

> It was unlikely that we would ever tackle anything heavier than a typewriter or sharper than a pencil. We fired M1s [rifles], charged strawbags, bayoneted them, uttering ear-splitting yells as we did so. We crawled through ditches and under barbed wire with live ammunition zipping overhead and shells exploding in the distance. There was little need for instructors to scream at us to keep our heads down. Mine almost became part of the landscape...but everything has a beginning, a middle and an end, and eventually we were released from the horrors of

" Dear Momma, in England they drive on the left side of the road . . ."

the course. We had, according to the army, 'been toughened up' and most of us by that time had learned how to clean a latrine, scrub a garbage can until you could see your face in it, make your bed so tight a quarter could bounce on it, keep your barrack window sill so clean a white glove could wipe it and stay white, force your eyes to stay open during lectures on venereal disease and never, never, never volunteer.

In 1942 it took exactly twelve months to train a division from scratch: forty-four weeks of individual unit training followed by eight weeks of exercises and manoeuvres. Then it was time to put into practice the first thing that a GI had been taught in the army: 'Hurry up and wait.'

From their training camps the soldiers destined for D-Day - and after - were sent to one of the hastily erected camps on the east coast which processed men for the insatiable demands of the war in Europe.

The Atlantic crossing was made in a merchant vessel, a Liberty ship, or an ocean-going liner - Churchill had offered Roosevelt the use of the two great *Queens, Mary* and *Elizabeth*, to speed the movement of troops across the Atlantic, as well as whatever merchant shipping was available. There was no such thing as a comfortable crossing as the soldiers sailed into war. The luxury peacetime liners were adapted with tiers of four bunks per single cabin and even so there were so many men travelling that they often had to sleep in shifts. 'It was a twilight world of multi-tiered bunks where the company had little room to move except in unison,' recalls an infantry officer, Charles Cawthon, and it wasn't much better for the officers either: 'A dozen of us were shoe-horned into double-tiered bunks in a richly panelled cabin originally designed for a privileged couple.' But it wasn't only comfort that was compromised: 16,000 men travelled in the liners that had lifeboats for only 8,000. 'If the ship had been hit', wrote a weapon sergeant with the 291st Engineer Battalion, Henry Giles, 'we would have drowned like rats we were packed so close.'

At a cracking twenty-eight-and-a-half knots it took an ocean liner like the *Mauretania* only about six days to cross the Atlantic whereas the Liberty ships, which had been developed as emergency freighters built in sections and welded together, the decks piled high with men and equipment, took nearer twice that time. But to the consternation of their military passengers, many of the ships travelled without convoy escort except in and out of harbour. A corporal from New York was horrified to realise that 'there is but three-quarters of an inch of steel now between me and the ocean: that the steel was made by man, and that other men in turn seek even now to break down that sheet and allow the sea to swallow all.' The ships steered a zigzag course changing direction every four and seven minutes. In fact troop ships were rarely attacked and continued to travel without convoy protection on most voyages. In June 1945 it was estimated that of the 4,453,061 soldiers sent to Europe, only 0.024 per cent had been lost at sea.

As they filed aboard their ships in New York or Boston, the troops were handed a letter that looked as if it had been personally written by the President on White House notepaper reminding them, if reminder were needed, that 'You are a soldier in the United States Army. You have embarked for distant places were the war is being fought,' yet the troops were still not told their destination as they sailed into that war.

> Since your ship left port you have been in a war zone…You will find that all Britain is a war zone and has been since September 1939. The British have been bombed night after night…thousands of them have lost their house, their possessions and their families…The British will welcome you as friends and allies. But remember, crossing the ocean doesn't automatically make you a hero…There are housewives in aprons and youngsters in knee pants who have lived through more high explosives in air raids than many soldiers saw in first-class barrages in the last war.

Ed Murrow, the CBS correspondent, broadcast nightly from London throughout most of the war. It was said that Murrow's words were an important factor in swinging American opinion towards the Allied cause and encouraging US involvement in that cause, but nevertheless the signs of war that they encountered the moment they docked at Liverpool, Belfast or Greenock shocked the GIs deeply. Ralph Martin, who had come to Britain as a combat reporter for *Stars and Stripes*, the newspaper distributed to the US troops noted the barrage balloons first 'hanging ugly in the sky, spoiling the picture postcard' and Robert Arbib, a US engineer, realized that he was in a war zone at last when he saw

> barrage balloons, moored to barges in the river. We saw a freighter with a gaping torpedo hole at the waterline. We noticed little camouflaged naval craft and one

large aircraft carrier moored at Greenock harbour…We looked for traces of war, and discussed the evidence of bomb damage that lay all around us…we hadn't heard that Glasgow had been bombed and we were not sure that the occasional open space between buildings, a gutted building, was a sign of the Blitz. We soon discovered that they were indeed bomb-damaged.

Bill Ong, who arrived in Britain in April 1942 to help build an airfield in East Anglia was appalled by what he saw:

> There is no way of describing to an audience who doesn't have the experience…I remember only too well how shocked we were when we disembarked at the sight of all that bomb damage. And if that wasn't enough, I guess it was the whole atmosphere of dirt and dinginess around the docks.

If the GIs had come from a country untouched directly by war damage, they had also come from a land of plenty. Food rationing had only begun to take effect in the States in the autumn of 1942 with constraints on the consumption of coffee and sugar. As their ships pulled into British ports they would often toss apples, oranges, chocolate and cigarettes down to those waiting on the quayside.

Clambering into the trains which were to take them to camps all over Britain, the GIs had time to consider what their *Short Guide* told them:

> For many months the British have been doing without things which the Americans take for granted…You are coming to Britain from a country where your home is still safe, food is plentiful, and the lights are still burning. So it is doubly important for you to remember that British soldiers and civilians have been under tremendous strain. Sixty thousand British civilians - men, women and children - have died under bombs and yet the morale of the British is unbreakable and high. A nation doesn't come through if it doesn't have plain common guts - you won't be able to tell the British much about 'taking it'. They are not particularly interested in taking it anymore. They are far more interested in getting together a solid friendship with us so we can all start dishing it to Hitler.

This 'solid friendship' was something that both the British and American governments wanted to forge, both because of the military co-operation which would be essential to 'dish Hitler' in a combined Allied assault, and also to ensure economic and political co-operation in the post-war world - an agenda particularly on Churchill's mind given the Allied wartime reliance on the Soviet Union and how that might translate into peacetime gains.

The impact of the GIs on British society was instant: as one of their number, William Bostick, wrote:

> To the British our mass arrival, however necessary, must have been a constant inconvenience. Most of us did not stop to realize this. At least, not often. We were in the main young, bumptious, good-natured, though demanding, dough-heavy, homesick, hitherto untravelled and in everyway hungry. We presented an acute problem in supplies, no less than space and hospitality.

'I opened with a gag I sometimes used to close with a story...you men know what a barrack is...it's a crap game with bunks'. Bob Hope toured US bases in Britain entertaining the troops, 'the American boys were so hungry for familiar faces...even if it was only my face...it was almost impossible not to please them'.

Accommodation needed to be found - or built - for the US forces, depot space located for storage and services, and hospitals, airfields and training assault courses constructed and it was these facilities that the first GIs had come over to prepare. Over a period of time the GIs came to occupy 100,000 buildings in 11,000 locations. At first the problem of supplies and accommodation was dealt with by taking over and adapting accommodation from the British Army and Air Force and erecting Nissen huts and bell tents around airfields in the course of construction, and supply depots. Officers often lived in private houses, but this was regarded as an emergency measure for enlisted men - though it became more frequent as the number of troops increased and particularly with the concentration of troops in the south of England as D-Day approached.

The assertion made by some GIs that 'we've come over to win the war for you,' was hardly popular, but it was what a lot of the British fervently hoped. Robert Arbib, who had come with the 820th Company Engineers to build airfields, recalls the delight of the locals in a small Suffolk village when they heard 'the work on our aerodrome is about to begin at last...we're going to have a great new bomber aerodrome, and thousands of American soldiers and airmen. And bombers flying right over Berlin to pay those Jerries back! Surely the tide of the war is turning today!'

The first priority of the US Army Air Force in Britain was to join in the fighting in order both to demonstrate the American commitment to the Allied war effort, to assuage criticism of Americans being 'armchair soldiers', late-comers to the war effort, and also to test the efficacy of daylight precision bombing in an attempt to knock out the industrial base of German war production and thus minimize the number of troops and matériel that would have to be thrown into ground combat. It was a policy diametrically opposed to that of the RAF who followed a course of night-time saturation bombing aimed at destroying German cities and destroying the morale of the people. To mount the USAAF raids into Occupied Europe and ultimately into Germany meant preparing the flatlands of East Anglia as a launch pad for the mighty US bombers, the B-17 Flying Fortresses and B-24 Liberators which would have sunk into the mud of the RAF grass airstrips. During 1942 £6,500,000 was spent on new airfields and rehabilitating and concreting old ones - a job which involved immense quantities of material and large numbers of men. Bud Hutton, a correspondent for *Stars and Stripes* reported: 'Across the green fields of England, from before dawn to late at night, US engineers are pouring concrete and steel and sweat into one of the most gigantic building projects ever undertaken anywhere.'

An airfield like the one at Thorpe Abbots in Norfolk took some thousand workers about seven months to complete at a cost of £1,000,000: it stretched over 500 acres; the main runway - there were three - was 6,300 feet, one of the longest in Britain: the 300 individual buildings, three-and-a-half miles of sewers, five miles of water mains and fourteen and a half miles of drains housed and serviced four bombardment squadrons consisting of 3,500 men. By 1944, on average, there was was an airfield every eight miles throughout East Anglia and over 100,000 acres of high-yield farmland had been commandeered in Norfolk alone.

Robert Arbib watched with regret as the countryside disappeared

> as a result of our relentless handiwork. As each new field was invaded by our crushing machines, as each new hedgerow was smashed and uprooted and shattered, as each great oak succumbed before axe and dynamite and bulldozer, we felt a pang. For there is nothing quite as final, as levelling as an aerodrome...Whatever had stood there before was lost...The war wrecked these...farmers' monuments just as surely as the bombs wrecked the monuments of architects and stonemasons when they exploded beautiful churches in London.

Training grounds for US forces were established along the Devon and Cornish coasts and the west coast of Scotland. Few parts of the country save the remoter parts of northern Scotland and north Wales escaped the impact of the 'friendly invasion'. Farmland was requisitioned in Hampshire and the Home Counties, buildings - suitable and less suitable - warehouses, barns, disused breweries, schools and country houses were taken over for men, a very few women, and supplies.

On his second visit to London in 1943, the American journalist, Ernie Pyle, was struck at the extent to which the capital

The wallpaper of war. A US 8th Air Force airman has a trim in a Nissen-hut barber's shop almost obscured by pin ups at the 381st Bomber Group base at Ridgewell in Suffolk.

was crawling with Americans, both Army and civilian...The section where American offices were most highly concentrated was a funny sight at lunchtime or in the late afternoon. Floods of American uniforms poured out of the buildings. On some streets, an Englishman stood out as incongruously as he would in North Platte, Nebraska...There were all kinds of cracks about the way the Americans had flooded the island and nearly crowded the English off...One said to another, 'The English are beginning to act as if the country belonged to them.'

The area around Piccadilly became a honeypot for GIs on furlough, because of Rainbow Corner, the most famous of all the 'Islands of Little America' established all over London and the rest of the country by the American Red Cross to cater for the GIs at leisure. It provided entertainment, American music and opportunities to dance US-style, jitterbugging to the music of the big band sound from Glenn Miller playing 'Moonlight Serenade,' 'Chattanooga Choo Choo,' 'At Last,' 'Don't Fence Me In,' 'When the Swallows Come Back to Capistrano'; Tommy Dorsey swinging with 'I'll Never Smile Again,' Jimmy Dorsey with 'I Remember You': the music of Benny Goodman and Artie Shaw: songs like 'Don't Sit Under the Apple Tree (with anyone else but me),' 'In the Mood,' 'All or Nothing at All,' 'Someone's Rocking My Dreamboat'.

Grosvenor Square was rechristened 'Eisenhowerplatz' since the headquarters of the European Theater of Operations United States of America (ETOUSA)was housed at number 20, whilst many of the elegant Georgian houses all around were commandeered as offices, housing and recreation facilities for US administrative staff. The English Speaking Union, housed an American Officers' club as did several other distinguished buildings nearby. The writers Robert and Madeleine Henrey lived in Shepherd's Market, just round the corner, which for them was still a village of shops and people they knew.

> The Americans came to our village in the chilly fogs of March [1942]. They wore battle dress and forage caps and hailed from anywhere and everywhere between Oregon and Maine and North Dakota and Texas. After dark they moved like shadows along Piccadilly straining their eyes, unaccustomed to the blackout, for a feminine shape to engage in conversation. They stood in little groups…humming tunes we Londoners didn't recognize. They talked in low tones, as if fearful to break the silence of the night, and their accent lingered in our ears.

GIs patronized British pubs with enthusiasm, despite their oft-stated contempt for warm, flat British beer, which vied with the weather, the mud and British food - 'Brussels sprouts, old mutton, Spam, powdered eggs, dehydrated potatoes and strong tea' - for top billing in the list of things the US troops didn't like about life 'over here'. To the chagrin of the local population the men would descend on the village pub and have drunk it dry by halfway through the evening and, an official report recorded, 'this is causing very considerable resentment' particularly among 'the agricultural workers who…are working long hours and cannot get to the public houses as early as the American troops.'

Not that there was often a great deal else to do, particularly in the early days before the American Red Cross Clubs had started up and British families had begun to issue invitations to the far-from-home soldiers and airmen.

Rationing had been a restraint to the generosity of many British families who recognized that the GIs were often very young men, as far as 6,000 miles from home, homesick and unsure of their future, who would welcome a dose of ersatz family life once in a while. And this was something that both British and US authorities were to encourage, both as a positive step towards better understanding in Anglo-American relations, and as a check on the young servicemen's propensity to drink too much and indulge in reckless sexual behaviour which sent VD rates soaring to a worrying level. GIs were encouraged to accept invitations into British homes, and the invitations were encouraged by enabling the men to turn up with tins of ham, canned peaches, candies, cigarettes and bourbon - and, of course, chewing gum for the children - bought from the PX or issued as 'hospitality packs' by the 'invaders'.

But for probably a majority of young women for whom the war seemed endless - and sometimes hopeless - the GIs were 'as good as a tonic'. A female Red Cross volunteer in Norwich remembers her feelings: the GIs 'brought with them colour, romance, warmth - and a tremendous hospitality to our dark and shadowed land.' A British serviceman, Eric Westman, observed:

> The Yanks were the most joyful thing that ever happened to British womanhood…they had everything - money in particular, glamour, boldness, cigarettes,

chocolates, nylons, Jeeps - and genitalia. The Yanks were sex-mad and countless British women who had virtually no experience in this line were completely bowled off their feet (and on to their backs, I suppose I should add). It was astonishing how such vast quantities of women of all ages and stations fell for them: almost every working girl aspired to 'have a Yank.' Apart from their Hollywood-style glamour which they played to great effect, they were stupendously rich by the British servicemen's standards and could treat girls to things that were beyond the Britons' ability...I think that never in history has there been such a conquest of women by men as was won by the American Army in Britain in World War II.

Most British women had never encountered a real live American before the GIs arrived: their images were derived from the films they'd seen depicting America as a land of chromium-plated sophistication and elegance. The GIs' smart uniform of pink and olive drab which 'fitted in all the right places' contrasted favourably with the ill-fitting, shapeless felt-like khaki of the British soldier's uniform, and exuded an air of confident prosperity which was reinforced by their relative wealth - in June 1942 a British private was paid 14 shillings a week whereas a private in the US Army received £3 8s 9d - nearly five times as much. There were, of course, deductions made, but no British serviceman received an overseas allowance when he was posted abroad, neither did he enjoy recreational facilities equivalent to the GIs' clubs and dance halls, nor the bounty of their PXs, where US servicemen could buy things like Camel cigarettes, whisky, candy, nylon stockings and scent. Such things had long ago disappeared from the shelves of war-rationed British shops and were no hindrance in the GIs' ardent pursuit of British girls and the good times they could give them at the innumerable dances held on bases and at church halls when local women were transported in US Army trucks - referred to as 'passion wagons' on such occasions - for an unforgettable evening of swing music and jitterbugging.

Over 80,000 British women were to become GI brides by the end of the war, and many more lasting friendships were formed. But an estimated 24,000 babies fathered by GIs out of wedlock were born during and just after the war. A rather bitter 'Lament of a Limey Lass' did the rounds:

> *Yanks say they've come to shoot and fight*
> *It's true they fight...yes when they're tight*
> *I must agree their shooting's fine,*
> *They shoot a damn good Yankee line.*
>
> *They tell us we have teeth like pearls,*
> *They love our hair, the way it curls,*
> *Our eyes would dim the brightest stars,*
> *Our figures like Hedy Lamarr's.*
>
> *And then he leaves you broken-hearted,*
> *The camp has moved - your love departed -*
> *You wait for mail that doesn't come,*
> *Then realize you're awfully dumb.*

Chorus
It's a different town - a different place -
To a different girl - a different face,
'I love you darling - please be mine',
It's the same old Yank - the same old line.

To which a GI responded:

The way we dance, the way we sing,
The way we do most everything,
The only thing we do that's right
Is spend our money left and right.

and crisply informed British girls:

With Yankee girls you can't compare,
The difference is, you're here, they're there.

Official US policy discouraged wartime marriages particularly if the serviceman was marrying abroad. A single man undistracted by family responsibilities was considered more likely to be single-minded in his war effort, and more likely to forge the strong ties with his 'buddies' that could generate the selflesss courage that war might demand. It was common currency, too, that wartime marriages were doomed to failure (in fact the evidence rather contradicted this: it was estimated that some eighty per cent of the 8,000 marriages contracted overseas during the First World War were successful - or at least had lasted). And there was public opinion back home, which was hardly enthusiastic about having the flower of American manhood return from foreign wars accompanied by foreign wives, at the expense of American women seeking husbands. In June 1942, the US War Department issued a regulation requiring troops stationed overseas to seek the approval of their Commanding Officer two months in advance of a proposed wedding. Larry McLaughlin, a US Captain stationed at Tichborn Manor, had the responsibility of interviewing any GI who wanted to marry a British girl.

We were directed to interview them together and explain to the girl that this man she was interested in marrying was going into combat and there was a good possibility that he might get seriously wounded or killed. And we wanted that fact brought very clearly to their attention. Most of the girls more or less said that they would still like to go ahead with the marriage.

Of course, there were cases of girls being shown photographs of 'sisters' who were really wives, and the personal effects of one man shot down on a mission were said to have revealed that not only was he married back home in Michigan, but in London and Kings Lynn too. It was clear that absence made the heart more accommodating, and for some GIs it was a case of 'If you can't be near the one you love, then love the one you're near.' 'We never had any cases of anyone trying bigamy in my unit,' says Larry McLaughlin,

but there were married men who played around, but we considered that it was their off-duty time and we didn't interfere. And there were sometimes pregnancies, of course. It put these women in a very difficult situation, but going into

Making it with the natives. A GI marries a local Cornish woman.

combat sort of resolved it. The problem became secondary in our objectives. Sometimes the parents of the girl would contact the Commanding Officer asking him to resolve the situation, but there was no easy way out. It was one of my most difficult jobs. I'd much rather be in really tough training for combat than having to listen to some mother or father who was upset about what had happened to their daughter.

The GIs' vade mecum to British life warned them:

You will naturally be interested in getting to know your opposite number, the British soldier, the 'Tommy' you have heard and read about. You can understand that two actions on your part will slow up this friendship - swiping his girl, and not appreciating what his army's been up against. Yes, and rubbing it in that you are better paid than he is.

The *Short Guide* stressed the importance of this in the context of fighting the war:

You are going to Great Britain as part of an Allied offensive - to meet Hitler and beat him on his own ground...America and Britain are allies. Hitler knows that they are both powerful countries, tough and resourceful. He knows that they...mean his crushing defeat in the end. So it is only common sense to under-stand that the first and major duty Hitler has given his propaganda chiefs is to

" Officer, how do we get to the native quarter ? "

separate Britain and America and spread distrust. If he can do that, his chances of winning might return...

There was distrust when it came to women: the majority of young British women's husbands or boyfriends were away fighting or posted on essential war work for at least part of the war, and there was natural anxiety - boosted whenever possible by salacious and threatening German propaganda - that the women left behind might do less to 'keep the home fires burning', and rather more to 'drift', in the language of the time, into collaboration with the friendly - and well-off - invaders. A nineteen-year-old nurse from Exeter had a typical story: 'Sometimes the hospital staff would put on a dance, but of course there weren't many of our boys left in town, so we invited the American soldiers...they were so friendly and everything turned into fun.'

And even those British men still 'left in town', or stationed nearby, could feel ousted from the centre stage of young women's interest. An ATS girl stationed in Wales recalls an evening when an American truck arrived at camp:

> About fifteen girls had primped themselves up - as far as khaki would allow - for the occasion. As we piled into the substantial truck there were, of course, catcalls from a few of our own soldiers who happened to be nearby and shouts of 'the Yanks have plenty of dough. No hope for us now!'

The GIs were in Britain to mount an Allied offensive and that meant US and British troops fighting together - or at least alongside - which is what happened. It was not a prospect which reassured either side in 1942.

There was a very understandable basis for animosity which was often reinforced by observation. Harold Nicolson recognized the heart of the matter: 'Whereas for us Anglo-American co-operation means security, for them it suggests danger.' Although on the whole entry of the US into the war after Pearl Harbor was welcomed by the British people, Mass-Observation noted 'a malicious delight that at long last the Americans would have a taste of war' and contempt for a nation that 'went to war when they are directly threatened, after a year in which they seemed content to let other people do their fighting for democracy'.

The historian Laurence Lafore who arrived from Washington to work for the US Information Service in London, offered a diagnosis : 'We were Johnny-come-latelies, that explained the peculiar form of self-defence against Americans that the British constantly presented to us: simultaneously to criticize us for not having arrived on the scene sooner while denouncing us for arriving at all.'

And in March 1942 a commentator for Mass-Observation added a further gloss:

> Americans are often regarded as a rather eccentric kind of Englishmen [and this] comes out in people's feeling that the Americans ought really to have been helping us right through the early part of the war, just like the Canadians and Australians...America is not really regarded as a foreign country to be wooed with praise, but as a close relative to be freely chided for her shortcomings.

The writer and journalist George Orwell regretted that he

> rarely saw American and British soldiers together. Quite obviously the major cause of this difference is pay. You can't have really close and friendly relations with someone whose income is five times your own. In the field this may not matter, but in the training period, it makes it almost impossible for the British and American soldier to fraternize.

This was true: but in addition neither side was inclined to trust the military capability of the other - and in combat that was going to matter. An infantryman from Chicago who arrived in Britain in March 1943 explained that though he felt great sympathy for the British, he had mixed feelings:

> They've taken an awful beating. And yet, nothing happens, day after day. If New York had been bombed the way that London has been, every man, woman and child would have been working day and night to whack whoever'd done it. I don't say that America takes the war more seriously than England does, but if that had happened in America, we wouldn't have taken it so quietly, we'd be yelling for their blood AND GETTING IT. The English have got so passive, I don't know how it is.

The GIs were apt to taunt the British about 'running away at Dunkirk' (to which they soon added the jibe about 'running away at Tobruk' too). A woman working in an office in Sutton Coldfield during the war recalls that whenever the immensely popular patriotic song 'There'll Always Be An England' was played on the radio, the Americans would intone 'As long as we're here to defend it for you.'

If the GIs thought that the British were passive soldiers, over-fond of teabreaks and with mindless deference to authority, Robert Raymond, a US pilot who had joined the RAF on the outbreak of war, was in despair at the effect, as he saw it, of the British class system on the military:

> I sometimes feel that Britain does not deserve to win this war. Never have I seen such class distinctions drawn and maintained in the face of a desperate effort to

preserve a democracy. With powers of regulation and control invariably centred in the hands of the few, abuse and preservation of the old school tie is stronger than ever on every side...It has well and truly been said that General Rommel of the German Army's Afrika Korps would never have risen above the rank of NCO in the British Army. The nation seems inexplicably proud of the defects in its national character.

If the Americans were wary about the British at war, the feeling was mutual. It was widely believed that America had been 'caught napping' at Pearl Harbor and Laurence Lafore discovered that

> the fact of being bombed generates a certain condescension towards those people who haven't. To this kind of condescension [the British] could add the pride of having Stood Alone plus their fully justified assurance that they knew a great deal more about the technical business of fighting a war than we did. We were automatically tenderfeet and due humility was expected of us.

On arrival in Britain the GIs did little to reasure many of the those who saw them as 'soft...degenerate...The hardship and conflict of war will do them a lot of good.' The GIs' 'unbloodied by conflict...armchair soldiers', appeared 'slovenly' to British eyes. Those who had watched them disembark had been particularly struck by the way 'the troops marched off in a curious silence on their rubber-soled shoes - it was more like a soft-shoed shuffle than a march.' The GIs' habit of chewing gum as they marched and 'even breaking ranks to pick poppies from the roadside', appalled British onlookers. The Americans' military bearing was particularly shocking to the older generation. An East Anglian woman recalls 'My father had been a sergeant in the 1914-18 war, and he was very disparaging when he saw them marching through our village street: "What a shower! They can't march to save their lives." '

Another complaint to compound the charge of being 'Over-paid, over-sexed and over here,' was that the GIs were 'over-medalled'. Jokes were made on the subject - 'Heard the one about the Yanks who went to a war film? One fainted and the other got a medal for carrying him out.' A soldier in the Queen's Own Royal West Kent Regiment thought that the GIs' uniforms were 'superb' and added that

> they even got a few medals for merely coming over; rumour had it they got them for using the jakes and for catching the pox [and, others claimed, for eating Brussels sprouts]...but they were certainly not soldiers. More goes into soldiering than wearing a fancy uniform: it is discipline and endurance among other things.

Jean Rennie Lancaster, who was able to observe the GIs at close quarters in the American Red Cross Club where she worked, tried to explain these misapprehensions

> ...We thought, 'They're too happy'...the British soldier always looks serious in his uniform: he knows only too well what it stands for. After all, we've been invaded before: the whole of the Empire is built on war. So it doesn't seem that these carefree, talkative, wolf-whistling GIs are going to be much use against the mad arrogance of Adolf Hitler.

Often there was no time to say goodbye...A GI camp hastily abandoned when the order came to move towards the embarkation area for D-Day .

And Margaret Mead, the anthropologist, who been sent to Britain by the US govenment in 1943 to try to explain the Americans to the British when relations between GIs and the civilian population were causing concern, tried to translate their body language:

> Americans don't set the same store that the British do on standing upright, and see no harm in taking the weight off their feet by leaning against the nearest wall. [The British] will judge the Americans they see leaning against a wall as undisciplined, spineless, low-grade people...but they would be wrong, because leaning against a wall doesn't mean the same thing.

This laid-back attitude seemed to affect the GIs' attitude to their superiors, to British consternation.

'They were all buddies,' recalls a Dorset woman. 'It didn't matter what rank they were, they were always friends. A private would go up to an officer and say, "Hi Bud, can I borrow your Cadillac?" and the officer would hand over the keys to his Jeep.'

A correspondent writing to a Cambridge newspaper after the war thought that this 'Hiya Sarge' attitude would have serious consequences: 'The GIs were cheerful, chatty, not over-disciplined - which we thought, morosely, would be a bad thing. Fancy going to war and treating your officers as "buddies".'

'Official Sources' sought to reassure: the GIs' *Short Guide* cautioned:

> Don't be misled by the British tendency to be soft-spoken and polite. If they need to be, they can be plenty tough. The English language didn't spread across the oceans and over the mountains and jungles and swamps of the world because these people were panty-waists [cissies].

A pamphlet issued by the Ministry of Information was - half - helpful: 'Unlike the German, in particular, who runs his "civvy life" as if he were in the army...the American soldier's mind is still in "civvies" even when his body is in uniform.'

Whilst the booklet *Meet the US Army* written by the poet Louis MacNeice for the British, recognized that 'while some...eyewitnesses...are somewhat shocked by [the GIs'] informality, it should be borne in mind that

> in action the US army is noted for its stern discipline...this army has a victorious history [which] has been unduly ignored in our schools, possibly because many of its victories have been won at our expense...Both the British and American armies are exceedingly tough...and when you meet a doughboy, don't be misled by his easy line of talk, his wisecracks...into thinking that he has any illusions about what he is here for. He regards your island as a halfway house to the front - and he knows what the front will be like.

The first 'front' that the British and American troops attacked in a combined operation was in November 1942, when the largest amphibious assault so far in the history of warfare deploying over 200 warships, 350 merchant ships, and 70,000 men, Operation TORCH, landed on the coast of North Africa. An American, General Dwight D. Eisenhower, was in supreme control of the landings; the commanders were all British - it was the same command structure that would plan - and execute - the D-Day landings.

CHAPTER FOUR

PLANNING AND DECEIVING

ONE SUNDAY EVENING IN early September 1943, Lieutenant-General Omar Bradley took a stroll through London's Hyde Park. The newly-appointed Commanding General of the American First Army in north-west Europe had arrived in Britain for the first time only a couple of days before, so he decided to 'see something of the British people.' Near Marble Arch, he came across the crowd around a soapbox orator at Speaker's Corner. A 'handsome but aged Briton appealed to his listeners to demand that England "open a Second Front".' Bradley turned away, reflecting 'how little comprehension the speaker had of what the "Second Front" entailed, of the labours that would be required to mount it.'

In January 1943 Roosevelt and Churchill had had their third meeting of the war in Casablanca in North Africa. The meeting followed the relative success of Operation TORCH, the first joint major Allied landing when over 70,000 British and American troops landed on the beaches of Oran, Algiers and Casablanca in November 1942.

It was a meeting that had two agenda. The British Chiefs of Staff were determined to follow up their incursion into North Africa with another stab at the 'soft underbelly' of Europe by attempting a landing in Sicily. For their part, the American military commanders were reluctant to countenance another 'Mediterranean side-show'. This divergence reflected the fundamental difference between the American and British views of how to win the Second World War. A cross-Channel invasion of Europe was axiomatic to US policy. The Americans demonstrated 'an impatience to get on with direct offensive action as well as a belief…that the war could most efficiently be won by husbanding resources for an all-out attack deliberately planned for a future fixed date, [which] was in contrast to British willingness to proceed one step at a time, moulding a course of action to the turn of military fortune,' in the assessment of the official American history of the Second World War. In addition Churchill's anticipation of the post-war spread of Bolshevism made him anxious to prevent the Russian Red Army from liberating, and thereby claiming to control, eastern Europe: his plan for a British and American attack through Yugoslavia, Greece and Italy would, he reckoned, have thwarted that possibility.

To the Americans, Churchill's engagement in a series of Mediterranean and Balkan excursions was a diversionary tactic which owed much to a political desire to preserve the British Empire. In practical terms it also endangered the success of the main military thrust by diverting men and resources that were essential to mount a cross-Channel attack at the earliest opportunity.

It was a delicate political situation as Henry Stimson, US Secretary of War, realistically recognized:

> We cannot rationally hope to cross the Channel and come to grips with our German enemy under a British commander. The Prime Minister and the Chief of the Imperial General Staff are frankly at variance with such a proposal. The shadows of Passchendaele and Dunkirk still hang too heavily over the imagination of these leaders of government.

However at Casablanca both sides made concessions: the Americans reluctantly condoned the launching of Operation HUSKY, an Allied landing in Sicily, and allowed for the possibility of further operations in Italy, whilst the British Chief of the Imperial General Staff, Sir Alan Brooke, pledged that 'We could definitely count on re-entering the continent in 1944 on a large scale.'

Lieutenant-General Sir Frederick Morgan was appointed to the newly-created post of Chief of Staff to the Supreme Allied Commander (Designate) (COSSAC) on 12 March 1943 and given the task of drawing up detailed plans to make the Allies' intention to 're-enter the continent in 1944 on a large scale' happen. He was well aware of Anglo-American tension in the wake of the Casablanca Conference.

The British, he wrote, were 'not pleased at having to commit themselves to the cross-Channel adventure more than a year ahead of time...sticking their necks out more than they had ever stuck them before.'

Whereas the Americans

> having decided to go to war [were] determined to fight a bigger and better war than had ever been fought before...[and] in certain American quarters there was...the gravest possible doubt about the honesty of intentions on the part of British strategists who kept nattering about Rome and all kinds of wildcat adventures to be based in the Balkans [whereas] their eyes were fixed on the German target...Their main idea was to hit quick, switch rapidly to deal with Japan and get back to business.

The last thing the Americans had crossed the Atlantic for was to get embroiled in a series of small-scale European adventures and they remained sceptical about the drain of men and matériel to the Mediterranean theatre, in their view at the expense of a cross-Channel invasion - though in fact the build-up of US troops, Operation BOLERO, had slowed down to something more like a slow waltz: by the summer of 1943 there were still only 238,000 American troops in the UK.

The balance was taut: the next time Roosevelt and Churchill met for a war summit was in Washington in May 1943. Here the Joint Chiefs of Staff agreed to allow for the possibility of troops being deployed in Italy following a Sicilian landing providing priority was given to Operation ROUNDUP (the original plan for an Anglo-American invasion of France in early 1943), a firm date for the cross-Channel attack was fixed and divisions were withdrawn from the Mediterranean Theatre for the purpose. The date was to be 1 May 1944: the operation was recoded OVERLORD, a name picked personally by Winston Churchill.

The D-Day Commanders. (Left to right, rear) Bradley, Ramsay, Leigh-Mallory, Bedell Smith, (seated, front) Eisenhower and Montgomery.

General Sir Alan Brooke, who was still writing pessimistic forecasts of OVERLORD's chances of success on the eve of D-Day, gave the forty-nine-year-old Morgan a terse directive: 'There it is...it won't work, but you'll bloody well have to make it work.'

To 'make it work' was a formidable task as Morgan settled with his Anglo-American team - his deputy was the US Army Major-General Ray W. Barker - into offices on the sixth floor of Norfolk House, a building in St James's Square on the site of the birthplace of George III, the monarch, who, the Americans would point out, lost the American War of Independence.

Decisions had to made about where the invasion would take place, what resources would be available, how these would be deployed, how the lessons of the failure of Dieppe could be implemented. The date of 1 May allowed just over twelve months for everything to be in place and COSSAC knew from the start that there was a major short-fall. It had been decided that ten divisions were required for the invasion, but there was only shipping to transport five.

The first question to be settled was where on the French coast should the Allied troops invade? The obvious place was the Pas de Calais: it lay only twenty-one miles across the Channel, which would make the vulnerable sea crossing short and the turn-around of landing craft quick. Landing at Calais would also offer the quickest route to Germany. But since Calais was the obvious place for a landing, the Germans had heavily fortified the port and the coastline bristled with pill boxes and gun emplacements. Dieppe had taught the Allies that they needed a harbour at least the size of Dover to land their troops and tanks, but the Wehrmacht had absorbed the same lesson and had worked to render Calais and Boulogne impregnable. The alternatives of Antwerp and Rouen were too far away to be practicable.

The COSSAC team plumped for a target further west along the French coast, the stretch of Normandy beaches around Caen which was much less heavily fortified and close to the major port of Cherbourg, allowing for easy access from the Atlantic for US troops to be transported directly once the area had been secured.

Working 'like beavers for months' and appalled by 'the paucity of resources we had to work with' but nevertheless aware that 'we went to Normandy or we stayed at home', Morgan and his team had formulated a plan by the time of the Quebec Conference in August 1943. A three-division seaborne assault was to be mounted along a thirty-mile front between Vierville-sur-Mer in the west to the River Orne in the east. Two airborne divisions would drop on the town of Caen as the tanks and assault troops were coming ashore. After securing the beaches the troops would wheel south towards Cherbourg which COSSAC targeted for capture on D-Day+8. By D-Day+14 there would be eighteen divisions fighting across Normandy, according to the plan.

Given the 'pitiful resources' on which the invasion was predicated, the COSSAC team recognized that the success of Operation OVERLORD depended on factors beyond their control. Enemy opposition had to be at a minimum: in Morgan's view 'German reserves in France and the Low Countries as a whole, excluding the divisions holding the coast...should not exceed on the day of the assault twelve full-strength, first-quality divisions.' So thinly spread would the Allied troops be that the calculation could be very precise. To make the whole thing feasible, Morgan cautioned, 'not more than twelve reserve, mobile field divisions should be available to the Germans in France - and...in the Caen area they should not have more than three of these divisions on D-Day.' ('What,' Stalin was to ask with heavy irony, 'if there are thirteen mobile divisions in France on D-Day - will this rule out OVERLORD?')

The realistic General Sir Alan Brooke applauded the plan, but considered that the rate of the projected troop advance inland was 'too optimistic', whilst Churchill conceded that his 'objections...to the cross-Channel operation were...now removed', but signalled the need to increase the landing craft by 'at least twenty-five per cent' for the first assault, and extend the front to permit landings on the eastern shore of the Cherbourg peninsula.

But Morgan and his team constituted a planning group: they had to operate within the parameters of existing resources. There had been reluctance to appoint a Supreme Commander a hypothetical exercise, but until that was done, there was no executive authority and Operation OVERLORD would remain an outline rather than a blueprint for invasion while German defences across the Channel strengthened month by month.

Throughout the autumn Anglo-American tensions over strategy simmered: the focus was Italy where only a heavy naval bombardment at Salerno had narrowly managed to prevent the US Fifth Army landings being driven back into the sea by German panzer divisions whilst Operation HUSKY in Sicily had been seriously threatened by bad weather and inexperienced air crews. These were all lessons that would prove useful in the planning for D-Day, but in the autumn of 1943 they epitomized the difference of approach of the Allies: for the British the very limited scale on which OVERLORD was being planned

**" I tell you, all this talk about
Hastings is deliberate bluff—I**

An Osbert Lancaster 'Pocket Cartoon'; drawn for the Daily Express *in spring 1944.*

made it imperative that the German forces should be drawn away from the Channel coast and engaged in diversionary battles in Italy and southern Europe: the US command drew exactly the reverse conclusion. OVERLORD would be in danger of failing if it was starved of the necessary Allied resouces because they were deployed elsewhere in Europe.

In November 1943, for the first time, the usual Allied wartime conference partnership of Churchill and Roosevelt was joined at Teheran by Stalin. And it was the Soviet leader leader, deeply sceptical of British intentions over the opening of the Second Front, who interrupted Churchill, as the British leader outlined his plans for southern Europe, to demand: 'Who will command OVERLORD?' and insist that until a Supreme Commander was appointed 'nothing will come of these plans'. He was promised that it would be settled within a fortnight.

It had already been agreed by Churchill and Roosevelt that the Supreme Command of D-Day was to go to an American. Britain might be the springboard into Europe: but it was the US that was the arsenal and would supply the majority of the troops - and the casualties - in the fight across Europe.

On 7 December 1943 General Dwight D. Eisenhower was summoned from Algiers to Tunis. He waited on the tarmac at Tunis airport for the Presidential plane, nicknamed 'Sacred Cow', to arrive from Cairo where Roosevelt had again been in conference with Churchill. Finally the US President - who had contracted polio as a young man - was hoisted in his wheelchair from the plane. Getting straight into the Presidential limousine, he turned to Eisenhower, 'Well, Ike, you're going to command OVERLORD,' he said.

'Just a co-ordinator, a good mixer, a champion of inter-Allied co-operation, and in those respects who can hold a candle to him?' Brooke scribbled in his diary, 'but is that enough?' Eisenhower was fifty-three at the time of his appointment; he was from Abilene, Kansas, and had risen from the rank of colonel to that of general in three years - without ever venturing on to the field of battle. It was not until he was flown over the Mareth line in North Africa by the RAF in the spring of 1943 that Eisenhower had ever seen a soldier killed in battle. He seemed to epitomize the American 'armchair soldier' who so unnerved the British and he was to be in charge of the most crucial military operation of the war. But over the next two years although there were always those to ready to snipe at him, Eisenhower, who defined his idea of leadership as 'pulling a piece of spaghetti across a plate, rather than trying to push it,' came in general to command the respect and admiration of British officers and men for his ability to work with an almost impossible power structure so that it could successfully mount an almost equally impossible military assault. Eisenhower arrived in London on 15 January 1944 with the unequivocal directive of the Combined Chiefs of Staff in Washington ringing in his ears: 'You will enter the continent of Europe and, in conjunction with other United Nations, undertake operations aimed at the heart of Germany and the destruction of her armed forces...'

How that 'entry' was going to happen, he had less than four months to finalize. From the start Eisenhower decided against locating the offices of SHAEF (Supreme Headquarters Allied Expeditionary Force) in central London. Instead he moved them out to Bushey Park near Hampton Court where a 'canvas city' had grown up, sheltering a variety of special services which soon totalled some 750 officers and 6,000 men at 'Widewing', the code name for Bushey Park.

The new supremo's first job was to get together with his Anglo-American team, sometimes a 'bunch of prima donnas' in his view, but also men Eisenhower had got to know during operations in the Mediterranean. The deputy Supreme Commander was to be Air Chief Marshal Sir Arthur Tedder, an appointment that reflected the crucial importance of air support for OVERLORD - a view held by Tedder himself who considered air power to be the decisive factor in the success for the entire war. For the past year Tedder had been Commander-in-Chief, Mediterranean Allied Air Forces, and had been responsible for the air operations in Sicily and Italy. Admiral Sir Bertram Ramsay, who had organized the evacuation of the BEF at Dunkirk and helped to plan the Allied landings in North Africa, was to command the Navy of the Expeditionary Force, whilst his opposite number for air was Air Chief Vice-Marshal Sir Trafford Leigh-Mallory who had been a key figure in the Battle of Britain and had been Air Force Commander of the Dieppe raid. Eisenhower brought the man who had been his Chief of Staff throughout the north African and Mediterranean campaigns, Lieutenant-General Walter Bedell Smith, to perform the same role in the OVERLORD operation, while Lieutenant-General Morgan found his position as COSSAC transmuted into that of a deputy Chief of Staff.

The person who was have the principal British role in OVERLORD was 'Monty,' General Sir Bernard Montgomery, the folk hero both of the 8th Army in the Western Desert and the British public too. The general who was an infantryman - 'a slight, erect figure in unpressed corduroys...and an unmilitary turtle necked sweater' - always wore the black beret of the Royal Armoured Corps and the cap badge of the Royal Tank regiment alongside his insignia of rank. It was Montgomery who was appointed Ground Commander of the Allied Armies - despite the fact that Eisenhower wanted General Alexander - but 'Alex' was said to be doing too important a job in the Mediterranean. The US First Army was placed under the control of Lieutenant-General Omar Bradley - who first knew of his appointment when he read it in the *Daily Express*. Its headquarters were located in Bristol, which Bradley noted, was 'the one-time maritime centre of the colonial slave trade'. The men lived and worked in an evacuated public school, Clifton College, where, inauspiciously, a statue of the First World War commander of the western front, Field-Marshal Earl Haig, 'overlooked the rugby field'.

Walter Bedell Smith, Eisenhower's Chief of Staff, had first learned of the proposals of the COSSAC plan for OVERLORD in November 1943 in Washington.

> Morgan gave the COSSAC plan. When he mentioned the puny little assault with three divisions, I nearly fell out of my seat. After all we had had more than that in all our landings. I told Eisenhower about it when I got back and he said, 'My God, if I were going to do it I would want ten or twelve divisions.'

The scope of COSSAC had to be extended drastically. Montgomery had been shown a copy by Churchill in Algiers on New Year's Eve 1943, and was of the same opinion. As Bedell Smith wrote: 'We were all unanimous. You might say that on the issue of broadening the base of the attack, the addition of divisions was accepted by acclamation. Freddy Morgan had wanted more but he had to work with what he had.'

When Montgomery went to St Paul's School, his alma mater and now his HQ, on 3 January 1944 for a briefing by the COSSAC staff, he effectively demolished their plan - or rather the scope of the plan - since the newly-appointed SHAEF commanders all agreed with Morgan that the area around Caen was where the invasion should take place. In essence Montgomery insisted on two things, and Eisenhower and Bedell Smith had independently come to the same conclusion - though subsequently Montgomery was to claim sole credit for the OVERLORD plan as it finally ran.

The assault was on too narrow a front - the stretch of coast between the Orne and the Vire was too restricted to allow the necessary landings to build up an Allied force in time to resist a German counter-attack - and the assault forces had be increased and better resourced. 'Give me five divisions, or get someone else to command,' Montgomery barked. As Bradley had observed the problem wasn't so much getting the men and tanks on to the beaches, it was making 'the invasion stick', and that was why it had to be possible to land many more forces across a wider front to permit the essential movement inland. The aim of OVERLORD was not to achieve a successful Dieppe landing on a grand scale - it was for the liberation of France and the defeat of Germany and that was the objective within which Allied strategy had to be framed.

Three weeks later on 23 January 1944 at a meeting at Norfolk House, Eisenhower accepted this logic. The assault force was to be enlarged to five seaborne divisions supported by three airborne divisions and two British Commando units plus two US Ranger detachments. The forces would land on a front extended westwards towards Cherbourg and including the planned parachute drop to the east near Ranville this would extend the front to nearer fifty miles rather than the original thirty envisaged by COSSAC. 'Nothing less', Eisenhower informed the Joint Chiefs of Staff in Washington, 'will give us an adequate margin for success.'

Once the blueprint for OVERLORD was in place, it became clear that more time was needed for the mammoth logistical task of marshalling the equipment and training the men for the assault, as well as filling in the fine brush strokes of the landings and building up as accurate a picture as possible of the situation the Allied troops would face on the 'far shore'. Eisenhower, anxious to campaign in France as much as possible before the winter closed in, was reluctant to delay D-Day but when the shortfall in landing craft, some of which were still deployed at Anzio in Italy, and many of which were, at the insistence of Admiral King, Chief of Staff, US Navy, in the Pacific, he realized that he had little option. At the end of January the date was put back a month until 1 June 1944 - though a close study of the moon and tides indicated that a date around 5 June would probably prove more propitious.

RAF Bomber Command and the US 8th Air Force which had been engaged in Operation POINTBLANK, the destruction of Germany industry in an attempt to paralyse the Nazi war effort, were switched in the spring of 1944 to attacking marshalling yards and railways that ran between Germany and France in an attempt to reduce the build-up of German forces and matériel in France prior to D-Day. The operations were very successful in these terms: by mid-May rail traffic between Germany and France had dropped by fifty per cent and low level strafing of trains and good yards in France further limited the rolling stock available to the Wehrmacht. But the cost in French lives was equally high - a factor which always influenced Churchill as he reckoned 'the cost to our Allies'.

D-Day was to be a joint Allied venture, but the US, British and Canadian troops were to fight separate battles on allocated beaches, establish a bridgehead and link up to fight inland. The US 1st Army would land furthest west, on beaches designated as 'Utah' and 'Omaha'; then would come the British 2nd Army which would land on 'Gold' and 'Sword' (the eastern flank) and the Canadian 3rd Army under the command of the British 21st Army Group was positioned for 'Juno' which lay between 'Sword' and 'Gold'.

'An operation of the magnitude of Operation OVERLORD has never been previously attempted in history. It is fraught with hazards, both in nature and magnitude, which do not obtain in any other theatre of the present world war,' Sir Frederick Morgan had written back in July 1943. Now there were precisely seventeen weeks from the acceptance of the final proposals for OVERLORD on 23 January and D-Day on 5 June to prepare the operation and anticipate and try to overcome the hazards. Enormously complex logistics were involved in equipping and transporting a force of nearly 200,000 men to land on the Normandy beaches. This first wave would be followed by deliveries of troops and resources to fight across France and into Germany. It seems now, as it must have done to the military planners in 1944, a task almost beyond human capabilities.

Not only was a vast assemblage of men, tanks, guns, and supplies of all sorts to be brought together for D-Day, but this had to be accomplished with the greatest secrecy. The Allies had two imperatives. The first was to try to find out as much as possible about what might await their forces on the coast of France: how effective was the legendary Atlantic Wall with which Hitler had protected his *Festung Europa*, fortifying it with bunkers, pill boxes and gun emplacements, which would be able to 'cover with fire the beaches and the sea off the beaches' so that when the expected invasion came it could be 'destroyed or thrown back into the sea by immediate counter attack'. The second was to ensure that although the Germans expected a cross-Channel invasion at some point in 1944, both the date and the location of the assault would take the German High Command by surprise.

Major-General Sir Percy Hobart, 79th Armoured Division, the man whose 'Funnies' were employed so effectively on D-Day.

The French coast had been under scrutiny since 1942. From the Bay of Biscay to the Belgian frontier British frogmen and swimmers slipped into the sea from small boats and clambered ashore to discover the ways in which the Germans were defending the beaches against an expected Allied invasion. Midget submarines and motor launches cruised the coast, too, collecting essential hydrographic information. At the same time high-flying aircraft took endless panoramic views of the French coast in a series of reconnaissance operations. When the films were brought back and developed, the details of rocks and sand dunes, breakwaters, gaps in the cliffs and what appeared to be pools of deep water, lighthouses and the spires of churches in the villages just inland, as well, of course, as of German defences and gun emplacements, were blown up so the planners could study every topographic feature that might help them.

Bunny Holden flew Spitfires with the No.16 Squadron on reconnaissance flights over Normandy for months before D-Day:

> I flew a Spitfire 9 which had square, sawn-off wings filled with petrol and no armaments and fitted with an large oblique camera pointing downwards which took photographs sideways so that we could get shots of the beaches...it was painted a salmon pink. The Spitfire 11 which were high-flying planes were painted sky blue, but salmon pink was reckoned to be the best colour for flying low along the beaches at different tide times and in different weather conditions. I used to like the low flying...we'd leave Northolt airport and head out somewhere between Beachy Head and Selsey and then just sit on the sea taking care that your propellor didn't actually touch the water. Then you'd make for the beach area along the Pas de Calais or wherever else was required, and you'd pick your starting point, pin-point that and then go down level with the beach and switch on your sideways camera and photograph the strip that was required. I'd probably be going about 200 miles an hour. I must have made over thirty trips and I seemed to concentrate particularly on the Pas de Calais area. I photographed it at all different tides, and sometimes I'd make a trip into the interior, a little bit back from the beaches - some of the pilots used to compete on these trips, come back with a tree leaf stuck in their propellor or something like that, but I just thought that was bad flying.
>
> I suppose that initially they wanted to find out which were the best areas to make a landing, and then once they'd decided that they wanted to take pictures to check what obstructions the Germans were putting there to prevent aircraft land-ing and boats coming ashore - but then we kept flying there to make the Germans still think that we were going to land in the Calais area. But I never thought that it would be the Calais area. It was far too risky, all the German divisions were there, and Dover, or wherever we'd started from would be much more at risk from retaliation.

The Intelligence unit studied German guidebooks, sea-faring manuals and tide tables and they quizzed professors of history, geography and economics to learn whatever they could about the French coastal zone. The public were called on, too. The BBC broadcast appeals for snapshots taken on pre-war holidays in France and the low countries - and several

One of Hobart's 'Funnies'. A Sherman 'Crab' tank with chain flails capable of clearing a path through minefields.

thousands arrived in the next morning's post. The press also took up the call and eventually close on a million pictures were collected from all over the world, and every out-of-focus Box Brownie family photo was scrutinized for the information it might yield to help the troops negotiate the Normandy beaches. A child standing eating ice cream in front of a sea wall in a holiday snapshot was studied to estimate the height of the wall, and one reconnaissance man was amazed to see when he landed on D-Day that a horse-drawn cart collecting seaweed on a beach he had located from a photograph was still in the same place - minus the horse.

This vital topographical and defence information was then fed back to the D-Day planners who could adjust their military dispositions in accordance with what the men would face on the far shore, and this was passed down the chain of command so that it was incorporated into the men's training. The Inter-Services Topographical Unit located at Oxford University began to construct detailed models on the basis of the photographic evidence and these were used both by planners and later by the assault troops to familiarize themselves with the terrain before they encountered it.

Sometimes the careful perusal revealed some surprises: the physicist J. D. Bernal, scientific adviser to the 21st Army Group, was leafing through a *Guide Bleu* to Normandy when he noticed a reference to peat-digging on the sands. He was alarmed at the implications for tanks becoming stuck on the beaches. Geological maps were smuggled out of Paris, a midget submarine was despatched and later Sam Basset, a colonel in the Royal Marines who headed the Oxford Unit with Frederick Wells, landed on a Normandy beach in the middle of winter clutching a trowel and a torch to check the situation for himself.

From within France itself, members of the Resistance played their part, too, in painting as full a picture as possible of the disposition and intentions of the German forces. They clandestinely took photographs with small cameras concealed in cases, clothing - even fishing nets and sketched whatever they could see of the fortifications and passed on any snippets of conversation they overheard among the Occupying Forces. They got the information out of France in smuggled notes and coded radio messages. The Chief Engineer of Roads and Bridges led a network of agents as he legitimately travelled the eighty-odd miles of coastline on his patch around Caen. Eugène Meslin and his agents - garage proprietors, electricians, plumbers and house painters - took responsibility for drafting maps, each one covering a thirteen-mile radius around the agent's home, noting any new features on cigarette papers and then transferring them to their own master map concealed at home under the chicken straw, buried in flower pots, anywhere the Gestapo would be unlikely to look. They measured distances between fortifications by pacing them out as they walked or cycled. An agent in Caen who had volunteered for air raid warden duty paced the bomb-damaged town of Ouistreham by night and noted every new ditch and casement on a pre-war map that had been issued in happier times by the local tourist office. And as fast as they compiled maps and filled in gaps in their knowledge of their occupied homeland, the British demand for detailed information grew even more voracious as D-Day approached. Meslin's staff sent off 'reams of typed reports on an area, with maps and photographs, and a few weeks later we'd be asked so many questions - queries like "What is the limit of the minefield on the beach at Honfleur? Are they anti-tank or anti-personnel? Give precise details of the seven blockhouses south of Morsalines" - that we might never have sent them.'

But it was not enough to find out what the enemy was doing. It was also necessary for the enemy not to know what you were doing, and it was here that deception played a vital part in the success of the D-Day landings.

It was a wartime rule that no code-named operation was ever to be instigated without a code name being assigned to a parallel operation to offer German Intelligence a choice of plausible threats if they manged to break the code. 'Truth', Churchill insisted in November 1943, 'is so precious that she should always be attended by a bodyguard of lies.' The Germans had to be misled about when the invasion would take place, and where it would take place. A deception plan named Operation FORTITUDE would feed the Germans a tissue of lies about Operation OVERLORD in all theatres of war.

If the Pas de Calais seemed the most obvious place for an invasion - though Hitler always suspected the Normandy beaches would be more likely - then it was essential that the Allies should contrive to see that the Germans continued to expect the landing there. This appeared to be the case: the building of the section of the Atlantic Wall around Calais was made top priority and seventeen divisions of the Wehrmacht's crack army, the Fifteenth, were stationed there. 'Nothing could persuade the Germans that we weren't going to cross the Channel,' says Professor Sir Harry Hinsley, employed by Intelligence Operations at Bletchley Park, where the 'Enigma' military code was cracked.

They wouldn't be fooled into thinking that we were going to Norway. What we had to try to persuade them was that it would be the Pas de Calais rather than Normandy. They couldn't be sure, so we could go on tickling their ignorance...after

D-Day they still thought that we might follow a couple of weeks later with an invasion in the Pas de Calais, and that kept them with one hand tied behind their backs, keeping more panzer divisons that they would have liked to have done in the Pas de Calais area.

If the Normandy landings could be seen as a mere diversionary tactic prior to the 'real' invasion, this would stop the Wehrmacht from increasing the strength of the eleven divisions of the Seventh Army currently stationed in Normandy in advance of the invasion, and would inhibit the movement of the Fifteenth Army as soon as the landings were reported.

So whilst every effort was made to keep the build-up of men and tanks around the embarkation ports from Sussex through Hampshire and Dorset secret, elaborate plans were made so that the Germans could 'discover' the concentration of forces in Kent poised to take off from Dover and Folkestone. Operation FORTITUDE was designed to mimic the preparations for Operation OVERLORD. The aim of FORTITUDE was both to deflect German anticipation of where the Allied landings would take place and to mislead them into thinking that a far greater force was poised to assault the French coast than was the case. 'If they thought that we had 80 Divisions, then when only 20 landed in Normandy, they'd think we still had another 60 left and that would give credence to the Pas de Calais follow-up theory,' says Hinsley.

FORTITUDE was an elaborate operation, masterminded by Colonel David Strangeways - now a Canon in the Church of England - a brilliant young man who had already been involved in deception Intelligence in the Western Desert and had won the DSO for shooting his way into the German HQ in Tunis, grabbing operational plans and shooting his way out again. He was gazetted under his correct name, so for the rest of the war had to operate as Colonel Culford 'which of course was terribly confusing'. Strangeways assembled 'R Force' - which some regarded almost as a private army, since he reported directly to Montgomery.

Dummy landing craft appeared in the Thames and Medway estuaries, whilst the airfields of Kent and Essex filled up with plywood gliders and inflatable rubber tanks, clearly visible to German reconnaissance planes as they combed the south-east of England.

The intelligence they brought back was reinforced by reports the Abwehr, the German Intelligence Agency, was receiving from its 'agents' in Britain. In fact this was one of the greatest success stories of the war: the network of 'turned 'agents co-ordinated by the XX (or Double-Cross) Committee chaired by an Oxford don, John Masterman, and counting the later-to-be-revealed 'fourth man', the art historian Anthony Blunt, as a member, who told the Germans what the Allies wanted them to hear.

Lieutenant Alex Lyons was recruited into 'R Force' from the early days. He'd been training in mine clearing with the Royal Engineers in Inverness in Scotland when he was sent down to Maldon in Essex and told that 'we were now called 82 Group Camouflage Company and that we were going to do something special, we were going to mislead the enemy.' They studied how animals and birds blended into the background and experimented using what was to hand, brushwood, chicken wire, leaves and netting. Lyons and his fellow soldiers tramped around endlessly in the grass to create the illusion of tyre tracks and activity. But of course in an operation of deception the camouflage must not be too good - it was no point in making a dummy tank and then concealing it so well that the enemy didn't notice its existence. Strangeways confessed that he was always 'annoyed that more airplanes didn't come over to see what we were doing...of course I was glad that our anti-aircraft cover was so good, but...'

Mary Reeve worked in a Nottingham factory that had produced silk stockings before the war. The factory had been in the process of being turned over to the production of nylon stockings and German workers were in Britain installing the necessary machinery. But when war broke out the half-ready equipment was abandoned and the factory equipped for war work, producing first silk parachutes and then barrage balloons and finally

> our immediate gaffer says 'we're going into a different product' and we had to sign a form saying that we wouldn't disclose to anyone what we were making in the factory and we started work on making artificial rubber lorries...the parts were cut out on a press and then you had to put on two coats of liquid rubber, and when it was tacky you rolled them with a metal roller and then the parts were taken away and all fitted together. You didn't completely make one - you did parts of it and then passed it on to someone else and when they were finished they were put on the floor where the barrage balloons had been tested and blown up...and they looked so real. From a distance you wouldn't have known they weren't the real thing. And in the lunch breaks at the factory we'd be shown films to show us how important the work we were doing was.

Strangeways had this view of people working in deception too: 'You musn't tell them too much except that it is extremely important and if they did the graft it was going to be very, very helpful to our troops going over to the other side.'

'We certainly didn't know what it was all about when we first got to the ordnance depot in Essex...we'd start getting these mysterious cases arriving - all different sizes...and we were told to take them out of sight of the main road and unpack them', recalls Arthur Merchant, a member of Strangeways' R Force, who had been stationed at Towcester but brought south in October 1943 to do a job he found pretty puzzling.

> The first one was about eighteen feet long and there were three iron poles in it, with some steel hoses coming out and a strip of rubber in the bottom, and when we lifted it out we still didn't know what it was. And in another box was a sort of pumping-up effort, a machine with two handles. And we plugged it in and stared blowing this thing up. It looked like a giant sausage to start with and then the ends became square at one of the ends and we suddenly decided that it was a gun bar-rel, a 75mm gun barrel and the square part was the breech...and we just stood and stared at it...still nobody told us anything. We didn't even know that there was going to be an 'R Force'. So we took this gun down and put it up again, and then we put nets over it. And then we moved it 200 yards away and looked at it again, trying to get it right. Then we moved on to rubber Sherman tanks. We got some more mysterious boxes and we had a go at them, but the Sherman tank was all in one piece that gradually flipped out and took shape. We didn't know what it was that we were blowing up. It was in four sections, we had to blow each one up and the idea was that if Jerry came over to take a look, if he decided that it was a

"There 'e goes—says he's going to get this ruddy invasion over, then get some leave.'/

Sunday Express, May 14th, 1944

tank and tried to have a go at it, and it was all in one piece, it would sort of splatter and the whole lot would collapse, but if it was in four pieces there was a good chance that it might stay upright and he'd still be fooled by it.

The men worked very hard to make the tanks look realistic - at extremely close range. Painted nuts and bolts had their own shadows painted on, men who had been upholsterers and tailors in civvy street fashioned hessian covers for the tanks, and the attention to detail paid to the *faux* leaves which were then strewn over the nets meant that like the real things they were painted darker on top with a paler underside.

All the men working on this dummy arsenal were sworn to secrecy - which could make going into the NAAFI or a pub an anxious occasion. 'You'd get at least a year's imprisonment if you were heard talking about what you did,' recalls Merchant. 'Loose tongues they used to call it.' And leave was no easier. Arthur Merchant's father 'was an ex-soldier, and he was interested in everything that I was doing. I just used to say, manoeuvres, that's all I've been doing, just manoeuvres. He probably thought I was a bit boring.' Not that the men seemed to know much more themselves: 'At first I thought the tanks were going to be used for target practice or something. I have to say, I couldn't quite see how rubber tanks and rubber guns were going to help us to win the war ...'

Lieutenant-Colonel White was a Royal Engineer involved with anti-aircraft when he was 'called to the War Office' and put on a special job that had nothing to do with building aircraft at all...

I was taken to a great big garage in Hammersmith and behind the garage was a shed and on the floor was lying a whole lot of bits of canvas and steel and bits of rope and things like that. And I was told they were landing craft. And I laughed - and so did everybody else. 'Well,' said the General who was running the show, 'you've got to put them together into landing craft...here's the book of words to show you how.' We had a year before D-Day to do it. We were going to build landing craft so we could put on a dummy invasion on a different part of the French coast and fox the Hun into thinking that we were going to land somewhere else.

The craft floated on oil drums, the framework was tubular scaffolding bolted together and the craft were covered in canvas painted the same colour as regular landing craft. They looked very real...I was driving past Buckler's Hard [in Hampshire] one day and I was half a mile away and I certainly couldn't tell them from the real thing. We had to work at great speed. There had to be nothing there when we started in the morning and there had to be the finished craft when we finished in the evening. We made them on land and then towed them to the sort of place you might expect a landing craft to be anchored, and left them there. It was all done at night. Sometimes launching them was hell. It was all right at Buckler's Hard but at Poole there's a very strong current and if you've got a thirty-foot length of very flimsy structure...and then of course you had to be careful, you wanted to have men moving about on them, of course, but the canvas top meant you didn't really want them putting their foot through it. We'd leave the LCs where they were for two or three days and then bring them back inland and dismantle them, so it looked as if the troops were moving around, I suppose.

But White was not as perplexed as some of his colleagues in R-Force because 'we'd done the same sort of thing in the First World War. We'd dropped dummy men with squibs behind the German lines then.'

Corporal Les Phillips was a OWL (Operator Wireless and Line). He'd been torpedoed in the Merchant Navy and asked for a transfer into the Royal Corps of Signals and from there found himself with R Force stationed at Guildford with the job of loading and broadcasting material he was given to lend authenticity to the activities of the Force.

It was a very secret organization with the right hand not knowing what the left hand was doing. You would be given certain instructions and a map reference and as an operator, you would take the truck to that spot and at a certain time you would broadcast the information that was on the tape according to a script that we were given when we arived at the location...It might be asking for reinforcements, it might be asking for ammunition supplies, all sorts of things. We'd perhaps pretend to be a whole corps. We had to look after our equipment and broadcast what we told to - the disinformation would usually be on tape. The timing was very important because it had to seem as if one tank in FUSAG [the First United States Army Group] was answering another. It was all very secret. If you asked a chap who'd been out that day in his tank, 'Where'd d'you go?' He'd say, 'I don't know. Somewhere up north, or some little village'. 'What did you do?' 'Usual, shoved out a bit of rubbish and came home again.'

"Listen, Jane—

I've found out the date of—

you know what.

Unfortunately I'm sworn to the most frightful secrecy—

so you'll just have to guess at it—

and I'll tell you when you guess wrong."

The men knew that they were involved in deception, but that was about the sum total of their awareness.

> We were practising enemy deception by radio coupled with visual deception. So that not only could the enemy see the tanks, but they could hear the tanks too. You had visual, you had audio and you had radio signals, all three combined to give enemy Intelligence the impression that there were real tanks in the area. We just hoped that what we were doing was effective.

Whilst some of the FORTITUDE reports were pure fabrication - like the US Division stationed in Iceland, and the huge fake oil dock designed by Basil Spence (later to be the architect of Coventry Cathederal) in Dover which was periodically 'inspected' by the King and Queen and General Eisenhower - some had some basis in truth.

The army supposedly assembling around the Kent ports was FUSAG, whilst the Third US Army was temporarily headquartered at Chelmsford in Essex, both under the command of the flamboyant Lieutenant-General George S. Patton Jnr, recently returned from Sicily in some disgrace for striking a shell-shocked soldier, who would threaten that when he got within sight of the Germans he wouldn't 'just shoot the sonofabitches - we're going to cut out their living guts and use them to grease the treads of our tanks.' In the eyes of the German High Command, Patton's involvement gave credibility to the Pas de Calais invasion force - he was in fact senior to, though of the same military rank as, Lieutenant-General Omar Bradley. 'He was a very colourful person. Everyone knew of Georgie P. His was a name you could catch very easily so it made good sense,' says Colonel Strangeways.

To Brigadier Sir Edgar Williams, Patton was

> a fairly senior chap who'd blotted his copy book...but had already shown himself particularly and obsessively as a very effective Commander. He was vainglorious, in a static position he was a perfectly bloody nuisance in battle, and in a pursuit battle he was unequalled. He was able to keep up the impetus and read a map as if it were a relief map. It was the most extraordinary thing. He was something of a cameraman and this played a large part in his verve and his topographical sense of what's-over-the-hill that he had. And of course he had a complete disregard for security.

But if FUSAG was an illusion, the 150,000-strong 3rd Army was for real, but it was quartered nearly two hundred miles away near Knutsford in Cheshire and wouldn't see the Normandy beaches until mid-July.

If there was one Patton in two places, the same was to be true of Montgomery. In an attempt to throw German Intelligence off the scent of an invasion date, 'Monty' conspicuously left for a 1,000-mile trip to Algiers and Gibraltar on 26 May 1944, less than a fortnight before D-Day. 'Since if Monty was in Gibraltar, he couldn't be about to cross the Channel.' In fact Montgomery was already installed at Southwick House, near Portsmouth, the HQ for D-Day. The man who flew to Gibraltar in a sheepskin-lined flying jacket wearing a raked-angle black beret and travelling wherever plausible in a highly-visible open car was a forty-one-year-old ex-repertory company actor, Lieutenant Meyrick Clifton James, who'd been in the Royal Army Pay Corps until someone noticed how well he'd serve as Monty's double and plucked him out of obscurity. He was to follow Montgomery around - on a fishing holiday in Scotland - and practice the Commander-in-Chief's nasal inflection, his nervous mannerisms and, for a time, emulate his non-smoking, teetotal, lifestyle with the compensation of a general's full pay for the duration of his 'command'. The only problem was that 'Monty's Double' had a finger missing from his right hand, which was very noticeable when he saluted. A bandage was substituted, so it looked as if the 'General' had had a minor accident. When 'Monty's' car stopped at a traffic light on the way to the airport, and a small crowd on the kerbside waved and cheered, Military Intelligence was able to relax. If 'Montgomery' fooled the British public, the chances of his fooling the Germans were good.

It was never posssible to know for certain how decisive these deception tactics were to the success of D-Day, though on occasions Ultra picked up messages that indicated that certain German actions were taken in response to the wiles of Operation FORTITUDE.

In Brigadier Williams's view if the Germans had been convinced that the Allied landings taking place on the Normandy beaches on D-Day were the full frontal and only assault and had consequently moved all possible divisions to the Cotentin Peninsula rather than continuing to hedge their bets in the Pas de Calais well into mid-June, this would have interrupted the Allies' build-up on D-Day

> very considerably, because we would have been tied to a very narrow frontage, and the presence of the enemy combined with these terrible storms would have meant that we would have had a very tricky time to consolidate the beach head.

'It was almost like a game of charades,' concedes David Strangeways,

> but the whole time you knew that there was somebody's life depending on it…[R Force's] importance was out of all proportion to its size…it helped the winning of a battle. And it certainly helped in saving lives. No question of it. In many ways we were weak, we hadn't got the good equipment that the Germans had. We never wanted to be outgunned and outnumbered. Our men's lives were very precious - the supply was not unending. So if you could reduce the effects of the enemy in any way, then that is what you did.

CHAPTER FIVE

PUTTING THE JIGSAW TOGETHER

'THE ATTACK WILL COME, there's no doubt about that any more,' pronounced Hitler decisively in December 1943. 'If they attack in the West, that attack will decide the War. If this attack is repulsed then the whole business is over...we can withdraw troops right away.'

Reconnaissance photographs taken by aircraft swooping as low as they dared, reports from agents and Resistance workers inside France, and news from the men who were undertaking the daring and hazardous familiarization of the beaches of France throughout the spring of 1944, showed that the German High Command was taking no chances in the West. It was a race against time - would the Allies be able to mount their assault on the Channel coast before Germany's much-vaunted Atlantic Wall sealed off France completely?

It was a formidable task. The entire western front ran for 2,500 miles from Holland to the Spanish border: the German High Command recognized that the most vulnerable section lay between Holland and Normandy - nevertheless that represented 800 miles of shoreline to defend. It was only in November 1943 that, a year after his defeat at El Alamein at the hands of Montgomery's 8th Army, Erwin Rommel had been appointed to take charge of Army Group 'B' which encompassed the Pas de Calais, guarded by the Fifteenth Army along the coast to Normandy and Brittany which was the territory of the Seventh Army.

Rommel had been horrified when he inspected his manor. He was convinced that the Allies must never be allowed to get ashore. 'We'll have only one chance to stop the enemy,' he admitted, 'and that's whilst he's in the water...everything we have must be on the coast.' Rommel had no time for the strategy of his superior officer, the elderly Field Marshal von Rundstedt, Commander-in-Chief of the German forces in the west, who recognized that the Atlantic Wall was no wall at all, but a series of heavily fortified concrete emplacements clustered around strategic points along the coast where the Germans anticipated an Allied landing - places like Cap Gris Nez and the mouth of the Seine, with long gaps with only desultory defences. It hardly measured up to the boast of Hitler's Chief of Propaganda, Goebbels, that it made Europe an impregnable fortress. It was an obstruction, not a barrier, predicted von Rundstedt, who believed in concentrating his troops inland, back from the coast. Indeed, it was more a wall to keep German morale up, some thought, rather than the Allies out - though at a cost of 3.7 billion Reichsmark.

"My nephew's expecting to invade the Continent very shortly."

The situation was urgent: to compensate for the lack of concrete fortifications which he found when he inspected the stop-go wall in December 1943, Rommel planned to make a killing field of the beaches. 200,000,000 mines were to be deployed in France alone - 65,000 mines per square kilometre to form a barrier six miles wide. He also used the winter and spring of 1944 to make the coastline bristle with improvised fortifications designed to repel and to snare enemy landing craft. There were what was known as 'Rommel's Asparagus': long mined wooden posts twelve feet high planted close together in rows, largely hidden at high tide and facing out to sea, whilst similar installations faced inland to snare retreating landing craft as the tide ebbed out. Iron gates, twelve feet high and with legs sunk deep into the sand to brace them against the incoming tide lined the beaches, designed to impede landing crafts and tanks alike; ramps were fitted with blades and mines and hastily dug into the sand; and tetrahedra, like truncated obelisks, were another obstacle that would smash to pieces a landing craft thrown against them by the tide, whilst hurriedly assembled rafts were mined and pushed out to sea to blow up the landing craft before they got near the shore.

Rommel was tireless in urging the German troops to work at a frantic pace to dig in the defences, travelling backwards and forwards along the coast with sharp words for the commanders and encouragement - and sometimes the gift of a harmonica or an accordion - for the men. It worked: on D-Day the Allied forces would face some 500,000 obstacles on the beaches of France as they struggled to come ashore.

But if Rommel and the German Army had spent a frantic spring erecting anti-landing hardware on the beaches of France, across the Channel the British were being equally industrious in developing tanks for the precise purpose of demolishing that hardware and forging ashore on the Normandy beaches.

In March 1943, Major-General Sir Percy Hobart, a pioneer of tank warfare since the early 1930s, was called from his post as a corporal in the Home Guard - the only role in which he could serve his country since being sacked from the command of the 7th Armoured Division in Egypt - to develop armoured tanks for use in the coming invasion. The unit he raised, the 79th Armoured Division, never fought as a division but was deployed on D-Day and after wherever it was necessary to overcome enemy tank obstacles.

'Hobart's Funnies', as the various tanks were called, were to play a crucial role in clearing the British and Canadian beaches on D-Day. General Bradley declined the use of most of them for the US Army since many of the Funnies were based on British tanks which it might have been hard for the Americans to service, and in any case Bradley thought the idea something of a Heath Robinson gimmick which did not fit in with the way he wanted to deploy his infantryman and tanks - an assessment he perhaps later regretted.

However, the centrepiece of the collection was an Anglo-American initiative, the DD Sherman tank. DD stood for Duplex Drive and its canvas flotation screen or 'skirt' both hid the tank and kept the water out, as did a specially constructed exhaust, making it a truly amphibious vehicle that could land with the infantry. The DD tank could enter the water quite a way offshore beyond the range of land-based artillery and its propellors would then enable it to 'swim,' camouflaged by its skirt, to land, where it would lumber out of the sea like some clumsy prehistoric monster, the screen would be collapsed and the tank would be able to start off up the beach. 900 DD tanks landed on D-Day and caused a terrifying shock to the German soldiers who had seen nothing like them before.

Jack Thornton, a driver in the 4/7th Royal Dragoon Guards, remembers being taken to a cinema in Keighley, where he was stationed in the winter of 1943.

> It was heavily guarded. We had to identify the men on each side of us before we were let in. And then they told us that we were going to be at the sharp end, we were going to be trained on a secret weapon. It wasn't good news. We were in Keighley near Bradford in Yorkshire, for the first time for a long time, and we were enjoying ourselves, we were in a town where you could go out and meet girls and go to pubs, we were having a good time, and all of a sudden the war was being pushed at us very hard. We were to go down south and start training. It was on the cards that we were going to work with 'swimming tanks'. We were lined up and asked if we had any seafaring experience. But only one man did, he'd once been on a trawler. But none of the rest of us had any experience of the sea at all.
>
> We went down to Suffolk and here we learned how to breathe under water wearing submarine escape equipment. Then we were taken to a local lake where the tanks were. We were shocked, horrified when we first saw the floating tanks. They looked so crude as if they'd been knocked together like Meccano...but they worked. We lifted up the screen and the tank floated. It was good fun, we played around with them, it became a lark.

*Field-Marshal Erwin Rommel inspects the Atlantic Wall in 1943, 'We'll only
have one chance to stop the enemy and that's while he's in the water...everything
we have must be on the coast.'*

As Group Captain Patrick Hennessey who was then a corporal and a Sherman DD tank commander in No. 4 Troop of the 13/18th Hussars explains: 'If you get a heavy stone, and put it in a canvas bucket, and put this canvas bucket in water, the bucket will go down a bit, but then it will float, so they figured that if they built a canvas bucket - a screen - around a thirty-two-ton tank which could be inflated, then when the screen stood up the tank would float in the water.'

But it ceased to be a lark on 4 April 1944 when the troops were in Studland Bay on an exercise.

> The ramps went down on the Landing Craft and we inflated the screen on the tank and went into the water. We formed up and headed for land. But within minutes, out of nowhere a storm suddenly sprang up, and the waves got bigger and bigger and they started to slop over the screen into the tank, and as the tank started to fill with water it sank lower into the water, so more water came in and we were gradually sinking.

Thornton managed to get his escape apparatus on and breathe oxygen, and when he got to the beach he deflated the screen

> and hopped out on to the beach...I looked behind and there was no one following. The tanks behind had all disappeared. But before I could do anything the CO drove past in a jeep and told my sergeant, who was still in the turret, to put me on a charge for not wearing my tin hat, that's all he was concerned about. We lost the two tanks behind me - I was the lead tank - and all the men out there. A tank crew's like a close-knit family, really. There were five of us in a tank. The men were my friends, and my particular friend was Corporal Park who lived just outside Lancaster, he'd died, and I was given the task of sorting out all his possessions, so I bundled them up and I was put on a train to Lancaster and I had tell his wife that her husband was dead - drowned. But I couldn't tell her how he'd drowned. I couldn't tell her that he was in a DD tank that had gone down, that was still top secret. All I could say was, 'I'm sorry, Arthur's been drowned on an exercise.' That was it. And I kept thinking about the driver, Trooper Petty, because when the screen collapses with the pressure of water it collapses inwards so the driver is really trapped and the tank sinks to the bottom and the driver puts on his mask and he's breathing the oxygen and it'll only last him about thirty minutes. Did he have to sit there breathing, struggling to get free for thirty minutes? I often think about that, it really upsets me.

These early DD tanks were Valentines: 'They were only a training tank, they were useless for battle. We went on to the Sherman which was much better equipped and much tougher.'

The 79th American Division had been formed to overcome obstacles that the forces were likely to encounter on the various Normandy beaches - like the tetrahedra, pill boxes, barbed wire, concrete reinforced houses, anti-tank ditches as well as minefields - so Hobart's collection also included a 'tankdozer', or armoured bulldozer that could shovel obstacles aside, a tank converted to carry a forty-foot-long box girder bridge for crossing ditches or mounting walls and a 'crab' tank, equipped with flailing chains to scythe a path through minefields.

Lieutenant Ian Hammerton was a troop commander in the 1st Troop 'B' Squadron in the 22 Dragoons who had five Sherman 'crab' flail tanks in his troop. 'At first we practised at Alford in Lincolnshire where they'd built full-scale replicas of parts of the Atlantic Wall with concrete bunkers and mine fields and wire entanglements, for which the crab was ideally suited, because of the cutters on the end of the drum which proved to be extremely useful.'

The Dragoons were originally a cavalry regiment 'way back before Napoleonic times,' but they had been reformed in late 1940 as a cruiser tank regiment,

> and they were all raring to go, scorching across the French countryside, or wher-ever we were sent. And then one day General Hobart called in on us at Stow-on-the-Wold and dropped a bombshell in our midst. He told us that we would not be going screaming across the countryside, but we were going to be using mine-clearing flail tanks, which we'd never heard of. The bottom fell out of the regi-ment at that point, I think. They'd all been trained to go dashing across the coun-tryside, whereas I'd had my training on infantry tanks, which were much slower-moving things. The flail beats a path [through minefields] about nine feet wide, which is not wide enough for practical purposes for another tank to follow through, so the idea was that you had at least two, possibly three, in echelon, with the driver putting the nearside track in the offside track mark of the tank in front, or the other way, round, depending. The only level ground in Stow-on-the-Wold where we could practise this was the cricket pitch, and much to the annoyance of the city fathers, I'm afraid we chewed that up rather badly.

A 'very democratic system' was introduced about this time in the tank troops:

> We'd have a weekly meeting of each troop and the men were encouraged to put forward ideas as to how these machines could be used, and whether there were any problems that we saw that could be overcome...of course no one was ever very happy at the idea of travelling at one and a half miles an hour through a mine field which has been put there specifically to enable enemy anti-tank gunners to more easily engage a target, it's not a very happy-making thought. But we had a job to do, somebody had to do it, and we did it to the best of our ability.

Then there were the 'Bobbin tank' which unspooled a canvas and coir matting to lay a path across soft mud or quicksands; a 'Fascine' (derived from *fasces*, meaning bundle, the same root as for the word 'fascist') tank which dropped bundles of chestnut palings to fill in anti-tank ditches and bomb craters, the Churchill ARK (armoured ramp carrier) and the AVRE (Armoured Vehicle Royal Engineers), which carried a powerful 290mm petard mortar, nicknamed the 'Flying Dustbin', that could blast through concrete pillboxes; and beehive charges that could be placed on the top of a concrete bunker. And there was the 'Crocodile', or flame-throwing, tank which could incinerate any obstacle within a 360-foot range.

Andrew Wilson, then a Lieutenant in the 141st Regiment, Royal Armoured Corps and now a journalist who has often written for the *Observer* recalls:

> The Crocodile was a very fearsome, secret weapon which was first used in Normandy. It consisted of a Churchill Mark 7 tank which was quite heavily armoured by British standards and behind the Churchill was a trailer containing some 400 gallons of the flame-thrower fuel which was something like napalm, as

we now call it. And there were also bottles of nitrogen under very high pressure in the trailer. When you went into battle the commander would give the order when the tank was about 100 yards from the target and the gunner who would be sitting up alongside the driver, would fire and a spark would ignite the napalm and a rod of burning fuel would shoot out. When this fuel struck it was very glutinous. Originally it was invented to assault the German pill boxes along the Normandy coast. But it was never used for this. The tanks were used against gun emplacements and houses and trenches. And sometimes the Germans would run away, and sometimes they wouldn't get away. Whenever we did catch the enemy with a flame it was a very horrible thing to see…as a tank crew member you were very well aware of the damage you were doing. If you were an artillery man you didn't always see the effects of the shells you launched at the enemy, but if you were a flame-thrower you sometimes had occasion to see directly what you had done, and it sometimes incinerated people in quite obscene ways. I think that those of us who took part in these operations could never quite forget what effect it was that you had achieved…it burned itself into your memory almost literally. But of course when we'd trained in the summer before D-Day…we were terribly impressed by the ingenuity of the equipment, the people who had been sent to instruct us from the factory had wonderful charts in different colours showing blue or red for the electrical system, and I was later struck by the contrast of these beautiful drawings and what happened when we claimed a German position.

Lieutenant Kenneth Macksey was a fellow officer in the same regiment as Andrew Wilson. 'The Crocodile flame-thrower was very secret…the people who were trained on it in England before D-Day were kept away from the rest of the regiment.' When Macksey first saw it he found it

very impressive. It was clearly a very destructive weapon and one way of dealing with things. What I was chiefly worried about was that it only had a range with the wind behind it of 150 yards and for effective purposes 800 yards downwards. So you had to get very very close to the enemy and therefore you stood a much better chance of being knocked out by a bazooka or something like that. They were usually used in set-piece attacks. You knew your objective before you started, so you had a plan and the most important thing was to keep the enemy quiet while you were actually giving directions to the flame-thrower gunner. You had to be very careful because he couldn't see after the first shot, he'd be obscured. So it became a very desirable thing to keep as far away from the enemy as possible and be supported by other tanks so that you couldn't be knocked off course while you were concentrating on flame throwing. If you fired into a house, the house went on fire, if you fired through the slot in the pill box it would probably destroy the oxygen in there and suffocate the people.

Macksey knows of 'no example of people being actually hit by it except our own troops sometimes…no one set out to set people on fire. The hope was that they would surrender before you did that. I don't think that anybody wanted to flame Germans in particular. It was a rather repugnant job, but it had to be done.'

FORTRESS EUROPE

The obstacles that faced the invaders on the far shore: net-camouflaged concrete tank obstacles - dragon's teeth - and steel objects known to the Allies as 'hedgehogs'.

As Intelligence gathering and reconnaissance expeditions came up with new information - like a problem of possible seams of soft clay - it was back to the drawing board for Hobart and his team.

Another team that had clustered round their drawing boards for many months before D-Day was also seeking a solution for what it knew lay on the far shore. If the Atlantic Wall was incomplete, the fortification of the French ports - Calais, Cherbourg, Le Havre - was not. It had been recognized since the Dieppe raid that the likelihood of being able to seize a French port on D-Day was effectively nil. Yet also since Dieppe, the military planners had recognized that in order to get the troops, tanks, guns and supplies ashore for an invasion that would be able to 'stick', in Bradley's word, and push forward inland, a harbour was essential - certainly until the capture of Cherbourg which had been pencilled in on D-Day+8. It had to be possible to supply eighteen divisions for a month. Captain John Hughes-Hallett Naval Adviser to Combined Operations, who had given the order to withdraw from Dieppe, reminded COSSAC of the solution: 'If we can't capture a port we must take one with us.'

The party that sailed on the Queen Mary to the Quadrant Conference in Quebec in September 1943 included Professor Bernal. It was the Combined Operations Chief of Staff, Lord Louis Mountbatten - anxious to convince the Allied Chiefs of Staff to press ahead with plans for 'a port to take across the Channel' - who had arranged his presence. After twenty-four hours at sea, the civilian Bernal was sent for by Mountbatten who told him ingenuously, 'I have just told them [the Chiefs of Staff] that, by the most amazing coincidence, the greatest expert in the world happens to be on board...It's you...Yes, I know you know nothing about it, but you are the world's greatest expert. That's an order!' And so the professor of physics found himself in the one of the liner's spacious bathrooms with a fleet of twenty ships made out of newspaper in the bath, and the Allied Chiefs of Staff gathered around with the First Sea Lord standing on a lavatory seat to command a better view. A young lieutenant obligingly created waves with a back brush and the 'fleet' sank. 'That, gentleman,' said Bernal dramatically 'is what will happen without an artificial harbour.'

He then borrowed a Mae West lifebelt and laid it across the shallow end of the bath (which was standing in for the coast of Normandy); launched another fleet of paper ships and asked for 'more waves, please' from the helpful young lieutenant and his brush. This time the boats pitched and tossed but didn't sink. The point was made.

It had taken seven years to build Dover harbour: the team of scientists and civil engineers who put their minds to the problem of designing a harbour with piers for landing ships that could ride the tides (up to twenty-two feet off the coast of Normandy), could cope with landing 2,500 vehicles and 10,000 tons of stores a day, stay afloat in a possible force six gale; and of building it undetected, had less than a year.

A civil engineer, Alan Beckett, who had the wartime rank of Major in the Royal Engineers, was involved in the design of a part of the Mulberry Harbours, the floating roadways that led from berthing dock to shore.

> We worked almost continuously except odd hours at night-time because not only was the design of the bridge required but the methods of placing it on the enemy coast had to be worked out in great detail...methods of towage, quick erection

*Training for D-Day: US troops march across Dartmoor in a simulation
of the exercise to 'seize Cherbourg'.*

and handling in difficult weather conditions under enemy attack, all those sort of things had to be taken into account. None of us realized how big it was because due to security the work was sectionalized and I was involved in the roadway, but I wasn't involved in the design of the caissons nor were we involved in the design of the breakwater...in total there were probably hundreds of people actually engaged in the design and none of them knew about the rest, that was reserved for the military and only the top military had the whole picture.

Brigadier Arthur Mervyn Walter was appointed Director of Ports and Inland Waterways 21st Army Group in February 1944 and was responsible for overseeing the construction of the British Harbours code-named 'Mulberry':

Mulberry was absolutely top secret. So secret that, as we used to say in the army, 'Burn this before reading it.' Nobody put the jigsaw together as a harbour. They thought that the roadway was for a bridge or something...and even the Intelligence people thought that the caissons were to be shipped over to Calais where it was planned to deceive the Germans into thinking that's where we'd land - they thought they were some sort of flak towers to help the invasion, nobody was quite sure.

But they might have been very sure, for one day 'after a series of tedious meetings' Brigadier Walter went to lunch with a colleague at a London club in Piccadilly and 'as was the custom you took your black bag safely locked and you put it under the table as you had lunch. That was the drill.' But when Walter got back to his office at Norfolk House

> literally just round the corner, I found that I had left my bag under the table. I thought that I would be put in the Tower...I got on to the phone and I shall never forget even to this day the calm voice of the Hall Porter saying, 'Yes Sir, a bag was found under one of the tables and I have it safe here in the lobby.' In that bag were plans which if found by the Germans would have disclosed where we were going to have the invasion...you can imagine my feelings...however it was safe and for some surprising reason they didn't execute me ...

The actual construction was done by 'goons',' men who had been suggested by their sapper units for this rather dangerous work. 'The RE units were asked to send their best and bravest, but the way the Army works,' says Brigadier Walter, 'is that it was an opportunity for every unit to get rid of the men it didn't want...so we did rather get the dregs...and when we sailed on D-Day+1 we had fourteen court martials pending...but they did the job wonderfully well.'

Kenneth Bungard was one of the 'goons.'

> I was a defaulter in the navy. I was adrift getting back to Chatham Barracks because I'd been with my girlfriend. And I was on Captain's report...so when they asked for volunteers I went as fast as I could to volunteer for something called Party Fun and Party Games. We were given the rig...sea boots, overall, lifebelt...and we were given a little red light and a battery to fit on to our lifebelt, so we began to wonder what we'd let ourselves in for!...We piled into a lorry and were taken to the Thames Estuary where we came across what I thought was an office block, with no windows or doors...And we were told to clamber up the iron ladder at the end, on to the top - which turned out, of course to be one of the caissons and this was towed with us on top of it to Dover...luckily the Germans didn't spot us. Occasionally they would fire across in the dark because they knew people were slipping things through...in fact Lord Haw Haw mentioned it, he said, 'Oh, I know what's going on, and if you try to get those things across the Channel, we will sink them before you ever get anywhere near us'...but I don't think that he knew any more than we did...We never knew what we were towing across the Channel...and we felt terribly exposed sixty feet up on a piece of flat concrete: we had no protection whatsoever. If we were hit by anything, we would have just gone down like a stone...When I got back to my girlfriend, I told her I'd spent my war sailing round the ocean on an office block - which is the only way I could describe it, really!

Eventually the plans were complete: the prefabricated Mulberry harbours were to consist of giant caissons or concrete boxes, called 'Phoenix', which would be protected by breakwaters called 'Bombardons,' with safe anchorage provided by a line of sunken blockships known as 'Gooseberry.' The floating 480-foot pier, surrounded by fifteen piers on 'iron legs' or 'spuds' anchored on the sea bed, where the ships would dock were appropriately called 'Whales,' and from them floating metal roads would lead ashore. Two harbours

"I'd like your opinion, Sir.   Naturally, we all think it's the prettiest assault course in Wales."

were to be built and then towed across the Channel for assembly on D-Day+1. One would be for the Americans and would be positioned off what had been designated Omaha beach on the west flank of the Cotentin Peninsula: the other, to serve the British, would lie off Arromanches.

The Mulberry harbours were designed for use for ninety days - but there were no guarantees and in the terrible storms that raged between 19 and 23 June the British Mulberry 'B' at Arromanches was badly damaged whilst the American Mulberry 'A' off Omaha was totally destroyed. Once the Allied troops had seized the major port the Mulberry harbours would become less important: supplies - and men - would be shipped direct from Britain and the US, but they would still need the fuel that would drive the advance inland. The major objective of the Allied bombing strategy in the run-up to D-Day was to wipe out the transport and supply depots in Occupied France - no one could tell what resources might be available to the Allies or how soon. Plans were made to run a pipeline - in the end there were four - along the Channel bed to pump petrol and oil to the Allied forces. PLUTO (Pipeline Under The Ocean) was projected to carry up to a million gallons.

The logistics of supply were daunting, but they would be totally redundant if the troops were unable to storm the beaches and advance inland. In the end - in the beginning - it was the soldiers who would have to do it. There was no way that they could achieve an assault of the scale envisaged by Operation OVERLORD without the military and supply back-up now being put in place, but without their courage and fighting skills, the invasion would be no invasion.

So whilst the strategists and the experts drew up their blueprints for success, the troops slogged it out in training.

Charles Cawthon was a Second Lieutenant of an infantry platoon with a US brigade famous since the American Civil War, the Stonewall Brigade. Knowing that he would be drafted, the young journalist volunteered and found himself in England. 'We marched away the winter of 1942-3...there were day and night training exercises.'

In the summer of 1943 the Stonewallers were on the move. They were ordered from the Salisbury Plain where they had been living and training to take a 150-mile march on foot to the west of England, to train on Dartmoor and join the growing number of US battalions which were scattered all over Devon and Cornwall: '[There was an] enormous concentration of troops and matériel for the invasion of the Continent, but we were not aware of this.'

The choice of training ground for the troops was dictated by several factors, but the most significant was the need to find terrain as similar as possible to that that they would encounter on the far shore; the other was the strategy for the landings which allocated the western beaches to the US 1st Army, whilst the British and Canadian troops would go ashore to the east. The transportation of 250,000 men from their training grounds to their ports of embarkation for Normandy was a logistical nightmare, and to compound this by moving battalions of men from the south-east of Britain to the west would have been total folly. In any case, the deployment of the troops around Britain had already been settled in broad outline by the historic circumstances of the war.

The threat of invasion in 1940 had meant that the majority of British troops had been moved to the south of England to be ready to defend the beaches of Kent, Sussex, Hampshire and the hinterland behind. When the Canadians started to arrive at the end of 1939, they streamed into the south of England, too. To the east, the flatlands of Suffolk and Norfolk, the counties on the most direct flight path to Germany, played host to the USAAF, whose massive airfield building programme stretched east into Cambridge, Huntingdon and Northamptonshire.

In January 1942 when the American soldiers started to come to Britain to fulfil the conditions of Operation BOLERO, they landed in Northern Ireland or on the west coast of Britain, at Greenock in Scotland and at Liverpool, Cardiff and Bristol, ports large enough to receive the ocean liners that transported them across the Atlantic, and also strategically placed so that the GIs could occupy the west side of this island to train in readiness for D-Day, for when that came, the US troops would make their assault on the west flank of the Normandy coastline. The beaches had been allocated their code names on 3 March 1944. The most westerly beach, earmarked for the US VII Corps, was a three-mile stretch now to be known as Utah settled on by Montgomery and Bradley to edge the assault a little nearer to Cherbourg; next came Omaha beach stretching the four miles from Vierville to St Laurent where, according to Bradley, 'the 29th Division had staked out squatter's rights before I had arrived in England'; going east came Gold in the British sector; then a four-mile beach, Juno, which ran between the small towns of St Aubin-sur-Mer and Courseulles-sur-Mer where the Canadian 3rd Division would land; the beach that lay the

US troops winch an 'injured' soldier up the cliffs during a D-Day training exercise.

furthest east was Sword beach, two and a half miles of coastline running from Riva-Bella to Luc-sur-Mer which had been decided on for the assault by the British.

On New Year's Eve 1943 the men of Cawthon's battalion celebrated with a certain sadness: there had been no Christmas presents from home that year: shipping from US was too urgently needed to transport the matériel of war for the space to be diverted. 'We knew that 1944 would be the year of the invasion, but we knew not where or when and had no idea at all of the cost. Had we been analytical, we would have seen that 1943 had belonged to the Allies.' Cawthon continued:

> The German Sixth Army had been frozen at Stalingrad, and the last German major offensive in Russia…had been defeated; Sicily had been secured and a hold established on the Italian mainland; the long, costly campaign to take Guadalcanal had been won; the air war had been carried to Germany.
>
> GIs' training had started off in a fumbling way, for there was only a vague idea of what we had to do. At first, it was all conducted on land, using homemade mock-ups of landing craft. Dartmoor was probably as good a land area for this as any, for it seemed afloat in rain. Its vast, rolling, pitching stretches of spongy turf were usually clouded in mist - a desolate, eerie, sometimes bleakly beautiful place. We came to know, but never to love, Dartmoor as we tramped across it, shivered in its cold winds and slept on its liquid surface.
>
> One attack called for overhead machine gunfire using live ammunition. We put wooden stops under the gun barrels to be sure they would not accidentally be depressed, but just as the firing started an umpire came along and kicked away the

Beached. A corrall erected to simulate conditions aboard an LCT so the soldiers could practice their embarkation and disembarkation drill.

stops, saying they ruined the realism. This particular bow to realism has played on my mind ever since, for somehow a muzzle dropped and a burst of fire hit in among some riflemen, killing one. It was the Battalion's first such death in training, but not the last; casualties rose as live ammunition and high explosives played a large part in training to kill...a British glider's training camp nearby appeared wasteful of life to the point of disregard; few days passed, it seemed, that a caisson bearing a flag-draped coffin, escorted by troopers in red berets, did not rumble by on the way to the British army cemetery.

Another GI, Bob Sheehan, who had landed in Britain in September 1943, started training in earnest at the end of April 1944. He had been working with the 60th Chemical Depot Company at Shepton Mallet in Somerset but now

> there was a feeling of destiny in the air. We knew from our 'homework' that the great invasion must start soon. Then the orders came. We said a sad goodbye to Shepton Mallet and moved on down to Salisbury. On that great English plain, we set about hardening our softened bodies. Our brains and wills had been lulled away from the war by the pubs, the chess, the ladies, the sleeping in soft and sometimes scented beds - and eating in a civilized manner from plates on tables

covered with clean linen cloths. Now we had to relearn that we were thousands of miles from home and here for a purpose other than loading and unloading railroad cars and loading their sinister contents into corrugated iron igloos. We had now become part of the 1st Army. To prepare us for what might lay ahead across the Channel they made us run, they made us climb, they made us crawl on our bellies - while real live bullets whined overhead and our instructors screamed impolitely at us to stay down. The days were long and our bodies cried out for mercy, as we pounded across the rain-softened fields or swung madly over water-filled ditches. When the whistle finally blew and the day ended, most of us were too bushed even to walk the hour to the local pub. We were still soft and flabby. Most of those evenings were spent in letter-writing, playing cards, conversation or just plain getting some sack time. But it was May in England. And it was breathtakingly beautiful. The weekends were times to grab and hold the beauty and peace which would soon be part of another world. We knew we'd soon be in combat amid the ugliness and desolation of war.

Donald Burgett, a member of the US 101st Airborne Division that would parachute into Normandy on D-Day, had had a pretty hard training before he ever got to Britain:

Everything was done at the double, but when one of the instructors wanted something done even faster, they would yell 'Hubba, hubba...'we were told that this was Yiddish for 'Hurry, hurry'...I had never done so many push-ups in my life... [one day] we were doing doing push-ups in one of the sawdust pits when the instructor...suddenly asked if we were tired. 'No! came the chorused answer, for we knew better than to say 'Yes'. 'O.K' he replied, 'let's keep going...'The afternoon was a close pattern of the morning training except that we were shown more about jumping and the equipment that would train us for our first jump. One ingenious device, called the plumber's nightmare, was a network of pipes built about twenty feet high and wide and about eighty feet long. The men climbed up one end, then across the top and wormed their way back and forth through it in a prearranged course that was said to work to the fullest every muscle in the body.

The British Commandos were undergoing a similar punishing routine designed to bring them to the peak of fitness, with daily forced marches weighed down with rucksacks weighing up to 90lb. They trained by scaling sheer cliff faces, fording icy streams and rivers, manoeuvring dinghies over rocks and white water, rope climbing, camping out and living rough.

It was necessary to train in conditions that most resembled those that would face the men when they landed in France. Beaches which had been prohibited areas, mined and ringed with barbed-wire when invasion from Germany threatened, were now cleared to prepare for the invasion of France. Charles Cawthon's battalion was one of the many that were sent to train on Slapton Sands in Devon where the cliff faces backed the beach much as similar chalk faces rose from the Normandy beaches.

The villages and hamlets in the hinterland of the 'invasion beaches' were cleared by government order - with some resistance. On 4 November 1943 the Chairman of Devon

County Council got a call from the War Office informing him that an area of South Devon known as South Hams was to be requisitioned under the Defence Regulations and Compensations Act of 1939. He called a meeting in the village hall to tell the local inhabitants that 30,000 acres comprising parts of six parishes, 3,000 people, 180 farms, village shops and other buildings were to be totally evacuated to make way for US forces' training. The 750 families affected had precisely six weeks to find somewhere for themselves and all their livestock to live, and to move all their possessions. Gordon Luscombe was a sixteen-year-old farmer's son living in Slapton in 1943, and he remembers it well. 'We didn't know where we were going and father had to find somewhere for the animals. As it was winter we had to take all the hay and straw for the cattle - the ricks had to be dismantled - all the farm implements, chickens, dogs, cats, everything had to go.' The Luscombe family found somewhere to live near Totnes, but they had to sell their dairy herd and sheep, because there was room for less than half in their temporary accommodation. Notices were put up all over the village and the WVS (Women's Voluntary Service) visited every home to make sure that everyone had understood. 'I said to my boy,' said one villager, 'if it'll help our chaps out there fighting for us then us've got to go.'

'There was a war on and we had to go,' says Luscombe stoically, 'the old people took it worst. Some of them had never left the village. A lot of them never got over it.'

The Admiralty informed the Ecclesiastical Commissioners that they could not guarantee the safety of the several pre-Reformation churches in the area, and an ecclesiastical sculptor from Exeter was dispatched to advise clergymen on moving their portable treasures to a safe place and sand-bagging those that could not be moved. A fifteenth-century chancel screen was found to be riddled with woodworm holes 'as brittle as gingerbread' when it was carefully dismantled and put into boxes. The Bishop of Exeter pinned a notice on the boarded-up and padlocked doors of village churches exhorting the GIs to respect the fact that

> this church, this churchyard in which their loved ones rest, these homes, these fields are as dear to those who have left them as are the homes and graves and fields which you, our Allies, have left behind you. They hope to return one day, as you hope to return to yours, to find them waiting to welcome them home. They entrust them to your care meanwhile...

The first villagers were not permitted to return to their homes until more than two months after D-Day. When they did they found that every window had been shattered, that Slapton Church had received a direct hit, and, despite being well sand-bagged, a historic stained-glass window had been completely shattered. They also found shell holes, rampant weeds, fields and buildings full of rabbits and rats and 'lots of live shells lying around, mortar bombs, everything'. The villagers would ring up the bomb disposal unit at Plymouth who would come along with lorries and take them away. But for a long time, farmers trying to get their land back into shape would turn up a live shell when they were ploughing. Meanwhile the war had moved overseas.

King's School in Canterbury had been evacuated in 1940 when raids over the city became heavy as German bombers dropped their load as they wheeled back across the Channel after blitzing London and other British cities and ports. The boys had settled into

A Sherman tank tears through the English countryside during training exercises.

a series of hotels and houses around St Austell in Cornwall, and on their walks on the cliffs and scrambles down to the coves and beaches they had a unique view of the American soldiers training for war. Brian Arnold, then a pupil at the school, recalls that

> the American Army were all around in great quantity, preparing for the invasion. Some of the boys - both senior school and junior school - were very keen on getting hold of some of their explosives, and keeping them. The Americans used to stack all the ammunition up on either side of the road. You'd walk down the road and you were walking through an ammunition corridor of explosives of all sorts. You'd just lean down and pick it up. It was as easy as that. We'd pick up blocks of gelignite which looked like packets of margarine, but luckily witout detonators, there were shells of every calibre, anti-aircraft shells, and quite a lot of this stuff found its way into school...One day we had a search at the school in cupboards and things and we amassed quite a considerable pile of weaponry...dynamite, shells, mortars, hand-grenades, small arms, these were all stacked - for safekeeping I suppose - under the bed of the chaplain - a man of considerable girth who we always called 'the tank'.

Sometimes the boys would lower their 'booty' on ropes down one of the disused tin mine shafts which proliferated in that part of Cornwall: 'they must have been full of explosives.' Another pupil, Paul Pollok, remembers the chaplain too.

> He called me into his study and held out something and said, 'Is this gelignite? What shall I do with it?' And I was a scientist so I knew that if there was no

detonator, it was perfectly safe, so I said, 'Well, in my opinion you should put it in a bucket and put the bucket in the Headmaster's study,' which he did...Then one time we were told that a boy in my house had stolen a very large anti-aircraft shell from a dump, so we had to search for it...and eventually we went to this hotel bedroom where Shirley had his bed and we tore the cover off and there, in the mattress, was the perfect impression of this very long shell - two or three feet long. But no shell. So I said to him, 'Come on, Shirley, that's where you had it, isn't it?' And he said, 'No, that's the way I sleep.' We never found it, but when Shirley left the school, he left in one piece!

'The area was guarded,' says Arnold,

but there just weren't enough guards. We used to have a whale of a time driving amphibious vehicles out to sea, and really enjoying ourselves knocking bottles off the top of barbed wire entanglements with American carbines. We saw the GIs practising with these DUKWS [amphibious vehicles] all the time - they're a cross between a land vehicle and a boat, in fact they are rather better in water. But you have to remember to take the bungs out of the bottom when you got on land to let the water out, and it was rather important to remember to put them back in again before you went back into the sea!

There was only one occasion when Arnold remembers a DUKW sinking on the beach, but that was nothing to do with the King's School boys:

an American soldier was showing off to his girlfriend. He dashed into the sea and went straight to the bottom instead of gliding across the surface. It caused an enormous amount of mirth amongst us boys, I'm afraid to say. He was okay, but they had to spend half a day fishing the DUKW off the bottom with a crane.

That sort of thing went on all the time. In their usual light-hearted way the GIs used to come dashing in and practise an invasion...big stuff...dash off landing craft and up the beach going full steam, and then they'd turn round and find that the tide had gone out and the landing craft was sitting on the sand and it couldn't move an inch.

The boys learned other things from the GIs too:

They used to go into the old iron workings around here with local Cornish girls, where conifer trees were growing, and they thought that they were well and truly hidden from the public gaze, but we boys used to crawl up and 'read, mark and inwardly digest'...It was all fairly graphic...it was the real thing. Once a large black gentleman suddenly realised that I was looking at him and he leapt up and proceeded to chase me like fury, leaving the poor girl just lying there on the ground. But we were quicker than he was through the conifers and down the shale slopes, so we got away.

An effective invasion force was going to depend crucially on military co-operation, both between the different services and also the different nationalities. For the former group training exercises were started, full-scale rehearsals involving foot soldiers, engineers and airmen simulated the different manoeuvres and command networks that it would be so crucial to get right on the far shore. And what might be called public relations exercises were mounted to reassure the British soldiers about the dependability of their US counterparts, and vice versa.

Stars and Stripes carried a pep talk on 5 May 1944:

> The Allied Force will be an army in which Yank and Tommy will work together. In the vocabulary of Supreme Headquarters 'We' no longer means 'Americans' or 'British'. It means the two. In preparation for the mutual job American soldiers have been on exchange visits with the British units and vice versa. What they have learned of each other has been healthy enlightenment.

And just to prove it, the forces' journal gave some examples: 'Because of the British soldier's extreme politeness, you would think he is a cissy, but he's far from that...he's a tough and rugged soldier,' said 'A Sergeant, Signal Corps'. 'A Staff Sergeant, Infantry' agreed: 'There is nothing strung out or freakish about the British soldier...overlook his accent, learn his way of saying things so you speak the same language and you will find the best fighting companion you'll ever want next to you in battle,' whilst 'a Corporal, Field Artillery', confirmed 'I can see that they are good soldiers to go into combat with.'

The British were not stinting in their praise either: 'a Private, British Infantry' was relieved to find on closer acquaintance that 'When one sees them at work, one realizes they are far from being the playboys they are thought to be,' and another 'Private, British Infantry' indicated that he would be 'perfectly confident fighting alongside them...they are some of the finest chaps I have ever met.'

It was just as well. On 19 May *Stars and Stripes*, invariably a sensitive barometer to these things, soberly suggested the reality, that D-Day would not be far away, when it carried a poem by Clement L. Luckwood which ran:

> *It isn't easy to say Goodbye*
> *When the parting time is due*
> *And to grin like hell*
> *When you know damn well*
> *You'll be lucky to get through.*
>
> *You know that you have to do it*
> *It's a job that must be done*
> *Across the sea*
> *With a world to free*
> *And a war that must be won.*

CHAPTER SIX

THE ARSENAL OF INVASION

'**W**E'VE GOT A FAIRLY BIG job on,' said a supply officer with typical British understatement when he was interviewed by the magazine *Picture Post* on 6 May 1944, a month before D-Day.

> Something comparable to the city of Birmingham hasn't merely got to be shifted: it's got to be kept moving when it's on the other side...we must take everything with us - and take it in the teeth of the fiercest opposition. We are, in fact, undertaking the greatest amphibious operation in history, so vast in scale and so complex in detail that the supreme consideration must be the orderly carrying out of a Plan.

The final unfolding of the plan for D-Day took place a week later, at the OVERLORD conference on 15 May 1944 at St Paul's School in west London. It had been called to explain the D-Day plans to the King and the Prime Minister and to demonstrate to the Anglo-British commanders that, despite difficulties and disputes, this critical Allied undertaking was on course for success. George VI sat in an armchair next to Churchill, whilst the rest of the military planners and commanders crammed on to tiers of hard narrow school benches in the school hall and craned to see a thirty-foot scale plaster relief model of Normandy and the Cotentin Peninsula. They listened attentively as the Commander-in-Chief of the Allied Ground Forces, General Sir Bernard Montgomery, sketched out the problems: 'The enemy is in position, with reserves available...there are obstacles and mine fields on the beaches...there are many unknown hazards...After a sea voyage, and a landing on a strange coast, there is always some loss of cohesion.'

There was an additional small triumph for Montgomery: many years before, he had been a pupil at the school which now served as his HQ, and he had taken the High (Head) Master's study, forbidden territory to him as a child, for his command post.

'But,' continued the general,

> we have the initiative...we can rely on the violence of our assault, our great weight of supporting fire, from the sea and air, the simplicity of our plan...our robust mentality and morale. We shall have to send the soldiers into this party 'seeing red'. We must get them completely on their toes; having absolute faith in the plan; and imbued with infectious optimism and offensive eagerness. Nothing must stop them! If we send them into battle in this way - then we shall succeed.

*February 1942. On a cold day 'somewhere in England', Eisenhower and
Montgomery watch US troops training for D-Day.*

The other OVERLORD commanders had already taken the floor. Lieutenant-General
Carl 'Tooey' Spaatz, Commander US Strategic Air Forces stationed in Britain, described
the unexpected success of the bombing raids on Occupied France over the last two
months. In fact Spaatz and his British counterpart, Sir Arthur Harris, in charge of RAF
Bomber Command, had been vehemently opposed to this strategy, arguing that whilst
they recognized the imperative of a heavy bombardment over France immediately prior to
D-Day, they considered that their planes were best employed until then in knocking out
German oil installations and reserves.

This strategy, the two 'bomber barons' believed, would, if employed single-mindedly,
bring the Third Reich to its knees within thirty days: a far more effective strategy than
being diverted to provide what Harris scornfully designated 'army support' by targeting
the transport system that could, if not largely destroyed, rush reinforcement troops to
Normandy once the landings started.

Harris spoke next, briefing the group on RAF raids to wipe out the V-1 flying bomb
installations known to be sited in France, Belgium and Holland, poised to send their deadly silent weapons across the Channel. He was followed by the Air Commander-in-Chief,
Sir Trafford Leigh-Mallory, who outlined the strategy that Dieppe had made obvious for a
successful landing, 'deployment of bomber aircraft to neutralize beach defences and act as
a screen for the invasion force'.

Then it was the turn of the Naval Commander-in-Chief, Admiral Sir Bertram Ramsay, who had the daunting task of assembling nearly 4,000 naval craft at present gathering to berth along the coasts of England and Scotland, to rendezvous at a point south of the Isle of Wight, named appropriately 'Piccadilly Circus', before setting off across the Channel on a precise course for the British or American landing zones.

Lieutenant-General Bradley sketched in the tactics for getting the US 1st Army ashore on Omaha and Utah beaches and, using a pointer, Montgomery traced the movements of the 21st Army Group on the plaster model of Normandy which showed the features the invading troops would encounter - the farms, villages and towns, the flat plains to the south of Caen, the bocage of hedges criss-crossing the fields behind the beaches where the Americans would land, and the Vire estuary where marshy terrain would prove so treacherous on D-Day. Markers indicated the fixed position of the German troops.

'He tramped like a giant through Lilliputian France,' Lieutenant-General Bradley recalled as Montgomery outlined the basic objectives of the ground forces. The British first-day objectives as they landed on the eastern flank of the invasion fronts, were to advance towards Caen and Bayeux, both vital communication centres. The US forces, landing to the west, were to try to cut off Cherbourg. Intelligence reports had already confirmed that the German commander whom the Allies would face on landing would be Rommel, Montgomery's old adversary in the Western Desert, and Montgomery was convinced that he was 'too impulsive to fight set-piece battles' and was doing his best to seal off the beaches. 'OVERLORD is to be defeated at the beaches,' predicted Montgomery, guessing his old enemy's strategy. Eight divisions were therefore to be landed on D-Day. By D-Day+1 the number would have risen to thirteen and then grow steadily until by D-Day+90 there would be an army of thirty-nine divisions in France. Montgomery was ebullient at the meeting, in full control of all details of the plan, and apparently totally confident of the ease and speed with which the invasion forces would advance inland. But he was also too optimistic about the rate at which the armies would be able to move through France - an over-confidence that would catch up with him later and diminish his military reputation.

When the military commanders had outlined their tactics and given their briefings, it was time for Britain's political war leader to speak. Churchill admitted that he had had doubts about the wisdom of OVERLORD, confessed that he was still haunted by the prospect of the English Channel 'running red with the blood of British soldiers, extinguished like the soldiers of the western front, the men of Ypres and Passchendaele,' but that now, less than a month before the off, the Prime Minister was 'hardening towards this enterprise' and felt resolute in banishing any doubt he might have entertained and in wholeheartedly committing himself to its success - indeed so confident was he of its vital importance that he wanted to be part of the action and asked Bradley if he could ride in the first wave, alongside US infantrymen.

It was Admiral Deyo, Commander of Bombardment Group for Force U, who summed up what everyone was feeling that cold bright May morning: 'It seemed to most of us that the proper meshing of so many gears would need nothing less than divine guidance. A failure at one point could throw the momentum out of balance and result in chaos. All in that room were aware of the gravity of the elements that had to be dealt with.'

As the King left, he spoke to Eisenhower, who assured him, 'Your Majesty...OVERLORD is backed by the greatest armada in history. It will not fail.'

From his headquarters in Bristol, Bradley took to the road, like a campaigning politican on the stump. 'To give the invasion troops the opportunity to see their Army Commander and demonstrate our interest in their training,' the US General 'toured south-west England...visiting the first eleven divisions scheduled to land in France. From the depressing moors of Dartmoor to the steep green hills of Cornwall [Bradley] tramped from division to division calling on each company and battery.' To avoid interfering with their training, he instructed division commanders not to alter their schedules 'in an effort to impress me'. One division disobeyed: 'A battalion commander had rehearsed his troops in a mock company attack. As I watched the men advance in suspiciously pat order, I suspected a rehearsal plan and questioned the battalion commander.' When the man admitted to having practised the operation, 'he was relieved by the division commander. Time was too pressing to be wasted on visiting top brass.'

Bradley had decided that he had to put his one experienced assault division, the 1st Infantry ('the big red one'), into the D-Day operation. The US 4th Infantry Division and the US 29th Infantry Division, which had been stationed in England, 'had both undergone extensive amphibious training, [but] neither had as yet come under fire.' Rather than chance a landing with two inexperienced divisions, he decided to include a veteran division in the line-up.

The 1st infantry had been fighting in North Africa and then Italy. 'They had swallowed a bellyful of heroics and wanted to go home.' When the division learned that it was to make a third D-Day assault, this time in France, 'the troops grumbled bitterly over the injustices of war. Among the infantrymen who had already survived both Mediterranean campaigns, few believed their good fortune could last them through a third.'

But Bradley felt there was little room for the niceties of justice in the business of warfare - his job was to 'get ashore, establish a lodgement, and destroy the German.' He felt 'compelled to employ the best troops I had to minimize the risks and hoist the odds in our favor in any way that I could. As a result the division that deserved compassion as a reward for its previous ordeals now became the inevitable choice for our most difficult job.' Whatever the injustice, the US General reflected, 'it is better that the war heap its burdens unfairly than that victory be jeopardized in an effort to equalize the ordeal.'

Eisenhower's naval aide, Captain Harry C. Butcher, was well aware of Bradley's anxieties - and in his view there was some cause for them. In March he wrote despairingly in his diary: 'The young American officers...seem to regard the war as one grand manoeuvre in which they are having a happy time. Many seem as green as growing corn. How will they act in battle and how will they look in three months time?'

So tall and courteous, and occasionally bespectacled, his combat jacket worn under a stained topcoat, his GI trousers stuffed into his paratrooper's boots, Bradley went around inspecting and reassuring his men. 'Tommyrot,' he told the soldiers of the US 29th Division when he heard that there was talk of ninety per cent casualties on D-Day. 'Some of you won't come back, but it'll be very few.'

On one of his visits to the US 9th Infantry Division in training, Bradley was accompanied both by Eisenhower and by Churchill. Churchill was very keen to try out the new

A line of DUKWs, two-and-a-half ton amphibious trucks, driving along the beach.

American carbines that he saw the troops were using. 'Targets were promptly put out for Churchill, Eisenhower and me. Mine was handicapped at 75 yards, Eisenhower's at 50. The Prime Minister's was placed at 25 yards. We each fired 15 rounds in rapid succession.' The targets were wisely hustled away before anyone could read the score.

Montgomery was on the D-Day trail, too. He had a routine. He'd walk slowly round the troops drawn up on parade, staring intently at each man's face. When he'd inspected every soldier Montgomery would return to his Jeep, pick up his loudspeaker and and call for the troops to 'break ranks and gather round'. The 5,000 soldiers would converge on the khaki army truck, and the birdlike Montgomery - he wore specially raised shoes to make him taller and was a 'blend of spinster and hawk who relished a grand occasion', according to Eisenhower's grandson and biographer - would address them through the megaphone. It was always the same speech. 'I have come here today, so that I can get a look at you and you can get a look at me...not that I'm much to look at...we've got to go off and do a job together very soon now, you and I...and now that I have met you I have complete confidence, absolutely complete confidence...And you must have confidence in me.' Stories about Montgomery's ability to talk to the troops abound. No matter how difficult Eisenhower and the other commanders found the often arrogant, opinionated and intransigent general, the soldiers bought his line of 'I know you and trust you and you must trust me.' If there was no opportunity to inspect the men personally, Montgomery would stand on a Jeep, or platform, anywhere where he could survey the men, and tell them to take their helmets off. His gaze would travel slowly over the soldiers, as if he was

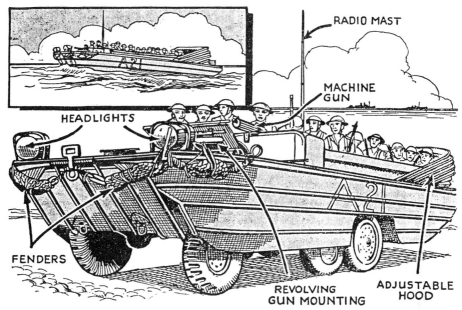

RADIO MAST

MACHINE GUN

HEADLIGHTS

FENDERS

REVOLVING GUN MOUNTING

ADJUSTABLE HOOD

THE DUCK, SIX-WHEELED, TWO-AND-A-HALF TON, LORRY AMPHIBIOUS JEEP

DUKWs: a diagram from The Children's Invasion Book *published by Faber in 1944.*

committing their features to memory. Finally he would nod, tell them to put their helmets back on and start up, 'Now that I know you...'

Montgomery, a strict non-smoking teetotaller, would offer soldiers one of the cigarettes ' my ladyfriends send me' or pass on a newspaper he was reading. The Ist Battalion Welsh Guards would always recall the time Montgomery asked one of their number at a crack-of-dawn muster, 'What's your most valuable possession?' 'It's my rifle, sir,' the soldier replied dutifully. 'No, it isn't. It's your life. And I'm going to save it for you. ..'

By D-Day Montgomery's pep talk had been heard by a million soldiers and he took his message not only to the troops who were preparing for D-Day. He made a pitch to boys who were still too young to fight, but had been training in the OTC and might before long be soldiers too. The boys of King's School, Canterbury, which had been evacuated to near St Austell in Cornwall, recall Montgomery coming to talk to them whilst on a tour of the troops training in the area. 'He was very self-centred,' recalls Harold King who was a pupil at the time.

> We all had to parade and then went into a huge garage which we were using as the
> school chapel at the time to hear him speak. He gave us a lecture on El Alamein:
> exactly how he'd planned it, how it had been fought, and as he spoke there were
> some road works going on outside, and suddenly a pneumatic drill started up, and
> he just stopped and he sent his aide outside, and just as suddenly as the drill had
> started, it stopped. There was a deathly hush...of course his name at that time
> would have stopped anybody doing anything.

'He was our hero.' Noel Osmond who was also a pupil at the school recalls Montgomery starting his speech to the assembled boys by saying, 'I expect that everybody in this chapel here this morning would like me to tell you when the Second Front is going to start,' and we all looked very excited and he said, 'Right, I'll tell you before I leave this hall.' And at the end of his lecture he said that the Second Front had already started, that the North African campaign was all part of the Second Front, and a landing in Europe wouldn't be the start...and we were quite disappointed...we'd really thought he was going to let us boys in on a secret no one else knew.'

As May - a particulary warm and pleasant month that year - wore on, Eisenhower was increasingly occupied at Norfolk House in planning and co-ordinating strategy, details and diplomacy. But earlier in the spring he too had been on the D-Day trail, trying to take weekly excursions away from his desk and the endless planning meetings that filled the thoughts and occupied the time of the Supreme Allied Commander, to visit both British and US troops in training and familiarize himself with the weapons and techniques of the invasion. It was an experience that was new to him. In the First World War, Eisenhower had been charge of a tank training centre in Gettysburg: when the war ended he had spent the next twenty years as a staff officer, involved in military strategy rather than with the day-to-day combat training of the soldiers. This was a source of some embarrassment to him. As his son diagnosed, 'He would have given a great deal for the prestige of having been shot at...' In his talks with the soldiers and in his rare public addresses, Eisenhower would emphasize his essential managerial role in a chain of command that he was confident would win the war: as Commander of the Allied forces he was always at pains to stress the common purpose of the British and the US troops - and how they could work together. For Eisenhower knew as well as anyone that the success of the battle for Normandy depended not only on the various services - air, infantry, naval, communications - all working well together, it also depended on the co-operation of armies on the ground, British, US and Canadian.

On every trip they made through southern and western England throughout May 1944 the commanders of OVERLORD had the satisfaction of seeing the 'remarkable conversion of the sleepy area into a busy cantonment of supply dumps, tent cities and vehicle pens stretching inland twenty-five miles from the coast.' By late February 150,000 American forces a month were arriving in Britain to join their British, Canadian, French and Polish comrades in the interminable wait for the decision to go.

By May there were 2,876,600 officers and men organized into thirty-nine divisions, plus air, medical, transport and communication units waiting 'as tense as a coiled spring' for the order to move. It was said that the British Isles were so laden down with men and equipment that it was only the barrage balloons that kept them afloat. Every week another trans-Atlantic convoy would arrive and crates of supplies of Jeeps, artillery shells, guns, K-ration packs, blood plasma and much more would be stacked on the quayside. The final plan for OVERLORD was that 175,000 men, 1,500 tanks, 3,000 guns and 10,000 trucks, Jeeps and other vehicles were to be landed in the first twenty-four hours, together with the supplies needed to support men and machinery - 1,000,000 gallons of drinking water, for example. To transport this formidable force across the Channel was the task of the Navy and, desperately relieved by the month's reprieve when D-Day was put back from 1 May to June, Ramsay was able to assemble a variety of craft developed for this purpose. Operation BOLERO had reached its climax.

'Let there be built great ships which can cast up on a beach in any weather large numbers of the heaviest tanks,' Churchill had decreed in July 1940. In addition, Landing Ship Tank (LST) had been developed to do just this: it was capable of carrying up to sixty tanks across oceans. There were also 837 Landing Craft Tanks (LCTs) which could carry three to five tanks and load and unload them through a ramp used on D-Day. The British version could land tanks in three feet of water. The LCT (R) was developed to support the troop landings with fire power: an LCT adapted to fire rockets, its potential was enormous and it could fire off 1,080 rockets in half a minute. There were also Landing Craft Guns (LCG) and Landing Craft Flak (LCF) equipped with quick-firing anti-aircraft guns. The troops would be put ashore from Landing Craft Personnel (LCP), Landing Craft Assault (LCA) or Landing Craft Infantry (LCI [L]), or a smaller version (LCI [S]). Another wartime invention was the DUKW, an amphibious vehicle - always referred to as 'DUCK' - which could float at sea and also be driven straight on to dry land. It had been designed for a US fruit importer who had had transport problems in South America, and it proved one of the most versatile of wartime vehicles, particularly in the first assault phase of D-Day when it was used to move between the landing craft and the shore.

There had been long-running battles over the number of LCTs available for the invasion landings but by D-Day Admiral Ramsay was able to rally 4,126 ships and landing craft that would be used in the initial assault and the follow-up. This D-Day armada was split in two: an eastern force commanded by Admiral Vian would make for the British beaches whilst the western force under Rear-Admiral Kirk of the US Navy would target those to the west. These main forces broke down into five smaller forces, each one heading for a landing beach, and each organized like a small armada with landing ships carrying infantry and tanks, hundreds of small landing craft including LCTs and LCAs and support vessels adapted for various functions such as that of carrying guns, cooking - including baking bread - and repair work. These convoys were to be flanked by destroyers and anti-submarine trawlers which would both protect the assault force and also pound the German concrete beach defences with mortar fire. 137 warships - including seven battleships from the Royal Navy - and the US Navy and a couple of Free French cruisers were to bombard the shore in advance of the landings.

On D-Day the minesweepers would sail across the Channel first, whilst the troop carriers and landing craft would anchor some miles out from the beaches. All the ships would be connected by radio communication to a headquarters ship, and when the order was given, the assault craft would be lowered and the men would scramble down the nets into the craft. Meanwhile far out to sea the warships would fire at pre-arranged shore targets, whilst nearer to the beaches the battleships and destroyers would splatter the beaches with shells. At H-Hour the first wave of assault craft would make for the beach. The LCTs would lead and release the DD tanks they were carrying a few thousand yards from the beach. The infantry would pour out of the landing craft and naval and marine demolition teams would have a short time to clear what obstacles they could before the next wave arrived. It was planned that all day wave after wave of landing craft would arrive on the beaches bringing tanks, a staged selection of 'Hobart's Funnies', engineers to clear the mines and other obstacles, and hundreds and thousands of men to try to breach the defences and carry the invasion inland.

By the end of May these immense naval forces were assembling in the ports of southern England. It was an awesome sight. 'No one…could believe that the invasion fleet would ever put to sea intact,' marvelled an American staff officer as he surveyed 'the tiny harbours along the south coast and the big sprawling harbour of Southampton packed like miniature Pearl Harbors, with ships stacked gunwale to gunwale.'

Apart from the armada around Britain's coastline, evidence of the coming invasion littered the south of England. At the end of May the roads of Britain were clogged with convoys of army vehicles, tanks, trucks and Jeeps as they streamed south towards the marshalling areas along the coast. Buildings had to be knocked down, roads widened or newly built, bridges strengthened, and hard-standing and lay-bys constructed to accommodate the huge amphibious trucks and giant transporters that poured into British ports, laden with tanks and bulldozers. In addition, some unexpected demolition occurred when transporters got stuck under road bridges, knocked down parapets and took the corners off innumerable buildings. A teacher in Dorset was alarmed at the sight of a truck carrying two Sherman tanks. 'It must have required tremendous skill, and a heavy engine, to drive this heavy load through our narrow streets. Our narrow country roads were unsuitable for Sherman tanks.' She found the noise of the tanks pulling up the steep hill deafening: 'It was impossible to speak…I arranged with the pupils that I would dictate until these tanks drew near, and then they should study their notes while we endured the deafening sound outside.' She recalls that employers gave staff an extra quarter of an hour for lunch because the town had become so congested with the convoys blocking the narrow streets that it took twice as long to get around.

Robert Arbib met 'his' engineers as he drove up the A1:

> Everywhere along that road, and all the others in England, there were endless convoys of army vehicles - miles and miles of them…moving along bumper to bumper - division after division. [The 820th Engineers] had pulled out of their aerodrome in Suffolk, and were headed south, to take part in the invasion. As bulldozers rumbled past, and the motorgraders and the shovels and the trucks, I stood up in the front of the Jeep and shouted and waved: 'So long, Pete! Good luck, Tommy!…Take it easy now John…Good luck, good luck!'

As the convoys stopped along the roads, women came out with cups of tea, cake and whatever they could spare for the soldiers, and gratefully the GIs would fling their small change to the local children who clamoured for gum as they moved off.

Bob Sheenan, a GI who had arrived in Britain in September 1943, found on his return to Salisbury from a week's furlough in London in May 1944, that some of his company, sensing the invasion couldn't be far off, hadn't waited for their official orders:

> In the small hours of one morning, they'd loaded up a Jeep with guns, ammunition and several cases of whisky. Thus equipped they sallied forth. Quite how they would join the invasion didn't seem to occur to them, for they had neither boats nor water-wings. They were returned to us next morning by the MPs with multiple hangovers - and minus stripes, Jeeps and whisky.

A rural arsenal. A cow interrupts its grazing alongside a tank parked in an adjacent field as part of the build-up to Operation OVERLORD.

Finally it was time to go and the convoy moved off.

> We would drive for five minutes at a time and then stop for what seemed like endless hours…It was a miracle that it all worked, as tens of thousands of men and their vehicles slowly funnelled down to the south shore to pick up the places assigned to them. To do it on time and then do it over and over again throughout the hours of daylight and darkness marked a major triumph for the bureaucratic mind.

Charles Cawthon watched as the Stonewall Brigade made moves to leave Dartmoor:

> The 2nd Battalion gave Bridestowe Camp a final raking and brushing, turned all excess toilet articles over to a nearby orphanage - soap was a scarce and valued wartime item in Britain - and left the moors. Watching the trucks pass out of the camp gate, I was impressed that the battalion was at its peak, as ready as an outfit can be. Its people, many of whom I knew by name, looked hard and fit; trucks, weapons, carriers and Jeeps, in dull olive drab, were spotless - and moved at careful sixty-yard intervals. I was not aware of it, but we were never to look exactly

*A world apart. By the end of May, troops destined for the first assault on D-Day were
interned in closely guarded camps around the south coast - and denied any outside contact.*

that way again. Battle turned sleekness to a wary, worn look; after D-Day, the
company became a kaleidoscope of changing faces.

All along the roadsides of southern England were parked tanks, trucks and Jeeps camouflaged with netting and foliage: piles of ammunition protected by corrugated iron stood in
serried ranks in fields, on commons, on the areas of car parks and hard-standing that were
not already occupied by tanks or trucks. In the woods, Red Cross ambulances were
parked, waiting among the bluebells to bring the wounded to hospital.

'Troops were everywhere...every leaf-roofed lane was parked with vehicles and supply
dumps; the air was charged with the vitality and power of all this restrained violence,
primed and ready to detonate,' recalls Cawthon.

At the end of May Mollie Panter-Downes noticed that

> There is a curious new something in [people's] expressions which recalls the way
> people looked when the Blitz was on. It's an air of responsibility, as though they
> had shouldered the job of being back in the civilian front line again. Stay-at-home
> Britons seem resigned to the probability that their Second Front will consist main-
> ly of humdrum hardships, including more inconvenience, fatigue and doing with-
> out. The idea that London, during the invasion, will come in for heavy air attacks
> seems to have faded away, oddly, and there is even less worrying over any secret
> weapon that might be up the German sleeve for D-Day. It is plausible to lots of
> English that the Germans may stage a token invasion or series of parachute raids.
> This would mean that, since the Army's attention would be engaged elsewhere,
> the Home Guard would be expected to take charge of the situation...the shadow
> of the Second Front falls across day-to-day happenings in even the smallest com-
> munity. One country-dwelling lady who recently decided that she must have some
> urgent plumbing repairs done in her home was warned by the contractor that he
> and his plumber's mates were all Home Guards. He pointed out that if anything
> happened (there isn't a village in England which doesn't proudly imagine that it's
> all-important to the Nazis), the boys would just drop her new water tank smack
> on the lawn and she would be left bathless until the fighting was over. It is often in
> just such a ridiculous way that English families begin to realize what it may be like
> to have the battle of Europe right on their doorsteps, involving not only big and
> historic issues but also small and homely ones like baths, trains, the morning
> paper, and the day's milk.

The 20,000 men working on the Mulberry Harbours which were to be towed across the
Channel knew that they were building something vital for the invasion. They had no idea
what it was. The 'Mulberry jigsaw' had become a metaphor for D-Day for most British
people: they knew that an invasion was imminent. The evidence of troop movements, the
build-up of the matériel of war and the increasing restrictions on information made it
unmistakable: many knew that they or someone close to them would have an important
role to play when the invasion happened, but until the very eve of D-Day only a handful of
top commanders knew how the pieces fitted together.

The Germans also knew an invasion was coming: German Intelligence had discovered
what they first decoded as Operation OVERLOCK (a misreading of OVERLORD) and
had predicted that 'for 1944 an operation is planned outside the Mediterranean that will
seek to force a decision and therefore will be carried out with all available forces'. It was
essential that they neither knew when or where it was coming. The element of surprise
was paramount if the Allies were to breach the German defences and establish a toehold
in Europe. That was another of the lessons of Dieppe. As COSSAC soberly assessed: 'If
the enemy obtains as much as forty-eight hours' warning of the location of the assault
area, the chances of success are small, and any longer warning spells certain defeat.'

Every effort was taken to misinform the Germans: RAF and USAAF planes bombed
the Pas de Calais and targeted the flying bomb launch pads sited behind Calais and
Boulogne - precisely the sort of 'softening up' exercise that would be expected before an

invasion. Enemy agents who had been captured and 'turned round' excitedly fed false details about planned invasions of Calais in July, information guaranteed to have been culled from 'sources in the know'. Whilst the build-up of men and tanks and trucks and boats in southern and western England was heavily camouflaged, the German Air Force reconnaissance planes found it surprisingly easy to fly over south-eastern England and see the massed landing craft in the harbours and estuaries there and the tanks filling the fields of Kent and east Sussex. Meanwhile the Abwehr found they were able to pick up 21st Army Group signals being relayed from Kent. In fact this was all part of FORTITUDE: the tanks were made of wood or rubber inflatables, as were the landing craft known as 'Big Bobs', and the Army signals, which originated at the Portsmouth HQ, were being deliberately fed across country before being transmitted from Kent.

Britain's island status had come to its rescue in the recent past: Hitler's tanks had not been able to roll across the Channel as they had rolled across the Ardennes into France in 1940. Now Eisenhower urged Churchill to turn 'our island fortress' to Allied account again: a cordon must be drawn tight around the British Isles to 'regulate all traffic from abroad, censor all communications, including diplomatic, by whatever means, and stop all air and sea traffic from the British Isles not under our direct control'.

Ireland, regarded by Churchill as 'a most useful base for enemy agents', was put under particular scrutiny: all mail was censored, all telephone calls to Eire were monitored; no flights were permitted to Ireland and the navy stopped and searched Irish shipping. On 17 April 1944 foreign diplomats were forbidden to enter or leave Britain and the diplomatic bag came under the eye of the censor.

It was, however, one thing to isolate Britain from outside contact, yet one of the motifs of the war had been the slogan 'Careless Talk Costs Lives'. It was essential, particularly in Eisenhower's mind, that the British people must be kept in the dark, too, for fear that German agents would be able to piece together any minutiae they overheard and build up a correct interpretation of OVERLORD. The British must not be able to see the build-up at close quarters, and so on 2 April those areas of training and armament storage from Land's End to the Wash and including a small belt round the Firth of Forth were designated no-go areas. Owners of ship and boats to be commandeered for the invasion were denied knowledge of where their craft were, what they might be used for and when they might get them back - 'Loose Lips Sink Ships', they were told. Once the troops were moved into the concentration areas, or sausages - so-called because of their shape - along the coast at the end of May ready for forward movement to the embarkation areas, security measures became even tighter. Barbed wire barriers were unrolled and 'perimeter and interior guards will be established by SOS and tactical units in order to prevent communication between briefed troops and persons not entitled to operational knowledge,' an order from the Chiefs of Staff to the War Office decreed. In other words, no contact with the outside world was permitted to the troops: letter boxes were sealed, public phone lines disconnected and the men entered a strange limbo land of waiting and uncertainty. Inevitably there were security scares - and what was most scary was that no one would ever know how real they were until it was too late.

At a cocktail party at Claridges Hotel in London in April a US general - a classmate of Eisenhower and Bradley at West Point Military Academy - was overheard complaining

"Yes, I shall be glad when they've passed—I have a bicycle under there!"

that supplies were not getting through from the US and would not do so until after the invasion on 15 June. Despite an 'old pals' plea, the man was demoted to colonel and shipped back to the US.

A man working at SHAEF HQ had sent a parcel to a Chicago Post Office for his sister to collect. The badly wrapped parcel started to come apart and a Post Office employee noticed that it contained documents relating to OVERLORD. The sender pleaded that overwork had lead him absent-mindedly to switch addresses on the two packages he was mailing out that day.

On 2 May a clue in the *Daily Telegraph* crossword puzzle had been 'One for the US' and 17 across had been filled in with the word UTAH. On the 23 May, the answer to 13 down 'Indian on the Missouri' was OMAHA. From 27 to the 30 May the words MULBERRY, OVERLORD and NEPTUNE all fitted the clues given. M15 officers paid a visit to the crossword's compiler, Leonard Dawe, a physics teacher from Leatherhead in Surrey, who,

*The world at war. Southampton householders go about their chores
as tanks awaiting embarkation for Normandy line the streets.*

with his friend, Melville Jones, had been thinking up clues for the *Telegraph*'s puzzle for over twenty years. Dawe had no explanation. Coincidence? Many years later a pupil of Dawe's, Ronald French, suggested an answer. The physics master had often enlisted the help of his pupils in compiling the crosswords, and at the time French spent a lot of time with American and Canadian soldiers at a nearby base and had absorbed the code words they used freely without realizing their full significance.

On 1 June men of the British 3rd Infantry Division, cooped up in West Ham Football Stadium and incensed when the beer ran out in their NAAFI, cut out of their confinement and, armed with the French francs they had been issued, swarmed into the pubs of East London. It took some time for Scotland Yard to round up the AWOLs and a couple of pub landlords who'd taken francs for beer, and no one could know what the men might have said - while under the influence - and who might have been listening.

On 3 June, a teletype operator at the Press Association in Fleet Street was routinely practising an information 'dry run' on a disconnected machine when she was distracted, and within seconds across the world had flashed URGENT PRESS ASSOCIATED NYK NEWS FLASH EISENHOWER'S HQ ANNOUNCES ALLIED LANDINGS IN FRANCE. Within seconds a colleague had intercepted BUST THAT FLASH...BUST THAT FLASH...BUST EISENHOWER. But already crowds in two sports stadiums in New York were observing a minute's silence to pray for Allied success.

Hollowood

"Well, are you going to let me get out? Or don't you WANT *a Second Front?"*

In Exeter a railway employee found an entire set of OVERLORD plans in briefcase left on a train; in Whitehall a gust of wind blew a dozen copies of the 'OVERLORD order' out of the War Office windows and into the street. The frantic civil servants could only recover eleven: two hours later the twelfth copy was handed in by a civilian. But could it have been copied?

There was a tragic security scare at the end of April. Operation FABIUS was a full-scale dress rehearsal for the Normandy landings for the landing forces destined for Utah and Omaha mounted off Slapton Sands in Devon - a shingle beach regarded as realistic as possible a simulation of what the Allied forces would encounter in Normandy. All the top brass were there - Eisenhower, Montgomery, Bradley, Tedder and Ramsay - all on separate crafts for security. The curiously named landing operations Duck, Parrot and Beaver passed off without incident, but Tiger was a disaster. The air cover never arrived to 'protect' the troops at H-Hour as they hit the beaches, when the troops did come ashore they seemed to have no idea quite what to do next, where to obtain ammunition or how they should form up to advance and, yelled the US 4th Infantry Division Commander Major General Raymond O. Barton, they were 'completely devoid of mine-consciousness, and a hell of a lot of you are going to get killed...'

In fact a 'hell of a lot' were already dead. Some 749 men, more than the entire losses on Utah beach on D-Day itself, were killed when nine German E-boats on patrol attacked a convoy of nine LCTs as they sailed through Lyme Bay heading for Slapton Sands. Many soldiers perished in the shell fire, others drowned as they obeyed the order 'Abandon Ship' for they seemed unsure how to inflate the Mae West life jackets they wore.

Eugene Eckstam, a doctor in civilian life back home in the US, was aboard one of the LSTs when a torpedo hit.

It hit midship, and the flames and the heat were separating the front from the back. There were twenty-two DUKWS on board and the men had been sleeping in them, and now they were ablaze...we could hear our small arms ammunition exploding and the men screaming. Navy regulations instruct you keep the integrity of the ship in any kind of an accident, and you have to close the doors to all the compartments to maintain air tightness so that the ship can float...and then people can hang on to it to be rescued. So I did what I learned to do while training in the Navy, I closed all the hatches. I don't know how many people were in there. I couldn't get in and they couldn't get out...I could just hear them. Then we went up on deck and even though we had really thick-soled shoes on the heat was coming through the decks and it was like walking on hot tar. We were all jumping or climbing overboard by the time the skipper gave the order to abandon ship. I didn't want to jump, so I eased down the cargo nets into the cold water which was forty-four degrees at the engine intake. The Channel's not the best place to swim - not out there in the middle. We were about twelve miles out from shore and we could see that the ship was burning brightly, and you could see the explosions from the gas tanks and the trucks on top. We were all anxious to get away from the ship, because of the suction, of being drawn down. And then we'd heard that Germans often tried to save survivors, came back for them, and that really scared us. We gathered round the life rafts, and there were some floats around too, but pretty soon some of the guys started to lose consciousness and float away, and I'd try to grab them, but I had no lines to hang on to, so they'd float away to nowhere. The water was so cold they were beginning to suffer from hypothermia. In the end I managed to get my hand round a rope that was on the side of the lifeboat, because I didn't want to drift off - and that's the last thing I remember...our ship had about 500 men aboard and we lost half...

Manny Rubens, a US Navy signalman, had been working on landing exercises for months.

It was weary work, we worked out of Falmouth and Fowey and it was very difficult because all the decent beaches were mined, so we'd go out into the Channel and work our way round the Cornish coast, and when the tide was out little coves were exposed at the foot of cliffs and we would take these GIs and land ourselves on the beach and land a few tanks and trucks and that was it, there was no place to go but up. So we'd get back on the ship and go back to port and get another bunch of guys and keep doing this day after day, month after month, just to get the men used to boarding the ship and leaving the ship.

On 28 April

after months of landing in little isolated spots where a real landing couldn't take place we were amazed to see that this was going to be a proper exercise of a task force of amphibious craft, LSTs, LCTs, all manner of assault craft on a beach that seemed to be miles long on the chart, and we just couldn't believe that a place existed in the south-west that wasn't mined…Our ultimate destination was Slapton Sands and it was supposed to be all pebbles…we had hours to spare, so, according to orders we had to spend the night circling round, and approaching H-Hour get in formation with other groups of ships and do a proper landing.

Things started to go wrong about two o'clock in the morning. I was sound asleep having come off the watch at midnight…and I grabbed my helmet and rushed up on deck at the same time as the Captain did and we both asked the same question, 'What the hell's going on?'

They were told that tracer fire had been seen two miles away, and concluded that it was all part of the exercise.

But suddenly all hell broke loose…we saw astern a gigantic orange ball of flame and you could see bits of black blobs flying off and you knew that it was men and parts of the ship, it was the most awful sight I had ever seen…moments later we heard an explosion and we realized that the ship had been torpedoed. We'd never carrried fuel on an exercise before…in fact most of the men thought that we were going to invade France because this time we were carrying live ammunition. All the men were carrying live ammunition and all the ships were carrying quantities of shells, fuel for the tanks and trucks and so on, so when the ship was hit, it just blew up like a fireball. Moments later we saw another explosion…we saw a sheet of flame, then a rumble and a couple of explosions and we realised that we'd been hit by a couple of torpedoes. By this time, the soldiers on the upper deck were getting hysterical..they were screaming…a lot of them were in open jeeps and half trucks and they were screaming 'Do something!' And there was nothing we could do. LCTs were not equipped to handle any sort of submarine or surface attack. We didn't know what to do…the sea was on fire, burning from the oil and the men were gone…there was no way we could get through that. We could see the bow wave with our naked eye…and a soldier with a heavy calibre machine - gun opened fire…and the Captain hadn't given the order to fire but the whole starboard side of the ship opened fire, all the 20- and 40-millimetre guns. Everybody was cheering because they were hitting a target. But I found myself screaming at the Captain and all the men on the bridge, 'It's too high'. We were hitting something that was thirty feet off the water instead of the torpedo boats that were very low…we were hitting another LST, one of our own ships, the LST 511. There were a lot of casualties…we didn't go on about liberty after that, the men were so ashamed. It was one of those tragedies of war. The E-boats went on strafing us, you could hear them, but you couldn't see them, there were terrible swells that night. The Captain said 'I'm getting the hell out of here…' and we headed for shore. The problem was we didn't know exactly where we were. We could have smashed into gigantic rocks…but anything is better than being a sitting target…that's what we were. We were like a covered wagon going very slowly with the Indians riding around and just killing us…

Nobody was killed on our ship…but we were numb with what we saw because washing in around the ship on to the beach were bodies. Some of the men didn't have a mark on them and they all hit the beach sitting up. They had their life pre-servers around their waists instead of under their arms and all these men had drowned sitting up. When they hit the beach depending on the force of the waves, some went on their face, and a lot just fell back and they had their full packs on and it was the worst thing I've ever seen. In the sea it looked like seaweed, where groups of men - three or four were literally burned together, as far as the eye could see there were these bodies. It was the worst débâcle, I think, that ever happened to the American Navy.

I've had nightmares for years. The sea was on fire, it was a surreal effect and you couldn't hear the men screaming out in the water, but you knew they were out there, and the wind was howling through the flag hoist and the rigging - to me it was just like something out of Hell...I don't know how many died, I've always reckoned a few thousand but I've seen a letter recently quoting 946, and a few years ago it was 700 and something. I don't know...the sea is their graveyard. All I know is that I never wanted to get close to anyone ever again. I had a lot of friends aboard the LCTs that died. All I wanted was to get married and have a family and live my own life with my family.

The deaths were kept secret: even Bradley was led to believe that it was 'a breakdown in command...a minor brush with the enemy that had delayed the men', rather than as he learned four years after the end of the war, '...one of the major tragedies of the European war'. A local girl who watched the burial of some of the soldiers was told she was 'never to mention what she had seen.' But though Manny Rubens was told 'under threat of court martial never to mention it to anybody, soldiers, sailors, family, to anybody, or there would be dire consequences,' he 'didn't give a Goddamn about it. I was mad as hell. I couldn't care less.'

But Eisenhower knew, and he was not only riven by the death of so many US soldiers and the disastrous loss of two much-needed LCTs, he was also well aware of the further risks. Ten of the missing men were officers of the 1st Engineer Special Brigade and they were classed as 'Bigots', top security, a category above even 'Top Secret' in Intelligence classification. Had they gone to a watery grave with the secrets they knew about the DUKWs, about the precise location and timing of the assaults on Utah and Omaha? Or had they been captured and were they at that very moment being subjected to a cruel interrogation which might lead them to put the entire D-Day invasion at risk? Eisenhower had his answer when the bodies of the officers were finally washed ashore some two weeks later.

CHAPTER SEVEN

TAKING TO THE BOATS

HENRY GILES WAS A WEAPONS Sergeant with the 291st Engineering Combat Battalion. He and his platoon had arrived in Britain in October 1943. Since March 1944 they had been intensively training for combat in the Gloucestershire countryside. By the middle of May, there was talk of little else but the coming invasion - 'when it's going to take place, where it's going to take place, how rough it's going to be, and of course, are we going to hit the beaches?...'

'God, yes! Bound to be. What the hell do you think we've had all this training for? They've got us pinpointed,' was the common opinion. 'Sure. We'll be the suckers who hit the beaches...they say Engineers will take ninety per cent casualties...Goddamn! Do you have to talk about it? Ain't it bad enough without bringing it up all the time?' Giles tried to reassure the men: 'This is the way I see it. Must be a hundred or two engineer outfits on the damn island. Say our chances of being picked are 150 to one. That's pretty good odds, I'd say.' One of the soldiers shuffled a pack of playing cards: 'If they was 1,000 to one, I'd still have the shakes,' he said.

Ralph Martin who wrote for the US Forces' newspaper *Stars and Stripes*, went to do a story about Liverpool at the end of May. He'd seen 'Liberty ships being loaded with equipment of war that could only be destined for one place.' So he hired a Jeep and toured around the south coast and found 'it was like watching an ant-hill, seeing the ever continuous flow of busy bodies rushing into the pinhead opening of the earth. These ports seemed to be the all-consuming centre of the world, with all the flocks running to get into the ark...our stupendous forces of liberation were on their way.'

Robert Capa, the photographer, was going to take part in the invasion too - he was on an assignment for *Collier's Magazine* - though as a Hungarian, Capa had been classified as an enemy alien and it hadn't been easy to get the necessary clearance to come to Britain, let alone be taken along for the D-Day landings. He remembers the 'immense concentration camps on the south coast of England. The camps were surrounded by barbed wire. Once you entered the gates you were half-way across the Channel.'

Yet Roderick Braybrook, who was a First Lieutenant in the first LCT to leave Southampton for Gold beach, found a loophole:

> They sealed us all off in the dockyard area around Southampton. We weren't allowed out or to make contact with anyone outside for at least three days before the loadings, but there was a telephone box on the quay and they'd forgotten to

disconnect it. You could ring anywhere in England...I used to ring up my girlfriend [who was a nurse] at the nurse's home and ask for her and I always got through.

Sealed behind the barbed wire of their concentration areas around the ports, the troops passed the time by honing preparations, trying to keep amused and just thinking. Henry Giles received several letters from the girl he'd met just before he had sailed for Britain: she told him that all his letters to her since 4 May had been opened by the military censor. 'That has never happened before, so she has her "alert" too.' After 18 May, no letters had been allowed out of the camp, and Giles reckoned that his girlfriend would know what that meant.

> She knows two other women with men in England. They have put their heads together and have come up with - invasion very near. Looks to me as if the top brass might as well have taken full page ads in all the papers and announced the news. Women aren't fools. Stop their mail and they begin to add two and two and come up with four. I think such close security is its own biggest gossip.

Joseph Martin was a sick bay attendant on a naval landing craft that was to bombard the beaches in advance of the forces' landing: 'We spearheaded the invasion, we were to go in even before the minesweepers.' He remembers

> we were in Southampton Water and I remember the Skipper calling everyone together and saying, 'Right, from such and such an hour the ship is sealed off.' That meant nobody could go ashore or nobody could come aboard, and then he said, 'There's one post going out now and there'll be one collection of mail.' Words to the effect that you'd better write your last letters. It wasn't quite as dramatic as that, but that's in fact what it meant...I wrote to my mother and father, and of course, my wife, Lisa...and I remember the difficulty that I had in writing those letters because you couldn't write home, 'Well, I'm going into battle. I'm going into the unknown. I might not come back.' You couldn't say any of those things. All you could say was, 'Well, we're off on an adventure, and I'm sure we'll be back, and when I get back we'll look forward to doing this and that. And you know what a wonderful mother and father you've been,' and that sort of thing without making it too sloppy or sentimental. At the same time you could imagine them receiving the letter and reading it. So I didn't want them to say, 'My God, you know this is the last letter we're going to receive from our boy,' so they were very difficult letters to write, there's no doubt about that. However they were written and sent and that was that.

Larry McLaughlin 'was single at the time, so I probably wrote to my folks, and whenever I wrote to them I tried not to be very pessimistic...I'd say that I felt that my Irish luck would hold out.' But McLaughlin was also concerned about one of his men:

> I had almost daily reviews of the men's equipment and told them to get rid of anything that was non-essential. But one of our medics had this huge Bible, it was his family bible and I told him, 'Can't you substitute a smaller book?' But he wouldn't budge, and so in the end I let it go. Ironically that boy was killed in Normandy...

'You write letters, play cards...' Canadian soldiers awaiting the order to join their ships.

Joseph Martin found it very difficult to look at his wedding photograph at this time. 'I kept it on board in my sick bay, and when times were really dodgy I had to put it away. It was a constant reminder that perhaps I would never see her again...so I used to have to put it out of sight then.'

The troops had plenty laid on to occupy the waiting time. 'Still sitting here,' Giles complained, 'No work, just a hell of a lot of recreation - baseball, volleyball, basketball, etc.' And double British summer time meant that 'the days are really long now. Doesn't get dark until ten o'clock.'

Some soldiers in the 4th Canadian Division whiled away the time in self-decoration. A member of the No. 7 Beach Group attached to the Division recalls:

> To liven matters up, they shaved their heads leaving tufts of hair as diamonds or squares, or sometimes they'd give themselves a Mohican cut or shave it in a line from ear to ear, or from forehead to nape. Next activity was to swap their cigarettes for 'Tommy Cooker' heating tubs - which were pure meths. It wasn't long before the craft was full of drunks, but within twenty-four hours, they were in the thick of the fighting all cool and calm.

Once they were sealed behind their barbed wire barriers with no one allowed in or out, the men started to receive their operational instructions and learned details of the great plan to liberate Europe. Smudged copies of combat instructions and detailed plaster models and photographs were pored over by the troops to discover what they would encounter on the far shore and what they would do when they did. 'We pounced on the

D-Day order [as if it was] "a second Book of Revelation" ', remembers Charles Cawthon. The whole operation was still couched in code: battalions were instructed that they would assault such places as 'Easy Green', 'Dog Red', 'White Queen' on stretches of beach dubbed Omaha, Juno, Sword, Gold or Utah. The soldiers studied natural features and man-made landmarks so that when they landed on the beaches these things would be already familiar to them. They were told by Intelligence Officers of the difficulties they would encounter, the obstacles to be navigated, the blocked exits from the beaches, the mines on the beaches and the guns on the bluffs. Then the battalion commanders would emphasize the overwhelming force with which the Allies were going to attack those obstacles: bombers would saturate all possible targets along the coast from the first minute after midnight: half an hour before the first landings were due, H-hour on D-Day, the beach fortifications and guns were to be bombarded from the air and sea in an effort to knock out their lethal fire power, force a way through the beach fortifications and also form craters or fox holes that the invading troops could use for cover. Volleys of rockets would be fired from inshore landing craft the moment before the invading force touched down on the beaches, the infantry preceded by tanks which would blast a way through according to Montgomery's masterful reversal of traditional tactics of assault.

The soldiers were well kitted out for this invasion. If the British infantry complained that they were always ordered to attack uphill and at the junction of two or more map sheets, the US Army, according to Cawthon, had a proclivity to oversupply itself and

> put too much of this surplus on the backs of its infantry…a special canvas assault jacket with large pockets front and back in which there were grenades, rations, mess gear, raincoat, a Syrette of morphine, toilet articles, motion sickness pills, water purification tablets, DDT dusting powder, a paste to put on his boots in case [the soldier] encountered chemically contaminated areas, a small block of TNT [though, Cawthon added, that of all the disturbing sounds he heard on Omaha Beach, there was none identifiable as from those blocks of TNT]… Around his waist was strapped an ammunition and equipment belt from which swung an entrenching tool, another first aid packet and a canteen. From his neck hung a special assault gas mask and extra bandoliers of ammunition. In addition, each man carried his individual weapon, and if a member of a machine-gun, mortar, flame-thrower, or demolition team, his part of that load.

The GIs were also issued with a new uniform impregnated with a chemical intended to neutralize the mustard gas that it was feared at the last moment the Germans might deploy. 'The uniforms felt constantly damp and gave off a sour odour,' says Cawthon. John Lynch, who was waiting with the US 30th Infantry Division in Portsmouth for embarkation, recalls, 'Our uniforms were regular fatigues that had been impregnated chemically against gas. They felt very stiff and uncomfortable and odoriferous. The old canvas lace-up leggings still worn at the time, received the same treatment. I reckon the Krauts would have smelt us coming, if it had been a night landing.' And the soldiers aboard the LCI [L] (Landing Craft Infantry, Large) on which a *New Yorker* journalist, A.J. Liebling, crossed the Channel, were taking no chances: when he went aboard on 1 June he found 'there were several groups of sailors on deck, most of them rubbing "impregnating grease" into shoes to make them impervious to mustard gas...our ships' rails were topped with rows of drying shoes.'

Joseph Martin was getting his supplies together, too.

> We'd been told by the skipper to be prepared for anything...so I looked at my medical supplies - of course every boat is given a medicine chest - and in this chest there's all sorts of bits and pieces and pills and so on, but of course the amount of first aid stuff that's shell dressings, splints, tourniquets, that sort of thing, was few and far between.

So anticipating that he 'might run into trouble,' Martin stopped at various points on the way down from Newcastle, where his ship had been berthed, to Southampton collecting supplies on the way.

> That enabled me to replenish what stocks I had, but of course the next problem was how was one man going to deal with several casualties if we got hit? So I decided to get together a first aid crew...the skipper thought it was a good idea: 'It'll keep them out of mischief.' There were a few volunteers and we trained and went through what to do, but of course, they all had their specific duties, so when we hit trouble they couldn't really help me, they had to man the guns and things like that.

As he was travelling with the troops Robert Capa was subject to the same regulations: 'We had to exchange our legitimate dollar bills and pound notes for invasion francs printed on flimsy paper.' The troops were issued with 200 francs in a special currency that meant that they could start trading with the people of Occupied France as soon as they went ashore. They were also issued with 'a little book telling us how to treat and address the natives there,' recalls Capa. It caused some derision: 'There were some useful approaches in French: "Bonjour, monsieur, nous sommes les amis américains." That was for addressing the men. "Bonjour, mademoiselle, voulez-vous faire une promenade avec moi?" That was for the girls. The first one meant "Mister, don't shoot me," and the other could mean anything.' Giles thought the leaflet was 'a real lulu. For instance, "Some French are good and some are bad"...what do they do? Put armbands on 'em so we can tell 'em apart?' Whilst *Stars and Stripes*, ever sensitive to its readers' concerns, reassured them, 'Don't be surprised if a Frenchman steps up to you and kisses you. That doesn't mean he's queer. It means he's emotional, French, and darned glad to see you.'

The troops were also issued with 'K-rations,' a small waxed cardboard box that fitted into the pocket of a fatigue jacket. It contained 'a packed tin of some sort of alleged meat or some cheese. Some contained chocolate or hard candies. There was synthetic coffee or lemon juice powder, a couple of biscuits and a small pack of cigarettes.'

The mood of anxious expectation was felt throughout the country. At the end of May Mollie Panter-Downes noticed that

> Although the British have had news from Rome to cheer them [the US 5th Army were advancing on Rome which was captured on 4 June] and the recent Churchill speech to puzzle them, the really big news for them is the fact that it's still C-Day and not yet D-Day. In the curious hush of the moment - a hush that isn't merely

*Fighting fit: US troops exercise on the quayside before joining their
ship ready for the cross-Channel crossing.*

figurative, since Londoners haven't been awakened by sirens for a month - it
seems as though everyone is existing merely from one ordinary day to the next,
waiting for the great, extraordinary one...Civilians have already had a foretaste of
the interruptions in the routine of existence which the invasion will bring, for the
railways, as was threatened, have been quietly withdrawing services here and
there under the very noses of commuters, who frequently arrive at the station in
their city clothes only to find that there are no trains to take them to the city.
Furthermore, over the recent Whitsun weekend, many of the determined holi-
day-makers who went to look for trains to take them out of London were disappointed...in coastal hamlets, where one can see the Channel simply by toiling up a
chalk track to the downs, the coming invasion is felt to be very much a local
affair...all the little churches will be open for prayers and improvised services
when the invasion signal is given. The local folk, especially in southern parts,
think that they will get a hint of what is afoot long before those slow London
chaps read it in their newspapers. It's true that the peace of the countryside is
rent day and night with every variety of loud noise, but they nevertheless expect
to recognize the real thing when it comes. Any particularly heavy coastal barrage
put up against the German reconnaissance raids these nights has wives excitedly

jabbing sleeping husbands in the ribs and saying, 'Wake up, Dad! It's started!' Tiny coastal communities, where cars never even bothered to stop in peacetime, proudly expect that when it does start they will find themselves in the front line, just as they have always been in the hundreds of years that Englishmen, in one pattern of warfare or another, have been slipping away across the Channel on other D-Days.

On 2 June the battleships and cruisers - the naval bombardment forces - had set sail south from their bases in Belfast, the Clyde and Scapa Flow.

On 3 June the troops destined for the first assault hoisted their invasion kit on their shoulders and set off from their marshalling camp for embarkation. Cawthon thought that the British cheer that went up as his US Battalion passed

> was for the departure of troublesome guests, and not for heroes leaving on a crusade...no bands played: no girls waved handkerchiefs while struggling to choke back tears. The closest to a send-off was a leathery old dockworker who croaked, 'Have a good go at it, mates.' It was like loading for a Slapton Sands exercise except for the pounds of equipment we carried.

Bob Sheehan's convoy had had a warmer send off when, on the trek to the coast, they had stopped outside a row of houses where a group of

> men, women and children all stood watching the never-ending column of tanks and trucks manned by their sweating crews. They waved now and then, but to tell the truth, they were waved out. Overcome by the awesome sight of this enormous cavalcade, they just stood still. We somehow became aware of their anxiety and feeling for us. It was as if we had assumed the object of all their hopes and fears for the coming struggle.
>
> Then from a house to our left emerged a mother-figure with bowls of strawberries and cream. She handed them to me and gave me a gulpy kiss to my forehead. 'Good luck,' she said, 'Come back safe.'
>
> The rest of the onlookers were then galvanized into action. Figures hurried down to waiting vehicles and the crews were invited to come in for a hurried wash, and in some cases, shave. Yet others brought out tea or lemonade. There was a kind of togetherness that I had never seen before. A sharing of spirit. It was no longer them and us. We were family and danger was afoot.
>
> It was a great consolation that these ordinary people cared. They didn't know us, had never met us, and would never see us again. But for that moment...we were allies.

D-Day was scheduled for 5 June 1944, the day when the tides and the moon would be most propitious for a landing. After a very cold and wet spring, the weather in late May had been beautiful. A record crowd had enjoyed cricket at Lords in brilliant sunshine - though as Mollie Panter-Downes pointed out newspapers were not

> alllowed to comment on the weather - at least until the information is too dated to help the enemy - but as a conversational topic in the countryside its behaviour

has recently run a close second to the invasion…a series of disastrous May frosts…wiped out the famous Vale of Evesham berry and plum crops and blackened the blossoms of what promised to be a record yield in Kentish orchards. The fruit growers regret that the official secrecy on weather conditions was not relaxed for once to give them a warning which might have helped save some of the fruit. The loss in this particular year, when all England is crowded out of both house and larder, is a serious one. Then to add to the joys of a…farmer's life the drought has damaged the hay crop, and this, in turn, will affect the milk yield. Although these headaches naturally figure in a good many of the discussions after opening time in the village pub, the one unfailing topic, as much there as in London clubs and bars, is the invasion.

By 4 June, a Sunday, everything was in place: the operational orders for the Channel crossing, Operation NEPTUNE, issued on 24 April ran to nearly 1,000 closely typed pages - a doorstep of paper three inches thick which detailed every boat's position, tasks and objectives. The US Western Task Force, consisting of Force O and Force U, was ready to leave from a coastal strip which stretched from Salcombe in Devon to Poole in Dorset, while Forces G, J and S of the Eastern Task Force were strung out along the Solent and Southampton Water. The tanks, weapons and equipment, waterproofed and camouflaged were stored aboard the troop-ships and landing craft, some covered with netting, which lay in wait all along the south coast in harbours, in inlets and on mud flats. The London railway stations stood empty except for a number of unfortunate would-be travellers, stranded when the trains had all been cancelled. Airfields all over the south and west flew the flag that informed planes 'airfield unserviceable: landing forbidden' above rows of waiting planes.

The men were already aboard the ships and landing craft. Cawthon and his battalion clambered into tugs to be ferried out to their transport, the SS *Thomas Jefferson,* where they found that 'the accommodations were spacious for a troop-ship', and the GI noticed for the first time 'that the oppressive crowding, so much part of army life, thins out markedly the closer the approach to battle'. Capa, on board USS *Chase* in Weymouth harbour, looked around him at

> battleships, troop-ships, freighters and invasion barges, all mingled together. Floating in the air above the ships were numbers of silver barrage balloons. The prospective tourists to France lazily watch[ed] the giant toys that were being hoisted aboard. For the optimists, everything looked like a new secret weapon, especially from a distance.

Capa divided the soldiers on board into three categories:

> the planners, the gamblers and the writers of last letters. The gamblers were to be found on the upper deck, clustering around a pair of tiny dice and putting thousands of dollars on the blanket. The last-letter writers hid in corners and put down beautiful sentences on paper leaving their favourite shotguns to kid brothers and their dough to the family. As for the planners, they were down in the gymnasium in the bottom of the ship, lying on their stomachs around a rubber carpet on

A heavy truck pulls a field kitchen up the bow ramp of an LST during invasion embarkation so that 'Invaders of Hitler's Fortress Europe won't go hungry'.

which was placed a miniature of every house and tree on the French coast. The platoon leaders picked their way between the rubber villages and looked for protection behind the rubber trees and in the rubber ditches on the mattress.

Henry Giles was definitely in the 'last-letter writers' category as he found himself writing twice a day; 'and I have an almost uncontrollable urge to write again' to the woman he intended to marry after the war was over - even though he knew the letters couldn't be sent, and he had already burned her letters to him since he had no way of keeping them. All around him, men 'who hadn't written a letter in months are suddenly as busy as beavers, coming in to borrow paper, ink, stamps, anything to get a letter off'. Was it last-minute conscience? wondered Giles; 'Could be, but I'd guess it's last-minute realization that the fun is over, that home is pretty good after all and a hell of a long way off.'

The one thing that wasn't going to plan was the weather. On 1 June it had broken, and now on the afternoon of Sunday 4 June Eisenhower watched the rain pouring down as he looked out of the window of Southwick House, a Georgian building perched on the hill just outside Portsmouth which was now the HQ of the Supreme Allied Command. The night before he had chaired a Supreme Commander's Conference when he, Montgomery, Tedder, Leigh-Mallory, Ramsay and Bedell Smith had heard Group Captain John Stagg, a civilian meteorologist now commissioned in the RAF, declare the weather over the next twenty-four hours to be 'untrustworthy'. It was possible that there might be gale-force winds off the coast of Normandy or low cloud cover, both of which would rule out the planned airborne operations and the air support that was deemed so vital for the success of the landings. There were now only twenty-four hours left to decide whether Operation OVERLORD should be postponed: Eisenhower ordered twice-daily meetings of SHAEF. Staggs's report at 4.30 p.m. on the 4th was no better: Leigh-Mallory, concerned about the very real threat that a 1,000-foot cloud ceiling and gale-force winds posed to the air forces, urged a postponement. Initially Montgomery disagreed, but when Ramsay pointed out that the Commanders had to make up their minds within half an hour or it would be too late and the main naval force would have set off, he concurred. OVERLORD was to be delayed for twenty-four hours. The pre-arranged signals for delay were sent: 'Bowsprit' to all naval forces, 'Ripcord Plus 24' to the airborne divisions. Not all ships received the message: at 9 a.m. the next morning 138 ships carrying the US 4th Infantry Division had not acknowledged that they had received the order to stand down and were still sailing towards the rendezvous point south of the Isle of Wight. A Supermarine Walrus amphibian bi-plane was sent out by Coastal Command to alert the lead ship and in desperation, when its radio signals were not acknowledged, dropped a canister on the deck. The task force turned back, narrowly averting compromising the success of the whole operation.

The weather had not improved by the morning of the 5th. A BBC correspondent, Chester Wilmot, wrote, 'The storm gathered in fury, and it seemed as if all the months of preparation would be nullified by the one factor that couldn't be harnessed to the plan.'

As a sideshow, Eisenhower had political concerns on the eve of D-Day too. Firstly, Winston Churchill had pronounced himself anxious to ride in the first wave of the assault force. Admiral Ramsay reported that the British Prime Minister was 'very set on the idea'. No one else was. If anything happened to the ship Churchill was on, at least five ships in the vicinity would be forced to alter course to come to its rescue - and that would be five ships lost to their proper tasks of bombardment and convoy protection. Eisenhower asked Ramsay to tell a disgruntled Churchill that his idea had been 'disapproved'. It was just as well since King George VI had subsequently informed Eisenhower that if Churchill went, the monarch, too, would feel under an obligation to indulge in heroics. In the event, it was fighting men who crossed the Channel.

The leader of the Free French, General de Gaulle, who considered that he, not the traitorous Vichy leader, Pétain, spoke for France, was deeply unhappy about the way he thought his country was used in the Anglo-American leaders' war strategy, and to find himself without a voice in their deliberations. Churchill had been well aware of this delicate situation when the decision was taken to bomb French transportation for months before D-Day. He knew that for every German killed, many French people would perish at the hands of their allies.

De Gaulle arrived in Britain from Algiers on 4 June aboard Churchill's private aeroplane. He was to be informed about the D-Day landings in his country, and urged to broadcast a message to the French people. When de Gaulle read the speech Eisenhower intended to make to the French people immediately after the landings he was angry: his name was not mentioned, nor was that of the Provisional Government of France of which he was President; furthermore, it implied that the orders of the Vichy government were to be obeyed until something more permanent was able to be arranged. To de Gaulle it appeared that France was not so much to be liberated as occupied by an Allied, rather than an enemy, invader.

Over a million copies of Eisenhower's speech had already been printed ready to be dropped over France in the wake of the landings: there was no way it would be possible to change it, even if the Supreme Commander had wanted it to be. The final compromise was that de Gaulle would record a separate broadcast to be transmitted on 6 June calling for orders given by 'the French government and by the French leaders that it has chosen' to be obeyed.

What would happen if the invasion was postponed yet again? The signs were not good for the 6th but the choice was either then or to attempt a daylight landing a few days later. The battleships would have to return to port and refuel as there was no hope that they could set off again after another day's delay. To wait for the right night-time conditions of tide and moon to come round again would mean a postponement of at least two weeks. The first alternative, a daylight landing, would lose the element of surprise and would have to rely on air and naval power alone. On the other hand, a two-week delay would lose the Allies valuable summer campaigning time, might even jeopardize the seizure of Cherbourg, and above all endanger security and the morale of the men - some US forces had already been incarcerated in their ships for seventy-two hours. The troops would have to be disembarked and returned to their marshalling yards along the south coast to kick their heels for another fortnight, or even a month. As Bradley, who was already on board the US flag ship *Augusta* in Plymouth harbour while these deliberations were going on, reflected, '…having been once briefed on the OVERLORD plan and destination, the assault troops would have to be locked up for totally incommunicado. The prospect was a frightening one: twenty-eight days of keeping a secret known to 140,000 men.' It had seemed inconceivable that an operation of the magnitude of OVERLORD had managed to stay hidden until now. The chances that the Germans would not divine Allied intentions if the concentration of troops, tanks and equipment remained assembled for more weeks were surely slight. In addition, the time delay would give the Germans time to proceed apace with their strengthening of the Atlantic Wall situated over the Channel - and what effect would the much-vaunted secret weapons have if they were allowed to be deployed unchecked? Would there not be a danger of them raining down on the assembled invasion fleet in harbour? And then there was Russia, already suspicious of Anglo-American intentions regarding a Second Front? How would the Allies' 'prevarication' appear to them?

For all these reasons, Eisenhower was well aware of all the desirability of going for the 6 June - as were the other commanders, but only if the weather allowed a 'window of opportunity', a break in the clouds. There would no second bite at this particular cherry. There could only be one cross-Channel invasion. It had to be right the first time, or the war would be prolonged - maybe for years. It was an onerous and lonely responsibility that Eisenhower as Supreme Commander shouldered that evening at Southwick House. He fingered the 'lucky coins' in his pocket that he had carried ever since the North Africa campaign.

At the 9.30 p.m. meeting that evening, Stagg had some cautiously good news: a cold front was advancing from Ireland. There could be a break in the storm for up to thirty-six hours starting at dawn on 6 June. Seas would be moderate and it was even likely that the cloud cover would lift. Stagg judged that the wind would drop so that whilst the landing craft would have an 'inconvenient time of it' getting to shore, it wouldn't be mayhem. 'I would say go,' Montgomery advised. For the Navy, Ramsay agreed: Leigh-Mallory and Tedder were more circumspect but Bedell Smith probably spoke for them all when he said, 'It's a helluva gamble, but it's the best possible gamble.'

Eisenhower reflected: 'The question is how long can you allow this thing to just kind of hang out there on a limb?' And he answered himself: 'I'm quite positive that the order must be given.' At the final meeting at 4.15 am on the 5th June, after a night when the storm that whipped the tent camp in the grounds of Southwick house convinced the US General that at least he had been right not to go on the 5th, he repeated his command: 'Okay, we'll go.' D-Day was on.

Aboard their boats the men had been told what was happening: they now knew - if any of them had doubted it - that this was no dry run, and that they were heading for France, that the code names that 'their' stretch of coastline had been given corresponded to a reality, to Port-en-Bessin, Merville, Ouistreham, Benerville...

Aboard the *Jefferson* Charles Cawthon had a 'last dinner that was quieter than usual, and there was no special talk of the morrow.' The Chaplain held a religious service above the throb of the ship's engine and 'there were probably more than the usual number of private prayers launched that night as the realization grew that this was not going to be another exercise, and that in the dawn, metal would be flying both ways.' Cawthon noted 'no bravado, or even the normal crap game. An engineer officer played an accordion, but there was no singing. Some of us talked with a British navy frogman who, several times, had gone in on Omaha Beach from a submarine to examine its rows of obstacles. He could tell us little that we did not already know from our study of the terrain model and aerial photographs,' but it was 'curious to talk with a man who had already trod with apparent ease the stretch of sand we were making such a titanic effort to reach.'

Lord Lovat, leading his No. 4 Commandos had given his men a pep talk: 'I ...took two minutes. It was simple enough, the message plain. I weighed each word, then drove it home. I concentrated on the task ahead and simple facts - how to pace the battle.' First he spoke in English and then to the Free French Commandos who were joining the exercise in colloquial French 'Vous allez rentrer chez vous. Vous serez les premiers militaires français en uniforme à casser la gueule des salauds en France même. A chacun son Boche.' Lovat reminded his own Commandos that 'they knew their job, and I knew that they would not fail...it appeared a tough assignment, but we held the advantage both in initiative and fire power...it was better to attack than to defend...The brigade was going to make history,' he said; he had 'complete confidence in every man taking part!' Lovat ended 'this harangue' with the suggestion that 'if you wish to live to a ripe old age - keep moving tomorrow. And so we stood across the sea to France...'

On the eve of D-Day Brooke was still profoundly dubious:

> It is very hard to believe that in a few hours the invasion starts. I am very uneasy about the whole operation. At best it will fall so short of the expectations of the people, namely those who know nothing about its difficulties. At worst, it may well be the most ghastly disaster of the whole war. I wish to God it were safely over.

US troops file down to the harbour to board their LCVRs 'as the second hand moves ever closer to H-Hour' as the contemporary US Office of War Information caption put it.

Churchill, that 'former naval person' deprived of a chance to go with the invasion, spent the evening in the War Cabinet rooms under Whitehall discussing the prospects for D-Day. When his wife looked in on her way to bed, he sipped a brandy and reflected, 'when you wake up tomorrow, 2,000 men may already be dead.'

It was that fear - with an additional focus - that was playing on Eisenhower's mind. Earlier in the day, he had slipped out of Portsmouth and headed off on a slow drive, in the opposite direction to the advancing embarkation troops, towards Newbury in Berkshire where the US 101st Airborne Division were stationed.

The US 101st and the 82nd Airborne Divisions had only been activated in August 1942 - less than two years before they were to be given a key vanguard role in the D-Day invasions. The romance of the parachute regiments was unassailable: men dropping rhythmically from their aircraft, the silent, silken umbrella of assault floating down to seize key positions by night. The successes of German parachutists had further fuelled the legend. General Bradley was adamant that the success of the US Normandy landings hinged on the use of parachutists to seize the exits from Utah Beach and make possible the advance towards Cherbourg. He proposed that the US 101st Airborne (the Screaming Eagles), a new formation commanded by Major-General Maxwell Taylor, for whom D-Day would be his first experience of combat, should be dropped during the previous night behind Utah Beach and detailed to hold the causeways, then advance south to link up with the forces coming ashore on Omaha. Meanwhile the US 82nd Airborne (All American), a more experienced group of men, commanded by Major-General Matthew B. Ridgway, who had seen service in Sicily and on the Italian mainland, were to drop further west - and take the small town of Ste-Mère Eglise. They were then to capture or destroy the bridges across the River Merderet, thus throttling the neck of the Cotentin Peninsula and isolating Cherbourg, and await the arrival of the overland forces which would have landed by sea in the early morning.

Bradley fought tenaciously for his plan: 'If you insist on cutting out the airborne attack, then I must ask that we eliminate the Utah assault. I am not going to land on the beach without making sure we've got the exits behind it,' he responded to the opposition of the British Air Marshal, Leigh-Mallory, who opposed the plan not for tactical reasons but because he believed that the cost in men's lives would be unacceptably high. 'Your losses will be excessive,' he told Bradley: 'certainly more than your gains are worth.'

Leigh-Mallory predicted that the airborne troops would lose eighty per cent of their troops in a parachute assault on Normandy. But this staggering prediction was low by comparison to the estimate the paratroopers themselves had had from their instructors during training: 'Most of you will die in combat. You haven't got a chance!'

The marching song of the 101st told it all:

> There was blood upon the risers, there were brains upon the chute.
> Intestines were dangling from the paratrooper's boots.
> They picked him up still in his chute and poured him from his boots.
> He ain't gonna jump no more.
> Gory, Gory, What a helluva way to die,
> Gory, Gory, What a helluva way to die,
> He ain't gonna jump no more.

The essential bridges over the River Orne and the Caen Canal at Bénouville and crossing the flooded River Dives on the eastern flank of the assault front were to be seized by the British 6th Airborne Division which had been raised in England in spring 1943 and was commanded by Major-General Richard 'Windy' Gale. The Division's additional D-Day task was to destroy the 100mm guns which combed the beach and shoreline from the Merville Battery at Franceville-Plage.

Despite Leigh-Mallory's opposition, Montgomery had backed Bradley's plan. Eisenhower had talked to the paratroopers, whose faces were camouflaged with a mixture of cocoa and linseed oil ('at least we'll have something to eat'), on the ground, and now at 11p.m. on the night of 5 June, when British double summertime meant that it was still light, he stood on the roof of the 101st's HQ building and watched as the C-47s (or Dakotas as the British called them) towing the gliders took off for France. A total of 13,000 American paratroopers would land scattered over the Normandy countryside on D-Day.

Each of the 822 aircraft used for the drop carried a 'stick' of eighteen fully-laden parachutists, along with the pilot, co-pilot, navigator and crew chief. It was a dangerous form of warfare. Pilots had to fly in close formation at heights of about 600-700 feet and at low speeds of 120 mph to allow their cargo to jump: this made them easy targets for anti-aircraft fire, yet they had been issued with instructions: 'Do not take avoiding action.' Many of the pilots who were to deliver the parachutists were, in the main, transport and carrier

"One more crack out of you about Kentucky Minstrels and someone's going to start an invasion right here."

Sunday Express, May 7th, 1944

fliers who had had no experience of combat flying and were totally unprepared for the barrage of flak that hit them. They were disorientated by the cloud cover and unused to flying at the slow and steady speeds required for a safe parachute exit. The main danger was not that the parachutes wouldn't open, for this rarely happened, and Major-General Gale was able to boast that he had got the casualty rate of the British parachutists in training down to 'a fraction over one per cent by 1942' (though 'to witness a Roman Candle, the term we used when a parachute failed to open, was a sickening sight'). It was rather that the parachutists would jump too close to the ground to be able to open their parachutes in time.

The men were so heavily equipped that it was only with the utmost difficulty that they were able to clamber aboard. Private Donald Burgett of the 506th Parachute Infantry, 101st Airborne Division, was wearing:

> one suit of olive drab, worn underneath my jump suit...helmet, boots, gloves, main parachute, reserve parachute, Mae West, rifle, .45 automatic pistol, trench knife, jump knife, hunting knife, machete, one cartridge belt, two bandoliers, two cans of machine-gun ammo totalling 676 rounds of .30 ammo, 66 rounds of .45 ammo, one Hawkins mine capable of blowing off the tracks of a tank, four blocks of TNT, one entrenching tool with two blasting caps taped on the outside of the steel part, three first aid kits, two morphine needles, one gas mask, a

canteen of water, three day's supply of K-rations, two day's supply of D-rations [hard tropical chocolate bars], six fragmentation grenades, one Gammon grenade, one orange smoke and one red smoke grenade, one orange panel, one blanket, one raincoat, one change of socks and underwear, two cartons of cigarettes and a few other odds and ends...Other things would be dropped in equipment bundles that we would pick up later on the ground. Torpedoes, extra bazooka rockets, machine-gun ammo, medical supplies, food and heavy explosives. When all the troops were aboard, a loudspeaker came on and the pilot read us a mimeographed message from the General wishing us Godspeed. A canteen cup of whisky would have been more appreciated....

Private Burgett was so weighted down that he had to be 'lifted bodily [by two US Army Air Force men who offered to help and who] with much boosting and grunting shoved me into the plane where I pulled myself along with the aid of the crew chief', and rode to France kneeling on the floor, which caused a journalist who was flying with the 506th to think that the men spent the crossing in prayer.

D-Day was fifteen minutes old when the first airborne troops were instructed to 'Stand up and hook up' and a few minutes later to 'Go'. Men started to drop at both ends of the fifty-mile assault front. Many had faulty parachutes, or were blown miles off course. Some landed in the sea and, weighted down as they were, drowned; some never left their planes which were hit by flak and plummeted to earth in flames; others were picked off by enemy machine-gun fire as they floated towards the ground; others jumped too late and too low with insufficient time for their parachutes to unfurl, and were killed when they hit the ground. Nineteen-year-old Donald Burgett was dropped at less than 300 feet rather than the specified 600-700; the hedgehopping of the pilot, 'to save his own ass,' in Burgett's view, meant that seventeen men 'hit the ground before their 'chute had time to open. They made a sound like a large ripe pumpkin being thrown to burst against the ground...I hope that [dirty SOB pilot] gets shot down in the Channel and drowns,' he wrote bitterly.

Others dropped into ditches or on the marshy land which the Germans had flooded as a defence precaution creating a five-foot-deep lake, and, unable to get free from their harnesses and burdened with 300 lb of equipment, many drowned; others were impaled on 'Rommel's asparagus', or dangled from the high branches of trees - or, in the case of Private First Class John Steele, hung suspended from the steeple of the church at Ste-Mère Eglise. If they could not be cut down in time by their companions they were taken prisoner or shot by the Germans: others were accidentally dropped behind enemy lines and either were never heard of again or spent the rest of the war as POWs. The US 101st Airborne Division landed over 300 square miles of Normandy instead of in the four groups planned. Only two battalions made a 'good drop' - that is they landed in the planned zone. Altogether 4,000 US paratroopers failed to join their units after the drop and, and in some cases it was several days - seventeen for one group - before they were able to link up.

'We all matured well beyond our years that day,' remembers Henry Lefebvre, a twenty-one-year-old First Lieutenant with 3rd Platoon 'A' company, 508th Paratroopers, 82nd Airborne Division on D-Day.

We saw not only our own platoon go, but so many others drown in the river.
They had so much equipment on them and no quick release 'chutes in those days:
if you landed in a flooded river you got drowned…Others got caught in the trees
and then [were] shot whilst they were hanging there…they were just left there
hanging; when the deregistration people came along, they were still there, just
hanging. It was devastating. We'd trained for twenty-one months as a unit, and
gotten rid of anybody that couldn't cut the mustard so we had a really fine unit.
We didn't think that casualties would happen to us, they'd happen to someone
else - of course you have to go in feeling that way, war has to be a young man's
game, you just figure it's not going to be you, it's going to be the other fellow that
gets it.

Meanwhile, those men who had managed to slash themselves out of their harness wan-
dered around clicking the metallic Christmas cracker 'crickets' they had been issued
with as a means of making contact with each other. The troops also had a password: 'The
password was "flash" and the counter-sign was "thunder".' So when Lefebvre 'ran into
another fellow, I said "Flash", and this other person said, "Jesus Christ, I'm American,
don't shoot". He'd forgotten the password, but it was all right - I reckoned no German
would say that.' Most had lost their radio sets and also found it difficult at night to follow the usual daylight procedure for linking up - that of watching the direction of the
aircraft stream.

As the 'pathfinders' had dropped in advance of the paratroopers and guided the planes
to land, so the third arm of the Airborne Divisions, the gliders carrying more infantry and
heavy equipment, including tanks and Jeeps, were to follow. The British favoured the
Horsa, a plywood monoplane nearly seventy feet long which could either carry a Jeep
(well lashed down to prevent it moving even the few feet that could unbalance a glider
and send it crashing to earth) and ten soldiers, or a full complement of thirty soldiers, or
the wooden Hamilcar, which could even carry a light tank. The US troops flew in
WACOs - none of which survived intact on D-Day. The gliders were towed by bombers
using a nylon rope, and when cut free they would glide up to six miles before coming to
earth. It was a difficult job even under ideal conditions, and hazardous in Normandy in
the pre-dawn hours of D-Day when it turned out that the hedges that had been so carefully studied in photographs and relief maps were considerably higher than had been thought
and the protuberant spikes of 'Rommel's Asaparagus' certainly seemed to have multi-
plied. 'They'd told us everything about everything,' recalls Lefebvre:

they'd talked about the hedgerows, but they hadn't told us about French
hedgerows…we'd practised in England, and the hedgerows that grow in England
are about two feet six high and a foot thick, and you can just shove your way
through and there's no big deal. But it's not so in Normandy, there are all these
little fields with a mound of earth about three feet high and then there's the hedge
growing out of that, and trees are growing out of it, and there's a great drainage
ditch at the bottom, so you could literally be dying in one field, and in the next
field people would be taking a break and having a smoke and never know anything
about you.

The gliders seemed to resemble nothing so much as orange boxes which invariably cracked and splintered on impact with the ground. A US officer reported that 'in all my time in Normandy, I only ever saw one glider that looked as though it could be used again, providing it could be towed aloft - otherwise they were all in various forms of destruction.'

The US 101st Airborne Division suffered twenty per cent casualties on D-Day - mercifully some sixty per cent less than had been predicted. Although they did not achieve all their D-Day objectives the exits from Utah Beach had been secured and what had appeared to be a disaster with men scattered so widely, proved rather to be a strength. It confused the enemy and engaged him in skirmishes rather than a co-ordinated counter-attack which could have massed towards the beaches.

At sixteen minutes past midnight on 6 June Major John Howard leading six gliders containing 181 assault troops of the British 6th Airborne Division was probably the first of the Allied troops to land in Normandy on D-Day as he came to a halt near the bridge over the Caen Canal.

Peter Boyle was co-pilot of the second glider in the formation.

> It was only the second time they'd put a lot of gliders into an operation [the first was Sicily] and we didn't really know what our chances were, but we'd been given to understand that they weren't very high, that we were on a one-way trip really. We were taught to do certain things without question. As our regimental commander would say, 'You, if you want to ask a question, ask it when the war's over.'

The glider pilots - who became fighting men again once their craft had landed - had been told some seventy-two hours before about their crucial mission.

> They'd shown us a sand table model and said, 'That's it.' It was a model of a bridge and then about twelve hours beforehand Major Howard spoke to us and he gave us the story. He said that it was vital that we took this bridge; the whole object was to stop the German armour coming in behind the seaborne troops once they'd landed. The airborne divisions would keep the Germans far back so that they couldn't shell the troops, but of course the problem is that an airborne division is so lightly armed when it lands, so unless it can be contacted fairly quickly, it's in trouble.

It took Howard and his men precisely ten minutes to capture the bridge intact with the loss of two men dead and five wounded: another key objective, the Orne bridge, was an even easier prize. When two more gliders landed nearby, they found that the German defenders had fled. The battle to hold the bridges was joined by airborne troops of the 5th Parachute Brigade and soon after noon the distinctive sounds of the bagpipe made the defenders realize that Lord Lovat's 1st Special Service Brigade had successfully landed on Sword Beach and were advancing. 'The paras expected us at noon,' Lord Lovat's piper, Bill Millin recalls,

> and I piped them all the way down to where the café is…the bridge was under fire. There were columns of black smoke coming up from a lot of small arms

THEY DROPPED FROM THE SKIES:
*Major-General Sir Richard Gale (top) briefs his men of the 6th Airborne Division on D-Day.
'The Hun thinks only a bloody fool will go there - that's why I'm going', he told them.
'Where are you from, soldier?' 'And you,soldier?' 'Good Luck, soldier'. Eisenhower (bottom)
pays an eleventh-hour visit to the men of the US 101st Airborne Division on 5 June 1944.*

fire...and Lord Lovat said, 'We'll cross over now.' So I had my pipes on my shoulder and just before we got to the other side he said, 'Now I want you to start playing and keep playing along this road till we get to the other bridge over the Orne.' So I kept playing, and the tune was 'Blue Bonnets Over the Border'; that was his favourite...

The 9th Parachute Regiment, commanded by Lieutenant-Colonel Terence Otway, a twenty-nine-year-old regular soldier, was given the 'grade A stinker of a job' of disabling the Merville battery for D-Day so that its mighty guns would not be able to blast the landing forces along the entire eastern flank of the invasion. Like the US paratroopers, the British were scattered over a wide area and of the 750 men and heavy equipment that had been detailed to attack the battery, only 150 of the men had arrived, vital heavy armour was missing and the gliders which were to have landed on the battery had been attacked by German anti-aircraft fire and forced to land in fields several miles away.

With insufficient men, lacking the anti-tank guns, flamethrowers and bangalore torpedoes that had gone missing, and with the bombardment of the battery having left it entirely unscathed, Otway led his men into a hand-to-hand storming of the enemy position with whatever small arms and bangalores came to hand. It was a costly venture: when, mortally wounded, Lieutenant Mike Dowling reported 'Battery taken as ordered, sir. Guns destroyed,' minutes before he died, over half the men who had stormed the battery also lay dead. The guns turned out to be older, less effective French weapons and not the powerful German 100mm guns that had been feared. But the massacre that would have awaited the troops on Sword Beach had been averted.

Before Eisenhower had waved off the first invaders late in the evening of 5 June he had sat down at his desk and scribbled a note which he carefully folded into his wallet; it read:

> Our landings in the Cherbourg-Le Havre area have failed to gain a satisfactory foothold and I have withdrawn the troops. My decision to attack at this time and place was based upon the best information available. The troops, the air and the navy all did the best that bravery and devotion to duty could do. If any blame attaches to the attempt it is mine alone.

As the boats carrying the first wave of the assault troops neared the French coast, the vanguard of the D-Day forces, the men of the Airborne Divisions, both British and American, had already made it seem that the note that the US Supreme Commander wrote as an insurance before every major operation, might not have to be fished out of his pocket this time, either.

CHAPTER EIGHT

THE FAR SHORE: UTAH AND OMAHA

'W'E WERE EXPECTING THE INVASION, we had had signs…we weren't surprised or frightened,' remembers Michel Grimaux, now Mayor of Graye-sur-Mer, on D-Day an eleven-year-old boy living with his mother and sisters in the seaside resort.

All night we went out into garden where we had a dug-out prepared and stayed in the dug-out for the whole night…we emerged from time to time, but there was intense bombing. After the naval bombing the planes came - it was tremendous, we thought the house would fall down, and every time we peered out we were amazed to see that the house was still standing. The planes stopped coming over at about six o'clock, and it was very quiet, and then a little bit later, perhaps about seven o'clock, we began to hear the noise of the guns. They were machine-guns, but to us it was a very sweet noise…the German Occupation had been very hard, we had been deprived of food, we used to go barefoot, we used to make sugar from beetroots and we got salt from seawater - we'd boil it up in a pail and extract the salt. We could do that as long as we could come to the beach, but after it was mined and all the obstacles were erected we couldn't do that anymore. We were always confident that the invasion would come - we just waited. But the Germans were taking more and more people away from our village, different categories of people. I'm not sure we could have waited much longer…

Elsewhere in Normandy members of the French Resistance crouched listening illegally to their transmitters: 'I am looking for four-leaved clovers;' 'The tomatoes should be picked;' 'The children are bored on Sunday;' 'The dice are on the table.' The BBC broadcast these cryptic messages just before announcing on the nine o'clock news that Rome had fallen, captured by Mark Clark's Vth Army. They must have seemed meaningless to most listeners, but to the Resistance workers they were a call to action. These were 'Code B' messages, transmitted in order to activate the carefully laid plan of sabotage which would disable the German war machine as much as possible in advance of the Allied landings. 'The Violet Plan' called for the destruction of underground post office cables to hinder communication; 'The Green Plan' was for mass sabotage of the railways. Coupled with the repeated broadcast of some lines from Verlaine's poem *Chanson d'Automne*, 'Blessent mon coeur d'une langueur monotone', between 1.20 and 2.30 p.m. on 3 June, the messages meant only one thing: the invasion was imminent. Stealthily, various members of the Resistance left their homes by foot and on bicycles and went into action: Albert Augé and his men destroyed the railway water tanks and steam injectors of the trains standing in Caen station; Yves Gresselin blew up the Paris-Cherbourg railway line near Carentan; other lines between Caen and various other key towns were dynamited; armed with shears and wire-cutters others hacked through the cables that ran vital telephone links along the coast and between the German army's command posts.

What the French Resistance could hear, their Occupiers could too. Von Rundstedt, Rommel and the Intelligence Chief of the Army Group 'B' were among those who could have taken the coded information seriously. But they didn't: there was a lack either of interest or disbelief. 'The immediate "invasion" is not yet apparent,' was the report from Rommel's Army Group HQ. Not that Rommel was there anyway: he had driven to Germany, mainly to see Hitler and try to convince the Führer of the need to move reinforcement tanks into Normandy, but he also planned to snatch a little time with his wife Lucie. It was her birthday and Erwin Rommel had bought her some particularly elegant grey suede shoes in Paris which he wanted to deliver personally.

The German commanders had been lulled into a false sense of security by the very factor that had caused the Allies so much last-minute anxiety: the weather. The usual reconnaissance patrol in the Channel, believing the sea to be far too rough for any force to risk attempting a crossing, had not gone out during the night of 5-6 June. This military complacency was to give the invasion forces the edge they so desperately needed. General Marcks, Commander of the LXXXIV Corps at St Lô, was about to leave at dawn for a *Kriegsspiel* - a 'war game' exercise - in Rennes. Ironically, in this war game Marcks was to take the part of the Allies mounting a paratroop attack followed by an assault from the sea. There was only one panzer division, the 21st, with 170 tanks and armoured vehicles, close enough to act during the early stages of the invasion - and by 7 a.m. its commander had still not received any orders from the German High Command other than being told that he was now under the command of Colonel General Dollmann's 7th Army.

Hans von Luck, a Lieutenant-Colonel in the 21st Rangers who was in command of regiments east of the River Orne, remembers that Rommel, on a visit to von Luck's regiment three days prior to D-Day, had said that he still believed that the invasion route must be Dover-Calais - 'but it could be here as well.' Meanwhile General Marcks had

> had a meeting with all his COs and he said, 'As far as I know the British, they will go to church on Sunday and on Monday they will come here'...and he was right...they didn't realize that Ike postponed for one day...the plan was for Monday for D-Day...but our Division was the only one here and we were here to protect the big steel factory and Caen. It was very important to guard the bridges over the Orne against the Commandos who would probably land.

The German High Command found it hard to give credence to the idea that an invasion force would brave the force six winds that were whipping the Channel as dawn broke on 6 June. They also clung tenaciously to the belief that when an attack came, it would come in the Pas de Calais and that the Normandy assault was a diversion to draw their forces west. This assumption was reinforced by the 'window' (thin strips of foil) that the RAF planes were scattering in the area to confuse the radar operators.

Springboard to invasion: The Chicago Tribune's *D-Day report.*

It was not until 4 a.m. on the morning of 6 June, 'three hours after I received the first reports of the invasion,' that Field-Marshal von Rundstedt, the German supremo, decided that 'these landings in Normandy had better be taken seriously.' But he could do nothing until he received the order from Berlin.

The D-Day armada advanced across thirty miles of the Channel. There were the huge command ships like USS *Augusta* and HMS *Scylla* which would keep radio contact with the shore, destroyers, channel steamers, white hospital ships, shallow, tray-like landing craft as long as 350 feet and, lying low in the water, minesweepers, tugs, and, out of sight, midget submarines too. Soon after 5 a.m. on 5 June the message had come to 'weigh anchor' and the first of the total of over 6,000 vessels began to move towards their allotted positions to sail across to France.

Very soon after that the naval bombardment began. At 3.35 a.m. a clanging bell had awakened Lieutenant-General Bradley aboard USS *Augusta*. He scrambled to pull on his inflatable Mae West life-jacket before going out on to the bridge. According to the log, the wind had dropped, but as he gazed into the tumultuous sea it didn't seem like it to Bradley. As he stood on the bridge

> 1,300 RAF bombers swarmed over the French coastline from the Seine to Cherbourg. An enemy AA battery stabbed blindly through the night. A shower of sparks splintered the darkness and a ribbon of fire peeled out of the sky as a stricken bomber plunged towards *Augusta*. It levelled off, banked around our stern, and exploded into the Channel. By 5.30, first light had diluted the darkness and three Spits whistled by overhead, the first sign of our air umbrella. High above the overcast, relays of American fighters formed a second layer of air cover.

This was the air fighter cover that was deemed so essential to the success of the landings: they were to bomb the beach fortifications and knock out the guns wherever possible, to make things easier for the troops when they landed. It was to prove a difficult and, to a great extent, fruitless exercise. Cloud cover hung heavily over the Normandy coast that morning, visibility was almost zero and the planes, which had all been painted with distinctive black and white stripes so that there could be no possible confusion with the Luftwaffe, had largely missed their targets and either dropped their loads miles inland to land on hedgerows and kill cows, or simply turned round and flown back to Britain. It was a closely timed operation: there must be no question of the bombs falling on the troops as they landed: pilots were given strict instructions: 'Bomb early, or don't bomb at all.'

H-Hour when the troops would storm ashore was set for 6.30 a.m. on Utah Beach. Bradley, whose flagship was moored off Omaha, was worried. His right hand man 'Tubby' Thorsen predicted ,'The DDs are going to have a helluva time getting through the surf.' But all the General could do for 'the next few tortured hours…was pace our decks and trust in the men to whom the Plan had been given for execution.'

At 5.50 am Bradley stuffed cotton wool in his ears as the *Augusta's* turret guns were trained on the shore 'and the ship shuddered as it opened fire upon its predesignated targets among the beach defences. The salvo coasted over the armada and we followed the pinpoints of fire as they plunged down towards the shore.'

It was the same all along the coast as, in advance of the troops' landing, the battleships and cruisers pounded the shore with 'blinding, breathtaking waves of fire…enough fire to avenge the Alamo,' thought John Mason Brown who was also aboard the *Augusta*.

HMS *Orion* found that she had much more room to manoeuvre than had been expected. The minesweepers had succeeded in clearing a wide channel and at 05.10 the *Orion* started to fire. 'Our shooting was very good,' recalls Ian Michie: 'we scored thirteen direct hits on the battery…the other cruisers were all ripping away - *Belfast* was firing tracer.' A pilot flying a Spitfire over the Vierville battery to target the great guns so that the fire assault from the ships could hit home remembers: 'a firework display as every craft opened up, viewed from 10,000 feet in the dawn light, is something I shall never forget.'

The troop ships had begun to arrive at their offshore assembly points just before midnight, and with lights dimmed they gathered to wait for the order to advance. On the way over towards Utah the men on USS *Bayfield* (which had been involved in the disastrous Operation TIGER exercise off Slapton Sands little more than a month before) had been made to feel even more apprehensive when they were gathered together on the deck for an uplifting service. After rendering 'The Battle Hymn of the Republic' the men sang 'Onward Christian Soldiers'; the words '...as God died to make men holy, let us die to make men free,' seemed both an exhortation and an omen.

Robert Edlin, a Lieutenant in the 2nd US Rangers detailed to assault Pointe du Hoc off Omaha Beach, was aboard a British ship, HMS *Prince Charles*.

> Some people gambled, some read books, some prayed. We had a Catholic priest, Father Lacey, who was quite a man [he was subsequently awarded the DSO for his bravery on the Normandy beaches]. He held three services the night before we sailed, a Protestant, a Jewish and a Catholic one. I went to all three of them. He asked me what my religion was, and I said, 'whatever works'; that's about the way I felt about it.

For Cawthon, who had been woken by the ship's gong sounding reveille at 2 a.m. 'breakfast in the ornately-decorated salon was unreal: bacon and eggs on the edge of eternity.' It was much the same for Robert Capa aboard USS *Chase*. He'd not even tried to sleep and the 2 a.m. ship's loud speaker broke up a poker game. 'We placed our money in waterproof money bags and went down to a pre-invasion breakfast served at 3.00 a.m. The mess boys...wore immaculate white jackets and served hot cakes, sausages, eggs and coffee with unusual zest and politeness. But pre-invasion stomachs were preoccupied, and most of the noble effort was left on the plates.'

By 4 a.m. the men of the 16th Infantry Regiment of the US 1st Infantry Division were assembled on the open deck with the invasion barges swinging off the cranes ready to be lowered. 'Waiting for that first ray of light, the two thousand men stood in perfect silence, whatever they were thinking, it was some kind of prayer.'

The US 29th Infantry Division, also bound for Omaha, helped each other into 'the open-topped, rectangular steel box that we were to ride to battle. It had a motor and rudder at one end and a hinged ramp at the other.' The men sorted themselves into their long-rehearsed places and then

> suddenly, with a rattle of chains and a screech of wire cable, the craft began to move slowly down the *Jefferson's* side. It was met by a rising swell that slackened the cables and dropped us with a crash as it rolled on. The next move brought us fully into the waves. By some miracle we were not slammed into the ship's side, the propellor caught, and we followed a shepherding launch out to join other craft, circling as in some strange conga line in the dark, with red and green riding lights appearing and disappearing in the troughs of waves that were four or five feet high...it seemed that we would surely swamp.

The men inflated their own life-jackets and those that protected such vital equipment as telephone wire, radio and demolition packs. Seventy-five inflated life-jackets were wedged tight in the already crowded craft, and the 29th rode 'packed like sardines in an open can, feet awash in bilge water and altogether uncomfortable.'

Anxious about the danger of fire from shore batteries, the US forces were decanted into their landing craft some eleven miles out to sea so that their journey ashore was even more hazardous and violently uncomfortable than that of the British who were lowered in their boats eight miles offshore. 'The men started to puke,' remembers Capa, 'but this was a polite as well as a carefully planned invasion, and little paper bags had been provided for the purpose.' But these proved entirely inadequate and soon the 16th were riding to shore 'ducked down in the pukey water at the bottom of the barge'.

The sea-sickness made men long for land - whatever they might find there. A Royal Navy Commando thought that the reason why the soldiers stormed ashore as they did was because they 'would rather have fought the whole German Army than go back on the ships and be as seasick as they were going over. My God! those soldiers couldn't wait to get on dry land. Nothing would have stood in their way...'

Ralph Ingersoll had been on one of the LCTs that had been called back when D-Day was postponed. That night he and a fellow officer had 'spread out our maps of the little section of Normandy which was going to be our world, and played soldier. Solemnly, we decided which routes we would take and marked our march route knowing all the time and very well that after the beach we'd take whatever road or field lay in the direction we wanted to go.' The next night as they sailed towards France again they

> had all night to ourselves to go over it again, and...that was what let fear in. You could count on your fingers the things that could happen to you and nothing could be done about any of them. There were the E-boats that had sunk our landing craft on manoeuvres the month before, no further from the English shore than we lay at anchor. There were the submarines that we knew the Hun might risk in the Channel if he knew this was the real thing. There were the mines. Most of all, on a crossing like ours, there was the air. No cover could wholly seal the air over the Channel and the long lines of landing craft would be bobbing ducks in a shooting gallery...On the far shore, there were underwater obstacles and the shore batteries...but most of all, for us, there was that damn strip of beach with the flooded area just beyond. This was the assault beach called Utah.

When the first troops went ashore on Utah beach many of them had already been at sea in a small, wave-tossed boat for over sixty hours, the worst experience at sea of any of the invasion forces. Force U, carrying men from the US 4th Infantry Division, had crossed the Channel from the harbours of Devon and Cornwall. They were intended to land on the smooth grey-sanded beach and link up with the airborne forces who would have already seized the causeways of the beach to enable the 4th to debouch across the Cotentin Peninsula. They were then to advance on Cherbourg with the objective of seizing the port within eight or so days of landing.

But it didn't work quite like that. For a start, the destroyer USS *Corry* suddenly spun sideways, broke in half and sank, having set off one of the oyster acoustic mines that the Germans had necklaced along the coast at that point and that lay on the sea bed, often undetected by minesweepers.

Then a quarter of an hour before the first men of the US 4th Infantry Division were about to go ashore, Allied planes swooped overhead, raining bombs on the beach

*US assault troops see the battle as they approach Omaha
beach in a landing craft on D-Day.*

defences. In the ensuing thick black smoke, dust and débris, the landing craft were unable
to see where they should be aiming for and missed their appointed place. The 8th Infantry
which was mapped to land opposite one exit was pulled by the current and, impeded by
the loss of one of their guiding craft, landed a mile further south opposite the Pouppeville
causeway.

Brigadier-General Theodore Roosevelt Jnr, son of the late President 'Teddy' Roosevelt
and distant cousin of the wartime US leader, Franklin D. Roosevelt, was Deputy
Commander of the US 4th Infantry Division. He was fifty-seven years old on D-Day and
leaned on a cane for support, but he had somehow managed to persuade his superior officer that he should join men more than half his age in the first assault, 'to steady the boys',
as he explained. Roosevelt realized what had happened at once: 'We'll start the war from
here,' he said decisively, walking up and down the beach waving his stick and indicating
that a new plan was now in place. The troops should advance up the beach from where
they had landed, and where the German defences were much lighter, rather than try to
reclaim their original position in the face of heavy German gunfire. The soldiers obeyed:
'If we were afraid of the enemy, we were more afraid of him,' an Arizona Infantryman
recalls. By nightfall over 23,000 men had landed on Utah. They made their way across a
narrow causeway or stumbled and swam across the marshy land behind the beach, which
Rommel had ordered to be flooded as a further defence measure, and started linking up

with the paratroopers who had landed near Ste-Mère Eglise. The 4th Division was to suffer grieviously as they fought toward Cherbourg - the death from a heart attack of Roosevelt on 12 July was a further blow - and by the end of the war, the Division had the heaviest toll of any US Division. But on D-Day itself, Force U was the only landing assault to achieve its objective and the price it paid for that success was less that might have been feared: 210 casualties including sixty men lost at sea.

Omaha was a four-mile crescent of sand backed by dunes, a gap in the sheer cliffs that commanded an excellent overview of the beach approaches and was only penetrable in a few places. It was an obvious place for a landing and the Allies knew that the Germans had heavy fortifications in place. Guarding the four exits from the beach were pill boxes manned by infantry equipped with machine-guns and grenades. There were heavy guns embedded in concrete, eighty-five machine-gun posts, anti-tank positions and rocket batteries, all linked by trenches manned by snipers. But what British-US Intelligence did not know was that the defenders were not a second-rate, demoralized army half comprised of reluctant ex-prisoners of war from the campaigns in Russia and eastern Europe. They were the crack 352nd Infantry Division, the only full attack division along the Normandy coast. The Division had been moved to Normandy at the end of May and had arrived in the Cotentin Peninsula only days before on an anti-invasion exercise.

The troops who landed on Omaha were the US 1st Infantry Division, 'the Big Red One', men who had fought in North Africa, Sicily and Italy - and in many of the bars on the way - and the US 29th Infantry Division which was as yet unbloodied by combat. The D-Day objectives of the Omaha assault were to occupy a bridgehead on the road towards Bayeux and capture the German batteries situated on the Pointe du Hoc, a sheer range of cliffs to the west of the beach.

Pointe du Hoc was a 100-foot-high sheer rock promontory - the equivalent to a nine-storey block of flats - lying between Utah and Omaha with a commanding view of the Normandy coast. It was thought that the casements set on top housed six 155mm guns with a range estimated to be 25,000 yards - enough to blast the invasion troops from north of Utah to Port-en-Bessin just west of Arromanches. These were to be bombed and assailed from the sea but they were regarded as so treacherous that if this failed they had to be put out of action by the infantry. The 2nd US Rangers, a tough Commando unit under Lieutenant-Colonel James E. Rudder, a thirty-four-year-old Texan football coach, had been given the job of disabling the guns before the assault troops started to come ashore on D-Day. Two LCTs carrying the Rangers had sunk with all men lost, before 225 rangers stormed on to the narrow shingle shelf below the cliff. The men had been training for a couple of months at Bude in north Cornwall. 'All we ever did was climb cliffs,' remembers a Ranger, Len Lomell; 'that and keep in shape and learn map reading so we could find our way behind enemy lines...so we were aware what was coming.' Lomell had had a head start, back home in New Jersey. When he was about fourteen he'd helped his house-painter father 'paint a water tower. It took me about two days before I had enough courage to get up those ladders, those water towers were pretty high. But my father was very patient and encouraging and soon I was running up and down like a monkey. So I thought I'd be all right when I got to France.' Bob Edlin, a Lieutenant in the 2nd US Rangers, recalls that we expected it to be easier than it was. The bombers were so close together it seemed as if the whole sky was covered with bombers, and we could hear them detonating on the coast and we could hear the terrible gunfire, and the flashes, and then the battleship *Texas* and the destroyers opened up and we thought that nobody could live through all that, so we actually thought that there wouldn't be any opposition - we'd just be able to walk straight across the beach.

But when his craft reached the beach, Edlin realized

I guess no war's like you'd expect it to be. Whoever planned the whole thing didn't take into consideration that…the bombers would have made holes in the beach where you could take cover, but when the tide came in the sea would cover the holes and they would become a hazard…Our part of the landing was delayed by about thirty minutes and by that time the Germans had recovered from the artillery and the bombing, and the navy and the fighter bombers couldn't come any closer or we'd be at risk, so when the ramp went down on the boat, I knew we were in trouble. The first thing I heard was like a woodpecker pecking on a tree. It was bullets rattling against the ramp of the boat and then big plumes of smoke went up and I saw that Lieutenant Fitzsimmons who was a good friend of mine, his landing craft was hit by an .88 or a mortar right on the ramp, and it just blew up, and I thought, 'There goes one platoon.' It was terrible…But the only thing we had in mind was to take those guns…when the ramp dropped we went down and the water was ice-cold. We had these big packs on, we were carrying three days' rations - not that Rangers carry much, only D-rations, little chocolate bars, and we were carrying ammunition and grenades and all these things along with a gas mask - which we never did need, fortunately. A lot of the men were wearing lifebelts, and they would immediately inflate them, but I think that most of our people were smart enough not to inflate them, because if you are wearing an inflated life-jacket when the waves hit you, you turn upside down in the water and drown…and you had to get off to the right of the ramp - I'd been trained about that for years - otherwise the boat could surge forward and run over you. The water was up to my shoulders straight away and I immediately dropped my gas mask, but I reckoned that I'd rather be gassed than drown so I just made for the shore and tried to get my men together because I figured I was the only officer left and I was trying to get the men off the beach and up to the rocks where we could reform and get after those guns because that was our job.

The Rangers had brought a firemen's sixteen-foot extension ladder to set against the rock to get a foothold but Rudder's men realized that it would be impossible to climb the rock face and so the men started to fire their rockets carrying iron grappling hooks to get a purchase on the rock for their ropes. But that wasn't easy as the ropes were wet and slimy from having been in the sea and often the grappling hooks couldn't get a grip. But once they did, the men started to shin up the ropes hand over hand. From the top of the cliff dislodged rocks came bouncing down, while the Germans rained grenades and rifle fire down on the assailants and cut the ropes they were climbing, plunging men to their death below. At last Colonel Rudder was able to flash the message 'Praise the Lord' to the battleship *Texas* moored offshore, meaning 'all men up the cliff.' But they weren't. 130 men out of the 240 lay dead or dying at the bottom of the rock face. And when those who did manage to scale the sheer face got to the top, they found the emplacements 'were all empty', according to Bradleys' aide Chet Hanson. 'One had a long wooden pole in it - it was obviously put there to fool the aerial photographers that it was a heavy-barrelled gun. There were no guns in any of the emplacements, they'd all been moved inland.'

Len Lomell and another Ranger, Jack Kuhn, found the five guns later in the day lying camouflaged in an orchard. They threw a thermite grenade at them to melt the metal of the breech blocks and render the deadly guns unusable.

Colonel Edwin Woolf, then an engineer with the 6th Special Brigades, had been involved with testing the amphibious DUKWs since their early trials . On D-Day his job was to bring the DUKWs ashore and in position for the 6th Brigade, but in the rough seas this was a difficult task. Woolf found the scene that met his eyes on Omaha

> indescribable…there were dead people everywhere, there were people floating in the water, there were wrecked tanks, there were wrecked jeeps, there were tanks that were supposed to be floating in water that were dead on land, and some of them had been knocked out by the .88 guns which were firing straight down the beach…we'd been told it would be a walk-over, we'd just walk on to the beach and the Germans would have been obliterated, the air force and the guns and the combat engineers, they'd make it so that the infantry could just walk ashore…but it wasn't like that. Not at all.

The German fortifications were hardly touched by the air support bombers, which, anxious not to endanger landing craft, flew inland and dumped their load well away from the beach, whilst the relatively short naval bombardment made little impact on the heavy concrete encasements and gun positions. Woolf saw 'a shell hitting one big gun emplacement and bouncing off the roof, literally bouncing off.'

The American preferred practice of transferring troops to the landing craft more than eleven miles out to sea meant that the men and their equipment had little protection from the waves that swamped their craft in the wide Seine Bay. When the DD tanks were lowered into the water 6,000 yards offshore, their waterproof 'skirts' soon collapsed in the heavy seas. Of the thirty-three tanks put ashore, twenty-seven were lost and tank crews drowned, trapped as their vehicles sank.

The US forces storming Omaha thus did so almost entirely without tank support. Hundreds of men drowned before they ever reached the beach, weak swimmers dragged down by heavy equipment - a radio weighed 40 lb - in the raging seas or shot by German snipers. Dead bodies floated in the sea, and the section known as 'Easy Red' was soon red with the blood of the dead and injured, but never anything approaching easy. The injured lay on the shore, whilst medics risked - and often lost - their lives to help them. The bodies were soon swept out to sea again on the ebbing tide which also drowned the wounded who were unable to move. Men who did manage to struggle ashore did so 'waxy ashen-faced' with seasickness, weighed down with by now often useless, water-logged equipment, and soaking, squelching wet.

Jeeps go ashore: a view from a troop transport on D-Day.

'Most of the men had sloughed off their packs,' says George Itzen, a platoon leader of the US 147 Engineer Combat Battalion, whose men were instructed to 'blow up obstacles and as soon as the beach was cleared and the small arms enemy fire was eliminated initiate the landing of cargo and the evacuation of the wounded.'

The .50 calibre and the .30 calibre machine-guns were left on the boat along with the bazookas and flamethrowers, there wasn't any question of getting them ashore - although they had been packed as floatable with extra life-jackets and large waterproof bags - we called them elephant's condoms. You could put a whole gun in them and tie the end up and keep it secure both from the water and the sand. Most of the chaps just got ashore with their pistol and cartridge belt and canteen and their rifle and perhaps their gas mask which was a helluva good piece of equipment to keep your head up.

As they tried to move forward, the troops faced machine and sniper gunfire that combed the beaches and the water, aiming at anything that moved. There were hardly any tanks to take cover behind, since many of the few that had made it ashore had received a direct hit and were now burning.

Bob Edlin was trying to get his men off the beach when

I saw one of my sergeants there and his left thumb was gone but he didn't look as if he was hurt too badly so I called his name and told him to get up and come with us, and I rolled him over and he was dead, and just in front of him was another fellow, Butch Blader, who was lying there so I hollered at him 'Let's get up and go'…and he kinda looked back over his shoulder at me and didn't say anything and when I got closer I saw that there was blood all over his back and he'd been hit in the stomach and the bullet had passed right through and come out of his spine, and so I started towards the sea wall…and then I was hit by machine-gun fire in the left leg and the pain was terrible. It knocked me down and I thought, 'Well, I haven't been here ten minutes and I've already got a Purple Heart' [an award for US servicemen wounded or killed in action] and I managed to get up, and then a sniper got me in my right leg…I started out to cross the beach with thirty-five men and only six got to the top, that's all. We asssumed that D and E and F company had been wiped out, and we hadn't heard from C company, and we thought that they might have made a landing on their own, and A company was just decimated, bodies were spread everywhere, you could hardly walk on the sand for bodies, and I thought, 'This part of the invasion's over, I just hope that they're doing better on Utah and the British beaches…'

'We had a perfect landing,' recalls Ted Lapres, another US Ranger. 'I didn't even get my feet wet. But when I looked at the beach I thought the world was coming to an end. There was no room on the beach. There was no room at the sea wall…there were just the dead.'

As the tide came in, the men who had made it across the beach - now, two hours after the first assault wave, a narrowing strip - crouched, trapped and unable to move forwards or back, beneath the sea wall.

Private First Class John Dandker was 'a sort of a time bomb' on Omaha:

I had 20 lb of explosives strapped to my back. I was supposed to blow up a blockhouse, and what with the TNT and everything else that was strapped to me, when I stepped off the LCT I went up to my neck in water. There were bullets pinging into the water all around me…and then I got on to the beach and I lay there right next to my company commander. He looked at me and he said, 'What are you doing?' and I said, 'Same thing as you, sir.'

*Members of a US landing party help a wounded soldier ashore from a
life raft after their landing craft was sunk by enemy action.*

Dandker was trapped for five and a half hours on the beach before he 'got the order to go across the open beach. They were shooting but we got the order, we just had to go, that's what we were trained to do. You are ordered to advance, and so that's what you do.'

As Cawthon and his battalion of the US 29th Infantry Division approached Omaha on the second assault wave at about 7.30 a.m. they were dropped on a sandbar 200 or so yards offshore since the coxswain of the landing craft was unable to get past the defensive obstacles - 'big, ugly structures of iron or logs, partly covered by the rising tide...There was no evidence that the engineers that had accompanied the first wave had succeeded in blasting paths through the obstacles.' Struggling to keep upright in the sea, his lifebelt lifting him on to the crest of a wave, 'the wave passed on, and in the trough, I touched bottom, to be lifted moments later and carried towards France. Such was the pattern of my advance in the greatest amphibious assault of history: propelled forward by a powerful, in-sweeping tide, regardless of any lessening fervour to open a second front in Europe.'

Charles Cawthon and his fellow infantrymen were washed ashore, where they lay, heads down, 'for Omaha Beach was obviously not a place to stand up and be counted' on the shoreline, looking their first on combat:

> It was now apparent that we were coming ashore in one of the carefully registered killing zones of German machine-guns and mortars. The havoc they had wrought was all around in an incredible chaos - bodies, weapons, boxes of demolitions, flamethrowers, reels of telephone wire, and personal equipment from socks to

toilet articles. Hundreds of brown lifebelts were washing to and fro, writhing and twisting like brown sea slugs. The waves broke around the disabled tanks, bulldozers and beached landing craft that were thick here in front of the heavily defended exit road...The beach rose above me, steep and barren. There was a wide stretch of sand being narrowed by the minute by the tide, then a sharply rising shingle bank of small, smooth stones that ended at the sea wall. Against the wall were soldiers of the first assault team. Some were scooping out shelters; a number were stretched out in the loose attitude of the wounded; others had the ultimate stillness of death; but most were just sitting with their backs against the wall. No warlike moves were apparent.

'My beautiful France looked sordid and uninviting,' thought Robert Capa as he left his landing craft. He hunched behind a tank for cover repeating a sentence he had learned as a photographer in the Spanish Civil War: 'Es una cosa muy seriosa. Es una cosa muy seriosa,' [This is a very serious business] as he found himself 'nose to nose with a lieutenant who he'd played poker with the previous night. He asked me if I knew what he saw. I told him no and that I didn't think he could see much beyond my hand. "I'll tell you what I see," he whispered, "I see my ma on the front porch waving my insurance policy."' Capa found it more than he could bear.

The men around me lay motionless. Only the dead on the waterline rolled with the waves. An LCT braved the fire and medics with red crosses painted on their helmets poured from it. I didn't think and didn't decide it. I just stood up and ran for the boat. I stepped into the sea between two bodies and the water reached my neck...I reached the boat. The last medics were just getting out. I climbed aboard. As I reached the deck I felt a shock, and suddenly was covered in feathers.

Capa wondered if somebody was killing chickens. 'Then I saw that the superstructure had been shot away and that the feathers were the stuffing from the kapok jackets of the men that had been blown up. The skipper was crying. His assistant had been blown all over him and he was a mess.' A barge picked Capa up and took him back to USS *Chase*, the ship he had left only six hours before.

The last wave of the 16th Infantry were just being lowered, but the decks were already full with the returning wounded and the dead...the mess boys who had served our coffee in white jackets and with white gloves at three in the morning were covered with blood and were sewing the dead in white sacks.

Aboard USS *Augusta* General Bradley's

worries deepened over the alarming and fragmentary reports we picked up on the navy set. From these messages we could piece together only an incoherent account of sinkings, swampings, heavy enemy fire, and chaos on the beaches. By 8.30 the two assault regiments on Omaha had expected to break through the water's-edge defences and force their way inland to where a road paralleled the coastline a mile behind the beaches. Yet by 8.30, V Corps had not yet confirmed news of the landing...It was 10.00 before the first report came in...it did nothing

Omaha Beach: 'We could see [the battle] dimly through the haze and hear the echoes of its guns...my worries deepened over the alarming and fragmentary reports we picked up of...chaos on the beaches.' General Omar Bradley on board Admiral Kirk's flagship USS Augusta, *6 June 1944.*

more than confirm our worst fears: 'obstacles mined, progress…slow…DD tanks for Fox Green swamped.'

Bradley could dimly see the battle on the beaches and 'hear the echo of its guns. The battle belonged that morning to the thin, wet line of khaki that dragged itself ashore on the Channel coast of France.' The staff officer Bradley, sent out in a DUKW to report on the situation at 9.30, came back an hour later sea-sodden and reporting that all was confusion with 'the 1st Division pinned down behind the sea wall while the enemy swept the beaches with small-arms fire,' while landing craft milled in confusion, unable to break through to the shore and raked by artillery fire.

At noon Bradley had to face the fact that of an assault force of 34,000 men and 3,300 vehicles 'only a portion had gotten ashore' and this might mean that the operation should be pulled and the second wave of men and vehicles bound for Omaha diverted to one of the British or Canadian beaches. But that would have meant Utah would have been isolated and the forces there could have been cut off by German reinforcements.

It was not until 1.30 p.m. that a terse message was received on the *Augusta*: 'Troops formerly pinned down on beaches…advancing on heights behind beaches.'

In fact small groups of men of the 1st and 29th Divisions had managed by acts of almost foolhardy courage to move up the beach around 10 a.m., exhorted by cries like Cota's which they'd heard so often in training: '29th, let's go! 29th let's go! They're murdering us here. Let's move inland and get murdered! 29th, let's go!' Colonel Taylor of the 16th Infantry yelled at his men 'The only people on this beach are the dead and those who are going to die…now get the hell out of here.'

By nightfall on D-Day, at a loss of over 3,000 men killed or wounded and an almost unaccountable loss of tanks and equipment, the three-mile stretch of France that was Omaha Beach had been 'liberated.' As reinforcements continued to funnel on to the beaches, struck silent by the terrible evidence of battle in the form of a confusion of bodies, twisted metal, burned-out tanks and abandoned and water-logged equipment, the men of the first D-Day landings had managed to push inland above the beach.

Surveying the beach at midnight Charles Cawthon had lost over half his ranks:

> Together we had been through months and years of wartime confusion and strains; marched countless tedious miles; lived in mud and dust, heat and cold. I knew their problems…and they knew mine…then it all came down to this brief first day of battle on the coast of Normandy, and, for so many of them, it all ended. For the rest of us, what has been since has not been the same.

'I don't think I knew what courage was until I was on Omaha,' recalls John Hamilton, a radio operator who was pinned down for three hours on the beach by gunfire. 'Our company commander was brought back and he had no legs…and he just asked the doctor, who showed up from somewhere, "I want to ask you a question, and I want you to tell me the truth. If I've got a chance, I'll stay awake, I'll fight. If I haven't, I'll go to sleep." I often wondered if he made it…I saw so many heroes that day, they just couldn't make enough medals for them all.'

CHAPTER NINE

THE FAR SHORE: GOLD, JUNO AND SWORD

H-HOUR FOR THE FIRST British troops to land in Normandy, dictated by the tides, was 7.30 a.m, an hour later than for the Americans. They were aiming to go ashore on the next beach going east from Omaha, designated 'Gold,' beyond the small harbour of Port-en-Bessin.

Max Hastings explains that the British plan called for each Brigade to land four LCTs each carrying four DDs each and to put these ashore at H+5; at H-Hour four LCTs carrying specialist armour - Crocodiles, Petards, Bobbin tanks, whatever was deemed most appropriate for that particular terrain - would be landed, and sapper groups would start trying to dismantle or incapacitate the beach obstacles. At H+7 eight assault landing craft transporting the two leading infantry divisions would land. A quarter of an hour later came another eight LCAs with two more infantry companies, then at H+25 two LCAs with the men of the Beach Group. At H+35 bulldozers and more specialist armour were landed to be followed within the next two hours by nine LCTs with self-propelled guns and then ten LCTs with a full squadron of tanks. The tenth wave brought more gunners and twenty-one DUKWs loaded with stores and ammunition. It was an ambitious timetable - COSSAC had predicted that ten per cent of landing craft would be lost and twenty per cent damaged. In the event that was an underestimate in some places where the seas were too rough, or craft had to mill around on the water's edge unable to beach: in some sectors, the prediction was over-pessimistic, but nowhere did the landing run to schedule.

Gold seemed to present many of the terrible hazards of Omaha. It was a smooth, flat beach heavily pocketed with mines and obstacles. The heights above Arromanches were dominated by heavy field guns and at both ends of the beach large calibre guns stood encased in concrete. The area around the beach was heavily populated - there was to be tragically heavy loss of civilian life in the battle for Gold - and many of the villas and small hotels overlooking the beach had been seized by the Germans and reinforced with concrete and equipped with guns. The area was defended by a second-rank division, the 716th, but also by men of the 352nd Division, the crack unit that was devastating the US forces further east on Omaha.

The men who came ashore on Gold were the British 50th Northumbrian Infantry Division followed by units of the 7th Armoured Division, the famous 'Desert Rats'. Their objective was to penetrate the German defences between the small seaside resorts of Le Hamel and La Rivière and advance inland to take Bayeux and also the small port of Arromanches - a vital first-day objective since it was here that the Mulberry Harbour was to be sited when it was towed across the Channel on D-Day+1.

The air and naval bombardment had only limited success against the Germans' bristling fortifications. Rough seas swept away many of the armoured support regiment tanks and prevented the DD tanks from being launched so they had to come ashore from landing craft behind the infantry. It began to look as if Gold could be a perilous copy of what was happening on Omaha - infantry without close support trying to make their way up a beach in the face a salvo of fire power. But it was on Gold that 'Hobart's Funnies' came into their own, with the 'crab' or flail tanks clearing a pathway through the mines and small obstacles with their five-foot chain swing, whilst other specialist tanks included one to lay matting across soft sand and the AVRE, whose petard was effective in shattering concrete pill boxes.

Company Sergeant-Major Stan Hollis of 6th Battalion The Green Howards won a VC for conspicuous bravery that day on Gold when he 'posted' a grenade through the slit in a machine-gun firing pill box which was part of the Mont Fleury Battery. He followed it up by firing his Sten gun repeatedly into the pill box and the surrounding trenches killing several Germans and taking others prisoner. Later in the day in the village of Crépon he disabled a field gun and crew and rescued some of his men under direct enemy fire.

Gold was not won easily: men drowned in the heavy seas, some entombed in their tanks; others were picked off by sniper fire, blown up by mines or caught in the cross-fire of heavy armour and machine-guns.

Warren, who landed on Gold beach with the 1st Battalion of the Hampshire Regiment, was a Company Commander, but when the Battalion Commander, Brigadier Nelson Smith, was injured by a bullet in the leg immediately on landing, he shouted at Warren, 'You'll have to take over. I can't go on.' He was put on a stretcher and loaded back into the landing craft he had left moments before.

> We'd landed a good two or three hundred yards east from where we should have been put down...and the leading assault company which was just ahead of us should have landed right on Le Hamel, and they were supposed to have climbed the sea wall and captured this gun position which was important because it was covering the whole beach. And because they had been swept down the coast, too, they hadn't managed to do this, so there was a lot of shooting going on and until the guns were captured no one could really use the beach. We'd hit a runnel - a sand bank - coming in in the landing craft, and so we went into four or five feet of water, and everyone was carrying a lot of equipment and ammunition which were very heavy, so quite a few of the shorter men drowned and others were hit by small-arms fire.

Warren managed to struggle ashore but 'what should have happened by this time is that the tanks, the AVREs, should have cut gaps through the mines and wire for the infantry

Sword Beach: Lord Lovat (to the right of the column of men) comes ashore with men of the 1st Special Service Brigade on Queen Red Beach near la Brèche d'Hermanville on D-Day.

like us to go through, but there was no sign of them.' Warren, with battalion commander responsibility thrust upon him at twenty-five, decided that he and his men would have to make their own way though the wire and minefield. The battalion would then storm Le Hamel from the rear rather than the seaward side as had been planned. 'This is the thing for this operation,' decided Warren when he came across an AVRE, 'which projects an enormous bomb [petard]…that can penetrate steel and concrete structures.' Under cover of the mortar bomb assault Warren and his men were able to surround and capture the strong point.

> The Germans obviously didn't want to fight. They came out with their hands up…they all came from the 91st Division and most of them were Poles or Czechs or Russians and a few Germans, and though they gave us a pretty rough time in some of our sector, generally speaking they caved in pretty quickly.

Gordon Tye was a Corporal with the 47th Royal Marine Commando that landed on Gold with the objective of taking Port-en-Bressin by D-Day+3.

> None of our boats got ashore. They all got shelled or a lot got holed, there were things like railway tracks buried in the sand and when it was high tide, the craft

just ran into them. There was water pouring in everywhere…we had a rough time getting on to the beaches…I reckon we lost about a hundred on the beaches…we never got to our full strength again after D-Day. Most of the men were drowned…at least I think they were, but at the time you don't get to look around you. You have your objective to get to, and it wasn't until we'd been ashore for some time that we realized that we'd lost our troop commander to start with, and a lot of officers. We were being fired on all day long…sniper fire and mortars. I've got to give them their due, the Germans were good mortar men. They'd put their mortar on a sixpence…you couldn't get out of their way. If one of your own soldiers gets shot, they just go down and you think to yourself, 'Well, that's that and there's nothing I can do about it.' It happened many a time: a man next to me would get shot and killed…they are your friends, your mates, but you gotta keep going, you can't stay. When you're shot nobody stops with you. You make them comfortable, you sit them up, and give them a cigarette and a drink of water if they want one, but you couldn't stay. There weren't enough men. Nobody would stay with the wounded, that was up to the medical orderlies, and the doctor and the padre. When you get shot you're on your own.'

Many of the troops felt they had no idea what was happening or exactly what they should be doing. 'Information just never got to the platoons.' They had to rely on news from despatch riders who happened to be passing, and impressions of the action from men from other units. But by mid-afternoon on 6 June Gold was in British hands, as was 'booty' as catalogued by the 10th Beach Group: '(Apart from what has inserted itself into pockets). Stocks of reserve ammo., grenades, rifles, LMGs, etc are being counted. It is estimated that there are sufficient supplies for the whole Beach group to blow itself up, if they go the right way about it.'

There were about 1,000 casualties on Gold, killed, wounded or missing. Some 500 German POWs had been taken, many French families were killed, wounded or made homeless. The 47th Royal Marine Commando were linking up with the straggle of US troops from Omaha and managed to take Port-en-Bressin on D-Day+1. The men of the British 50th Infantry Division had taken Arromanches and were advancing on Bayeux. 'We are at last liberated,' wrote a young French woman in her diary that night. 'It is just 7 p.m., the weather is lovely - we only hope other villages will soon be liberated.'

Juno, the beach on which the 3rd Canadian Division were to land, was three miles east of Gold. It was a holiday area, and the beach was edged with small resort towns linked by houses and villas set back from the shore, most of which had been requisitioned and heavily fortified by the Germans, swathed in barbed wire, littered with mines and backed by anti-tank and machine- guns. The 3rd Division was linked to the British 2nd Army for the assault phase of the Normandy landings and would return to the Canadian Army when a sufficient number of their fellow countrymen had arrived in Normandy. In fact on D-Day the 3rd Division consisted of 15,000 Canadians with 9,000 British troops and Royal Marines in support.

The tides were such along this stretch of coastline that the 3rd Division was scheduled to land some ten minutes later than the troops on Gold, but in the event they were delayed by heavy seas, and by the time many of the landing craft arrived on the shoreline,

The beaches of Normandy. A German propaganda photograph warning of the mined sands that awaited any invaders.

many of the obstacles were covered by the advancing tide and proved a lethal menace, blowing up craft with the mines, impaling some and causing others to overturn. As on all the beaches of D-Day, but perhaps most on Omaha and Juno, the sea that delivered the crafts and men was relentless in its advance, which meant that unless they were able to penetrate the Atlantic Wall and get off the beach, the assault troops were trapped on an ever-narrowing, ever-more dangerously congested strip of sand or shingle with tanks piling up, their waxed waterproof protection being discarded, and landing craft jostling the shoreline with no place to land. The men had to make the decision whether to be gunned down if they stayed at the shoreline, or risk the mines if they set off across an uncleared beach.

The resistance the Canadian and British support troops encountered on Juno was formidable and, again, many had to advance unsupported by tanks or heavy fire when pounding seas made it impossible for DDs to be launched; if they did they were in danger of overturning and being lost under the waves.

Grant Suche was a twenty-two-year-old Rifleman with the Canadian Royal Winnipeg Rifles who felt

> very fortunate that we landed that day without getting swamped...but then I was so seasick that I didn't care what happened. I was no sailor. I was real seasick. And when we did land everything seemed so mixed up. The first thing we saw were bodies, and parts of bodies, our own people, and this country that was strange to us, and all these pill boxes everywhere. But I guess you didn't have time to think about anything but your own neck...I can always remember seeing the steeple of

this church, and there were snipers up there zapping us with lead flying all around. They were there all night on 6th June and the 7th and the 8th too…

'We'd worked out roughly where we were going,' according to Ian Hammerton who was a Troop Commander in the 1st Troop 'B' Squadron, 22 Dragoons, on D-Day, and for whom the rough sea crossing to Juno beach was 'the worst journey I have ever taken in my life…words fail me. I was sick all through the night, everyone was sick except the skipper. All I wanted was dry land. I didn't care two hoots about the Germans.'

The Tank Troop went ashore at Bernières-sur-Mer intent on clearing two exits from the beach. They tried to petard the concrete wall that faced them and knock holes through it, but they found that there was a concrete ramp up from the beach to the top of the sea wall and on top of that was a huge gate built of railway lines welded together. Hammerton drew his tank to the foot of the ramp and shot, sighting the gun through the barrel as they were so close to the target. That was successful so the tanks started up the ramp but by that time the tide was rising and Hammerton and his men were forced to abandon their tanks and try to get ashore.

> It was very difficult because the undertow was very strong, and there were several dead bodies and wounded men and we had great difficulty in pulling ourselves out…but we were under strict instructions that under no circumstances were we to stop and help the wounded men. The essential thing for us to do was to make an exit for the follow-up troops who were coming ashore. We were not to stop for anyone, which was rather hard - but necessary.

Whilst two of his tank crews were repairing their flail chains, Hammerton walked along the sea wall:

> I saw a wounded Canadian with most of his face blown away, and a padre was try-ing to comfort him, and the chap wanted a cigarette, but there was nowhere to put it…it wrings you seeing things like that and not being able to do anything to help. The next thing I remember seeing was half a dozen Germans with their hands up and a big Alsatian dog waiting to surrender and that pleased me enor-mously…when I got back to the tanks, there were two Frenchmen coming towards us, and they said 'Bonjour…vous êtes bienvenus en France.' But I'm afraid I wasn't in a very sociable mood at the time, I was too busy, but I shook hands and that was it…

The Canadians were driven by a fierce determination to avenge their losses at Dieppe. They were also helped in this populated area of Normandy by the actions of the French Resistance, who, alerted by an invasion message from the BBC on 5 June, 'Le champ du laboureur dans le matin brumeux,' and the sound of offshore gun fire, hurried to their task of felling trees and scattering nails in the path of advancing German reinforcements. As night fell on Juno Beach on 6 June the Canadian forces had advanced further inland than any of the other assault troops that day. They had linked up with the British 50th Northumbrian Infantry Division from Gold to establish a fifteen-mile-long, seven-mile-deep beach head and had begun the advance towards Caen nine miles inland - originally, and as it proved, unrealistically, a first-day objective for the Allied forces. The cost had

French civilians give information to British soldiers as they proceed inland from the beaches. A photograph taken on D-Day by a British soldier of the 4th S.S. Brigade at St Aubin-sur-Mer.

been over 1,000 Canadian casualties - a precursor of the many more that were to result from the 3rd Division's slow and bloody fight through Normandy.

The final beach of the Allied assault, west of Ouistreham at the mouth of the Orne, was code-named Sword. It lay five miles from Juno along a rocky stretch of coast that the D-Day planners had felt would prevent a successful landing. The gap would be closed by assaults from the 4th Commando Brigade landing on either side. Many of the soldiers who stormed Sword were returners: men of the British 3rd Infantry Division that had been driven from France at Dunkirk. Arthur Robson, a Sapper with the Royal Engineers, had a number of Dunkirk veterans in his unit: 'I think one reason why they were put in was to boost the morale of the younger men - not that they were much older, probably only about five years or so, but these were men who'd seen action, they knew what it was about and they could show you the ropes. They escaped from Dunkirk, they'd seen it all...'

This time their objective was to liberate Caen and link up with the 6th Airborne Division that had parachuted on to the Orne bridgehead.

In peacetime the beaches where the troops were disembarking in heavy seas at 7.30 on 6 June were where French families holidayed, and the shore was ringed with hotels and boarding houses. ('It looked astonishingly like Blackpool,' marvelled a South Lancs soldier.) But this particular summer the family holiday accommodation housed a deadly arsenal of machine-guns, Sten-guns and fortifications which were linked along the coast making a formidable addition to the Atlantic Wall.

A German blockhouse knocked out in the battle for the Normandy beaches on D-Day is inspected by men of the 4/7th Dragoon Guards.

Colonel Patrick Porteous was with No.4 Commandos. He'd been on the Dieppe Raid - which is when he was awarded his VC, and he had thought that was 'the biggest disaster that had ever happened,' but he was eager to get back to France again.

> We were on top of the world. We were all looking forward to it like mad. We were all picked men, the Commandos, and we'd been training and training in the UK and getting absolutely fed up with it and we wanted to see if all this hard work and training would really work.

It was the same for Lord Lovat's 1st Special Service Brigade.

> Hell's bells, we'd joined up, gone places and grown tall together...and this was a special, almost festive, occasion. It meant a long haul for most of that great brigade, chosen to spearhead the BEF's re-entry into Western Europe. If the men had seen much fighting in different theatres they surely knew that now they faced the clincher.

With the Commandos went the irrepressible Free French under Philippe Kieffer '...their eyes were bright, for they were going home. Each wore the Cross of Lorraine with his shoulder titles.' 'L'audace et toujours de l'audace summed them up' - as was to be shown when Kieffer and his men battled to seize the heavily defended casino 'where I've lost many a fortune' at Ouistreham late on D-Day.

But things started to go wrong for Porteous as soon as he and his company transferred to their landing craft:

As we were lowered from the parent ship, we took a large wave into the craft and we found that the bilge pump wasn't working, so we had to start baling water out with our tin hats which wasn't very easy in a confined space on a choppy seat with men being seasick all around you. Finally the boat sank, but it was only in four feet of water, so we were able to scramble ashore.

As Porteous reached the beach

there was another landing craft coming in on our left. One of the subalterns stood up to get out and he was absolutley bowled over by machine-gun fire and he was cut to ribbons. It was very frightening. And then a flail tank on the beach just in front of us was hit by a shell or something and just blew up, and there was machine-gun fire all around, and there were bodies washing about in the engine oil at the water's edge, and men kneeling in the water trying to fire, and then they'd get hit.

When Porteous finally did manage to make it up the beach he was 'carrying this very heavy load, about 90 lb on average, and was soaking wet'. He reached down to unzip the map pocket on his leg 'and out came a great sodden mess of paper, quite useless'.

The Commandos' task had been to seizc the gun battery overlooking Sword Beach, but when his men finally managed to climb up there, having dumped their heavy equipment in a château garden on the way, they found that

the guns were dummies, they'd been replaced a few days before and the real guns had been drawn back, and they were using the battery as a defence to draw the Allies' fire power so the best thing that we could do was to get the hell out of there as fast as we could and fulfil our secondary objective which was to link up with the 6th Airborne on the other side of the Orne and hold the left flank.

But Porteous never entertained the idea that D-Day could turn into another Dieppe, with the Allies thrown back into the sea: 'We'd obviously learned lessons from the Dieppe raid, and the various Combined Ops in North Africa and Italy and Sicily, and we had the whole thing sewn up as far as it possibly could be.'

Towards the end of May Group Captain Patrick Hennessey, who was then a tank commander of No. 4 Troop 'A' Squadron, 13/18th Hussars, was briefed that

in a few days we would be heading for the shores of France to spearhead the invasion...we were shown maps with no names and aerial photographs which showed a line of white houses along the beachline and we were told that those were our targets...they were enemy gun emplacements, and there would be firing coming from there. Once we were on board ship we were called for our final briefing and shown maps with names on so that we knew that we were to land on a beach code-named Sword, at the little town of Lion-sur-Mer, and we were to be the left flank of the assault...The journey over was absolutely horrible. The LCT is a flat-bottomed ship with not much to it apart from a large deck which was the tank deck. There were five Sherman tanks on each LCT, and they weren't built to accommodate so many men and tanks so there was nowhere to sleep and we bedded down on the hard iron tank deck...we had been issued with hammocks, but very few soldiers knew how to swing a hammock...It was very exciting for the first hour or so whilst we watched the armada assemble, but gradually the sea got rougher, and in the next hour or so we began to get very seasick, and this went on for several days. Hardly a man aboard wasn't very sick. We had sea-sickness pills and a certain amount of rum went round, but it didn't really help...When we got about 5,000 yards from shore, our flotilla stopped and we mounted the tanks, put up the screens [on the DD tanks] and got everything ready. And one by one we launched off through the doors and out into the sea, and a force eight wind was blowing and it was very rough indeed, and we could feel what that was doing to an LCT that weighed hundreds of tons, so what was it going to do to a poor little DD Tank with a screen round it? But it was a matter of drill: once the ramp was lowered there was only one way to go and that was out. The waves must have been five or six feet, and we went right up and then right down into the trough of a wave, but then slowly we could feel the Duplex Drive propellors biting into the water and we started to make way. It took us well over an hour to cover the four miles to the beach and a couple of tanks were lost. The screen tore on one and it went down and one was run over by its own LCT which should have stayed back because of sea conditions, but it was moving forward. All the crew went down, except the captain - he managed to get free. We had to take it in turns to work the bilge pump - we'd thought it was a piece of Meccano, but it worked, and we were baling water out with our tin helmets all the way to the shore.

The opposition started before we got ashore, they must have woken up with the naval bombardment and the aerial bombardment and they started to retaliate, so we were under fire for the best part of 1,000 yards coming in. But from the German point of view there was very little to see...all you could see from the shore of the DD Tank afloat is a little piece of canvas floating on the water, so if our security had worked, they weren't even aware that these were tanks until we came out of the water and dropped the screen.

We came out of the water, and dropped the screen and within a minute of landing the first shot had gone off. The plan was that the tanks would get to the waterline, stop and start firing while the assault engineers who'd come in right behind us would go ahead and clear the minefields, and then we'd follow the engineers and start making paths through the mines, and we'd hoist a windsock which was our signal that there was a path.

But it wasn't like that. The water was getting deeper, the Royal Engineers were having great difficulty getting through themselves so Hennessey had to decide whether to stay at the water's edge as the tide came in or chance it through a minefield. At that point

the problem was solved for us, because a big wave broke over the stern of the tank and swamped the engine which spluttered to a halt and we had no power. We

Long-hidden flags were waved from windows of French houses as Allied troops passed through liberated French villages. A photograph taken on D-Day by a British officer.

couldn't have moved that thirty-two-ton tank even if we'd wanted to. We stayed there keeping our guns in action as long as we could, but the tide comes in very quickly in that part of the world. It was flooding the tank and the driver and the co-driver had to evacuate because their compartment was full of water and the sea was beginning to creep up through the turret, and eventually we had to give up. We took the machine-guns and ammunition and tripods and inflated the rubber dinghy which we had for emergencies and all five of us got in that with our guns and ammunition and using map boards we started to paddle to the shore...we hadn't gone very far before we were hit by by a burst of machine-gun fire and of course the rubber dinghy was punctured and collapsed and turned over. The co-driver caught a bullet in the ankle so we had one wounded man, our tank was flooded, our dinghy had sunk and we'd lost our guns and somehow we had to get ourselves and the wounded man ashore. It was surprising how deep the water had got by that time, but by swimming and scrabbling and helping each other we finally got to the shoreline. All around the shore were stakes of wood and metal. These were anti-invasion devices and on top of each one was a black Teller mine which exploded if you happened to touch it in the wrong place so there wasn't much chance of stopping for a breather. We were all five of us pretty exhausted when we dragged ourselves ashore, and in the meantime the infantry had come ashore and there was battle going on all around with the Germans retaliating with mortar and shellfire and altogether it was a fairly unhealthy place to be.

The morning after. German soldiers being marched along the beach on 7 June 1944.

Hennessey and his men lay on the beach

> puffing and panting and soaking wet and Gallagher with his wounded ankle and at
> that moment another DD tank of ours drove up and the Commander shouted out,
> 'Can't stop I'm afraid,' and he threw us a tin of self-heating soup. They were
> rather like tins of baked beans, and you pulled a lever on the top of the tin and the
> soup began to warm itself. It was mulligatawny soup and I've never forgotten the
> taste to this day. So we shared this soup between the five of us, lying soaking wet
> and shivering on the Normandy beach...we were a bit forlorn because our tank
> was no use and we had no weapons apart from our pistols and the battle was going
> on all around us. We were wondering what to do and a Captain of the REs came
> up to us and he was very angry and he said, 'Get up, Corporal; this is no way to
> win the Second Front.'

So 'rather shamefacedly' the five made their way across the beach and joined up with
some infantry 'but we weren't a lot of use to them because we had no weapons and they
were very busy.' So Hennessey found a Royal Navy Beachmaster,

> a Lieutenant Commander in the Royal Navy trying to organize the beach. I
> reported our presence to him and asked him what he'd like us to do? And his
> answer was 'Get off my bloody beach.' He was a very busy man...So we did...we
> felt rather like lost souls at that stage...the war was going on. There wasn't much
> we could do to influence the course of the battle and nobody wanted us to join

*Another war. The 13/18th Hussars pass a memorial on D-Day to those killed
in the First World War at Hermansville-sur-Mer.*

in…we felt a little upset until we stopped to think well we had done our part. We
had swum a thirty-two-ton tank through 5,000 yards of savage sea in a gale, we'd
landed on the beaches on time and we'd supplied that vital fire support to enable
the infantry to come ashore and do their job…so we had done what we'd trained
for all those years.

D-Day was the first time that many men had experienced combat. 'Your first experience
of combat is a very shocking thing. You never get over it. You might learn to fire better, to
operate better under attack, but you never get over it.' For those who had already seen
battle, the beaches on D-Day were nevertheless an experience without compare:

You can never quite believe it, when someone's firing at you…it's a sort of cold
feeling: 'He wants to kill me, he really wants to kill me'…I had no fight with
German soldiers…we only killed them to save our lives…It's another human
being - they were such fine soldiers. I'm speaking of the Infantry, I'm not speaking
of the Nazis or the SS. I'm speaking of some guy like myself that was conscripted
to come and fight for his country. I still have remorse that I had to take his life.
You don't get any joy out of it - but at the time I was glad that I fired first…They

call it the longest day, but to me it was the shortest day that I'd ever experienced...the hours seem to go so fast, all we saw and heard...There are an awful lot of sights I'll never forget. There was an American soldier on our way to Vierville lying in the middle of the road, with his legs like spaghetti, and there was a hole in his head the size of a fist, and it just happened that we had to slow down just there, and I said, 'Oh my God...this is what war is about.' I shall never forget one fella that transferred into our outfit right before the invasion - he was an engineer. Didn't have time to get friendly with anyone...we didn't even know his name...he just got transferred...I reckon we were low on men. And when we were on the beaches, he put his head over this hedgerow and he got a bullet right in the middle of his head: he just stood up and slid down...he didn't say anything. I think of him still today. He wasn't friends with anybody, and he got killed as a stranger...The first dead American I saw was a boy out of our company. I wasn't particularly close to him. You don't get close to your men - well, you shouldn't anyway, but I felt I knew him quite well from censoring his mail. He was perhaps twenty-one, twenty-two, and I knew he had a wife and he had children. I felt awful about him, but after that, the more dead Germans I saw, the better I felt...I remember steeling myself to reach down and take this pistol from the German's holster and it was all congealed with blood. I felt I was under test and it was a most vivid picture. I compared these Germans who were really so handsome with the average British soldier who were all shapes and sizes - an absolute Sergeant Major's nightmare, and yet we were the ones who achieved victory, and the handsome Germans were the ones who lost. I grew up in Normandy. I really grew up. They make a lot about counselling nowadays. Nobody ever counselled us. We'd say, 'Poor old Charlie's caught it. Yes, it's lucky he didn't burn.' That's how we'd look at it. The worst thing that could happen to a tank man was that he would be caught in his tank and burnt. If a Sherman tank was hit it burst into flames. The Germans used to call them 'Tommy cookers'...Staying alive on those beaches, wasn't training or skill, or even courage, or anything. It was just luck, pure luck. One man might be all right and the man next to him would be killed. There was no sense to it. It was just luck.

Frank Svoboda was a Chaplain to the 79th Infantry Division and he went to Omaha beach with them on D-Day. In a lull in the fighting he would gather a few men around for a communion service - with grape juice representing the Blood of Christ, and crackers His body. 'It didn't seem to matter...when a soldier died, when he was breathing his last, he'd always say something like "Tell the people at home not to forget us. Don't forget us." '

CHAPTER TEN

A NATION WAITS

B EFORE DAWN ON 6 JUNE 1944, Anona Moser, who had come to Britain with the American Red Cross, pulled back the black-out curtains at the Swan Hotel in Bedford where she was billeted to see what it was that had awakened her so early. Below her window stood the hotel's night porter, a veteran of Dunkirk. He, too, was gazing up at the still-dark sky where hundreds of aircraft seemed to be having a rendezvous. He looked up at Miss Moser. 'This is it,' he said (as Miss Moser reports) in a 'husky whisper', 'we're going back.'

A night sister in charge of a ward at Brighton Children's Hospital in Sussex, was watching the planes too:

> We'd felt for days that the invasion was imminent, but about 4 a.m. on 6 June 1944, there was no doubt that this was 'it' ; there was a constant drone of heavy aircraft overhead, I had a quick check on all the children under my care, most of whom were sleeping peacefully. The bottle-fed babies had not yet started their 'dawn chorus' for their early morning feed, so I decided I'd call our Resident Medical Officer, a brilliant Czechoslovakian refugee. I told him that the invasion had started. He grabbed a coat and a splendid pair of Zeiss field glasses and together we hastened to the roof of the hospital.
>
> From there in the pale dawn light we saw the entire invasion fleet, with protective barrage balloons stretching out across the Channel towards the French coast. It was the most awe-inspiring sight - I'll never forget it. If I'd been C-in-C of Allied Forces I could not have had a better view of those dramatic events.

A WAAF radar operator, whose underground operations block was at the tip of the Isle of Wight, thinks that she was 'probably as near to the invasion of France as any woman.' At 22.40 hours on 5 June the crew of twelve set out for 'B' watch duty. Wearing headphones she 'observed' at the 'tube.'

> At close range it was saturated with 'echoes' from hundreds of craft. Slowly, they started to move, and we relayed all information to Filter Room at Stanmore where it was linked to that of other radar stations.
>
> Gradually, the massive area of vessels progressed across our map. As the leading edges neared the Normandy coast, everyone was at fever pitch. Throughout the night we continued to observe. In the morning, towards the end of our watch, our plotter called out excitedly, 'We're there!'

The continual drone of planes overhead had meant that a Cheshire woman had had a sleepless night and as she worked at a war production factory, she had to be up by 4.30 a.m. to catch the 5.15 bus.

We were all so excited at home, even though I had no brothers. We were going after 'that man' at last and we'd show him what we could really do.

The atmosphere on the bus stays with me today. We sang our heads off - mostly the dirtiest ditties we knew - it was our compliment to the boys in the battles to come.

When I arrived at work, I didn't feel the least tired and even the most notorious slackers were working like hell that morning. We were on the smoke group and we meant that stuff to really screen our lads. I think we all said a prayer as we worked. This was IT and we meant the enemy to know just what we intended to do, I still remember that day.

Despite the secrecy surrounding the invasion forces' departure, it had been almost impossible not to read the signs - particularly in the south and west of England where the men and their machinery had been stowed for weeks.

The Sussex woods around Newhaven had been teaming with thousands of soldiers living in tents beneath the trees and all waiting for action. On the early morning of 6 June, a Lancashire man stationed nearby walked through the woods and found them

silent and deserted, the tents were empty, lines of washing strung up between the tents fluttered in the morning breeze, a few personal possessions were scattered around on the ground...It was so silent, it was if the whole country had upped and gone off across the Channel to settle with Hitler once and for all.

A sixteen-year-old girl living in Boscombe

heard a rumour on 5 June that there were a lot of ships in the bay, so my mother and I went to the top of the cliffs between Boscombe and Bournemouth. I will never forget the sight that met our eyes: the bay was filled with ships of all sizes packed tightly together so there was no sea visible between them. It was a clear, peaceful evening and I remember my mother saying, 'We're sure to be bombed tonight - the Germans couldn't miss such a target.' But there was no raid that night.

Next day at lunchtime I decided to cycle home along the cliff road. It was a beautiful day but this time there was nothing to see but an empty bay. There was not one ship in sight. I remember that as I propped my bike against the wall at home, my mother called from the kitchen door, 'It's D-Day. We've landed in France. The invasion has started.'

For the boys of King's School, D-Day meant a certain loss: 'Suddenly the place was empty,' recalls David Moreau. 'The Americans in Jeeps with white stars on and a special device in front of the windscreen to cut the piano wires that the Germans stretch across the road, they suddenly all went. And the DUKWs disappeared like a vanished breed.'

A Devon woman knew that the invasion was on when the postman called out, 'Happy Birthday, missus' as he handed her a card when she left for work. 'But I was not born on 6 June. This was a private sign from my husband in the RAF that IT had begun.'

A Bradford woman who had two sons in the army, realized that 'something big was going to happen' when the younger one came home from Southampton where he was stationed on a twenty-four-hour pass, and as he was leaving said 'Goodbye'. 'That was the only time he ever said it,' his mother noted; 'usually it was cheerio.'

A VAD billeted in a convent on the outskirts of bombed Plymouth was sent on a special mission to collect group O blood from surrounding factories and villages. As the blood in unprocessed form would not keep fresh for more than a week 'we knew that D-Day was imminent.'

Others heard about it at work, too, or as they went about their daily chores. A woman in a small village in Kent was getting on with the housework,

> half listening to the voices of my two toddler sons, to the radio and still an ear pricked for the whine of a 'scalded cat' Nazi plane. Then came the radio announcement. D-Day was on. Allied forces had landed in France. Tears flowed at the immediate hope that this was the beginning of the end of fear and horror. Tears and a prayer for those doomed to die, but also tremendous excitement that needed sharing.

She rushed outside

> but the only sign of life was a woman cleaning her windows. I tore across and babbled breathlessly, 'It's D-day. The Second Front has started.' No response... 'Don't you understand, our troops have crossed the Channel and the war may soon be over?' Still calmly polishing her windows, she looked at me briefly and said, 'Well, I hope it doesn't upset the bus service. I've got a dental apointment in Ashford this afternoon.'

'Mum, it's started - they're off.' The sky over East Anglia was black with planes from before dawn as the RAF and USAAF took off from the chequerboard of airfields. 'These were "our boys",' recalls a woman who lived in a village just outside Norwich;

> By the marks on the tail-planes we knew them. We waved, we shouted. 'Good luck, St Faith's, Rackheath, Attlebridge [the names of various bases].' A neighbour was waving a child's Union Jack...We dashed down the garden and frantically waved white tablecloths. Who knows if they were ever seen? By breakfast time it had quietened. You wouldn't have known anything special was on, although we had lost our voices. 'Let's turn on the radio, and see if here's any news.' Not that we needed to be told. WE KNEW.

Esther MacMurray was working in a big aircraft factory and in the lunch hour all the staff, technical and clerical as well as the works staff, had gathered in the canteen, which held 4,000 people, to watch a lunchtime concert.

> Suddenly the Managing Director came on to the stage and everything stopped. 'Ladies and Gentlemen,' he said quietly, 'we have landed in France.' There was a stunned silence, then a quavering voice started to sing 'Land of Hope and Glory'. In a moment everybody had joined in a great crescendo of sound...some of the women who had sons and husbands away were singing with the tears running down their faces, while the men were trying to control their emotion. Then we went quietly back to work - for victory.

A NATION WAITS

J. C. Potter worked in an aero engine factory that employed many thousands of workers - a very large percentage of them women. The tannoy suddenly crackled to life

> with the news we had all waited for for so long...'Allied troops have landed in France...we will keep you informed.' There was immense cheering, singing of patriotic songs, much laughter and not a few tears. About two hours later, the tannoy crackled to life again and everybody listened with bated breath for further news of the great landing but the voice said, 'I am very sorry to say...' and paused. Everyone thought of Dunkirk; our blood ran cold. After what seemed an age, the voice continued, 'I am very sorry to say that some employees are leaving their work to go to the canteen ten minutes before the appropriate time; this must stop.' Loud yells of disgust, mingled with relief ensured that the 'voice' was consigned to the care of Mephistopheles.

Peggy Cornish was working for a Government ministry in a typing pool with thirty other women. There was a teleprinter in the same room.

> When the news of the invasion came through, the girl operating the machine screamed with excitement. This upset the rhythm of the clacking typewriters, and the head and shoulders of the supervisor, an absolute dragon of a woman, rose above her frosted glass screen to see what all the noise was about. When she heard the reason for the uproar, her fury abated and she allowed a twenty-minute break. Cigarettes were lit and we all left our desks to talk about the exciting news. At the end of the allotted span, the 'dragon' rapped on her glass panel and work was resumed.

In a butcher's shop in Glasgow the news passed quickly along the queue waiting to be served. When it got to the butcher he stood up, beaming and smiling, and announced that only coupons were required for meat that day, not cash. So Helen Davidson's memory of D-Day was of 'bangers and steak together on one plate' for dinner that night.

The Red Cross was having a flag day on 6 June and a part-time member took up her pitch outside Hammersmith Underground station from 6.30 in the morning. Business was fairly good with people dropping in pennies and the odd sixpence. But when Miss Sullivan returned to her pitch at 8.15 having been back to the office to get more supplies, she noticed that now nearly everyone was stopping to buy a flag, giving a shilling or two, or even half a crown. 'I remember one person remarking, "You'll need all you can get now" ...my tin was soon full and people were putting money in the flag tray.' It wasn't until she had sold out again and returned to base to get more supplies that she was told that it 'had been announced on the radio at 8 o'clock that the Second Front - which people all over he country had clamoured and hoped for for so long had started that morning.'

Not everyone was so enthusiastic. Some remained sceptical of the news all day, others could think only of the terrible losses that would be involved, others simply seemed to have other preoccupations. There were also many who feared that the Germans would wreak a terrible retribution on British civilians.

A British Army Major was waiting to embark near Hastings where the inhabitants had 'for months been in direct contact with the massive military build-up which was to be the

"Didn't I tell you it would start on the sixth?"

defeat of Nazi Germany.' They had from dawn onwards that day witnessed 'aircraft roaring across the Channel and convoys of troops rumbling along the road.' News flashes came every half an hour, but when the major dropped into a hotel lounge early that evening he overheard one old lady sitting there say to another, 'It's been a funny sort of a day, hasn't it?' 'Yes, dear,' her friend agreed, 'I quite expected it to rain after lunch but it never did.'

A twenty-year-old Battalion Intelligence Officer was on an advanced course at Matlock in Derbyshire 'studying Invasion Intelligence techniques'. But on 7 June he opened a newspaper at breakfast and exclaimed, 'Good heavens, D-Day has taken place already!'

Evelyn Waugh, who was behind with his writing of *Brideshead Revisited,* heard in Devon

> that the Second Front had opened. I sat down early to work and wrote a fine passage of Lord Marchmain's death agonies...I sent for a priest to give Lord Marchmain the last sacraments. I worked through till 4 o'clock and finished the last chapter - the dialogue poor - and took it to the post, walked home by the upper road. There only remains now the epilogue which is easy meat. My only fear is lest the invasion upsets my typist at St Leonard's, or the posts to him with my manuscript.

Another novelist, Bryher, the friend of Gertrude Stein and H. D. [the writer Hilda Doolittle] felt curiously uninvolved too.

> How does one feel about an important date in history? I fear nothing at all. On June 6th I went to the bank in Sloane Street to get a weekly supply of petty cash. 'It's started,' the cashier said, and although I had listened to the trucks passing at night for weeks, I wondered what he meant. We've had so many alarms and inconvenient surprises. 'The Invasion,' he added, noticing that I looked puzzled. I walked back to tell Hilda but there was no stir in the streets, many had not heard the news, others could only think about the inevitable losses.

And far away from where it was all happening, Naomi Mitchison was on her farm in the Scottish Highlands.

> Got the news from Angus as soon as I went over about 8.30. All the men talking about it, more or less, especially Fred Browne who was a volunteer in the last war...I went around all day in three layers of consciousness, partly fidgeting about this and being so remote and out of it, partly thinking of all the funny jobs we have to catch up with now, and partly thinking about a book which I read rapidly today - largely in the loo as I think I have a touch of this enteritis germ - Stapleton's *Sirius* which he sent me and which I like...

Though a couple of days later, some neighbours of hers were not 'feeling out of it' at all. 'Veronica and I are gloating over the stories about Shimi,' wrote Joan Wyndham, a WAAF stationed near Inverness who had discovered that she was 'a sort of distant cousin' of the Lovat family and frequently spent her free time at Beaufort Castle, and with Simon ('Shimi') Lovat's sister, Veronica.

> His Commandos refused to wear helmets and went into the attack in their green berets, with Piper Wlliam Millin leading the way. 'Give us "Highland Laddie", man!' Shimi yelled as he plunged into the sea up to his armpits.
>
> Once on shore the piper paraded up and down the beach playing 'Road to the Isles' oblivious of the shells and shouts of 'Get down you silly bugger!' Relieving the bridge over the River Orme, he strolled along in his plimsolls, as if he were inspecting a herd of bulls, with his inevitable pipers - who, I think, really deserve a medal - playing 'Blue Bonnets over the Border'.
>
> The Scottish papers gave him a colossal spread on the lines of 'Tall, handsome Lord Lovat, a leader any man would die for, strolled up to the bridgehead in an open-neck pullover,' and so on. Veronica and I are, of course, lapping it up. It even consoles her for the awful fact that she has got piles!

Many, of course, also had their own personal, heart-stopping reasons for the intensity with which they followed the news broadcasts that day, 6 June 1944.

Mrs Mundy's soldier husband had been sent to the south coast 'and we both knew why. Tension rose over the next six months, when would the fatal day come?' She had her own hairdressing salon at the time and

> always had the wireless on listening to every news bulletin. On 6 June when the news came that the first British troops had landed on the Normandy beaches I had a client having a permanent wave. In those days perms were 'cooked' under a machine that got terrifically hot and if great care wasn't taken, the scalp could get a nasty burn...when I heard the news I just left my client sitting there all strung up under the electric perm machine and ran round to tell my mother who was as anxious as me. By the time I got back, the lady was well and truly 'cooked' - her hair was just a mass of fuzz. Oh, was she annoyed! Needless to say she was one client who never came back again. But, thank goodness, my husband did after active service through France, Belgium and Germany.

Jessie Mosley was twenty years old and had been married for only two months to a para-trooper. She was doing war work in a local factory when, on 6 June, the radio programme 'Workers' Playtime' was suddenly interrupted soon after 10 o'clock and news of the D-Day landings was announced. Everybody cheered - including her. It was only later that she learned that by the time she heard the announcement her husband was already dead.

Mrs F. Jones of Birkenhead was married to a Corporal and she and her husband wrote to each other every day during the war. Suddenly the letters stopped coming.

> I knew something desperate was happening and wasn't surprised when the radio announced landings on the Normandy beaches. It was D-Day. I felt sure that my husband was in that terrible affray...we were told on the radio that we would receive a card from the troops who had gone over on D-Day. The next day all my husband's letters that had been held up arrived. In one of them he begged me to keep writing. I wrote to him every day for three anxious weeks. Every day I wait-ed for the postman to bring me that longed-for card. The card never came. Instead a letter arrived from the War Office telling me that it was their 'painful duty to inform' me that my husband had been killed on D-Day.

Margaret Whittlesea was in the WRNS, billeted in Weymouth. On the morning of D-Day she was with a bus-load of other Wrens going to work at Portland dockyard.

> We were going on the early morning watch and all along the route we could see the activity of troops marching to the landing craft. That was the first we knew that this must be THE day, D-Day. As we waited in the bus to be searched before we were allowed through the dock gates, one of the Wrens, Eileen from Bridport who had recently married a GI saw her husband. Against all the regulations she dashed off the bus and scrambled across the pebbly beach to kiss her husband goodbye as he got on the boat. We all looked the other way...not many hours later we saw ships bringing the wounded back to Weymouth, and the same ships reload with replenishment troops. I felt very humble. I still wonder whenever I look at a photograph I have of those troops boarding the *Consul* how many of them came home? It was only a couple of days before we heard that Eileen was a D-Day widow. And we all shared her sorrow.

For Staff Nurse Maureen Gara who had volunteered for the Queen Alexandra Imperial Military Nursing Service in 1943, D-Day meant a high degree of preparation:

> I'd trained at Bury Infirmary and we were being blitzed day and night, and then mobilization started for what they called the Second Front, and so several of us said, 'They'll be needing people,' and we thought, 'Well, this is an opportunity to do something about it,' so several of us went and signed on the dotted line, and I was called up two months later and got a letter asking me to report to the 79th General Hospital. When I got there, it was buzzing with soldiers - and what struck me on that first day was that everything had to be done at the double...We had lectures on chemical warfare and gas warfare, that was the main training. The other training we did - if you can call it training - was tent pitching. We had to put up fifty-bedded marquees, pull them down and put them up again until we knew

exactly how to...So the time came when they told us, 'Now you have to pack a hospital. You've to pack 1,200 beds', 800 were for immediate use and 400 for reserve. So we did the beds first. The mattresses were narrow, and we put two sheets and two blankets on each mattress; two pillows, a pair of pyjamas; and a soldier's shaving kit, soap and towel. That was rolled up very tightly and tied with a particular type of knot, that we knew how to pull, and the bed was already made. So we packed 800 beds. We then packed all the medical equipment; each sister and group of orderlies knew exactly which number ward they would be located to within the hospital. I was to be in the casualty, the resuscitation ward, and we knew exactly what equipment we were going to need for that ward. We packed it into crates and had to memorize what was in each crate. I would be asked, 'Sister, what is in the right-hand side of crate 58?' 'Syringes.' 'What is in the left-hand side of crate 16?' And you had to know. It was for speed of opening when you got to the other side. We didn't know where the other side was going to be then, but when we got there it wasn't going to be any good shuffling round opening the wrong crate...and again there might not be any lighting, we just didn't know what circumstances we were going to face...We knew that wherever the men were going to land, it was going to be very heavily fortified and that there would be terrible injuries...

Nurse Gara left for the Normandy beaches on D-Day+6.

At 6 a.m. on D-Day the operating theatre door swung open at a north of England hospital and 'the only doctor' spoke urgently to Sister Holmes: 'A twenty-five-year-old woman is bleeding profusely internally. You'll have to take a pint of my blood. I'm group O, I'll risk giving it.' 'This was not normal procedure for nurses,' recalls the Sister,

but in those days of depleted doctors, we did many tasks outside our province. Soon the precious blood was flowing, when the anxious doctor appeared again to say that the woman was unconscious. 'I'll have to risk operating.' It turned out that the woman was pregnant. From the ruptured womb [the doctor] extracted a baby boy who took much reviving, but left us crying lustily. Later as the mother gazed adoringly at the infant she said, 'I never thought I was pregnant. George had embarkation leave last September, now I have a bit of him.' One week later she heard that her husband had been killed in action on D-Day. Never were we so thankful that a splendid doctor had taken his calculated risk.

Mrs Tannahill's most treasured memory of Day-Day was 'the birth of my daughter. It was her father's birthday too, but he never saw her. He'd been killed in action just before then. I called her "Norma"; it was the nearest I could think of to "Normandy."'

A man who is now a journalist on the *Guardian* newspaper was also born on D-Day. His father was flying with the RAF and as his mother went into labour she could 'see all the planes flying very low overhead with special Allied markings on the wings'. In the labour room Mrs Norton-Taylor

woke to hear on the one o'clock news that we had landed in France. At 4.14 p.m. my son was born...I was worried, though, as the matron kept coming in to

The aftermath: Montgomery conducts Churchill on a visit to the Normandy beaches six days after D-Day.

inquire what I was going to call him. I thought that something must be wrong - but the Press had been calling to see if any boys had been born that day, and was I going to christen him Bernard or Dwight?

The baby was named Richard.

Harold Nicolson went to the House of Commons,

arriving there about ten to twelve. Questions had ended unexpectedly early and people were just sitting there waiting for Winston. He entered the Chamber at three minutes to twelve. He looked as white as a sheet. The House noticed this at once, and we feared he was about to announce some terrible disaster. He is called immediately, and places two separate fids of typescripts on the table. He begins with the first which is about Rome. Alexander gets a really tremendous cheer. He ends with the words, 'This great and timely operation,' stressing the word 'timely' with a rise of the voice and that familiar bending of the two knees. He then picks up his other fid of notes and begins, 'I have also to announce to the House that during the night and early hours of this morning, the first of a series of landings in force upon the Continent of Europe has taken place...' The House listens in hushed awe. He speaks for only seven minutes and then Greenwood follows with a few words. We then pass to the Colonial Office Estimates Committee of Supply.

Churches opened their doors for short impromptu services of prayer and thanksgiving. Margaret Watson was working in a bank opposite St Anne's Church in Manchester where

> services were being held every half hour and as midday approached queues formed outside - the workers of Manchester were waiting to spend their lunch hour today in prayer, myself and my colleagues included. Just a simple service, a hymn, a prayer, private meditation and the National Anthem. For me that simple service stood for unity, faith and the willingness to help in the fight for freedom

A Lincolnshire vicar,

> Felt that I ought to do something at the church...so I put up half a dozen notices to say that there would be a short service...the people started to come, and by 6.45 the Church was more than half full. The service was very simple...confession and absolution...a few verses from fortieth chapter of Isaiah, the hymn 'Lord While Afar Our Brothers Fight.' A.&M 743. Some wartime intercessions, a prayer for the forces with the names of all those who are serving from the parish read out, just under 200, and we finished with the blessing. It took twenty-one minutes. We are having a similar service every evening this week.

An East Anglian clergyman

> seized the initiative. He borrowed the police loud-speaker van, the only vehicle then permitted to use a public address system, and toured the streets. Instead of the usual 'Police calling!' surprised townspeople heard, 'This is the Church calling. I invite you to a special service at eleven o'clock.' The response was magnificent. The great church was filled to overflowing and during the moving service tears trickled down many faces.

A Sussex woman found it 'rather tantalizing that the weather was fine on the evening of D-Day,' for she 'badly wanted to go over to the allotment especially to see how my new plants are doing before the slugs get at them. But I felt Church was the first duty this day.'

But a Coventry woman found that the choice was not hers: she heard the news about the invasion whilst out shopping so she 'went into a local church to pray for victory. The Vicar asked why we weren't wearing hats. We put handkerchiefs on our heads. "No woman comes into my Church without a hat," he insisted'. The woman asked him quietly, 'Your Church or God's? Have the men out there today got hats - or heads?'

'Newspapers are snapped up the moment they appear on the streets,' Harold Nicolson noted. An Epsom man working in London went out into the Strand at lunchtime.

> Every news vendor had a waiting queue. On my way back the papers had arrived. The vendor outside the Waldorf had an orderly queue plus a crowd around him. Being typically British I stayed put whilst the papers were being gobbled up under the vendor's eyes. I thought that one crowd by the kerb was a man selling them. I inched my way through. It was a man reading one...

'Freedom to worship...' French families walk to mass in the village of Creully in Normandy with US and British troops in the background.

A Yorkshire man, who did manage to buy an evening newspaper in Hull, was impressed at the size of the type which had obviously been dug out specially to set the headline on this auspicious occasion, but disconcerted to read in huge letters 'TROOPS LAND IN NOR-MANBY' - a nearby village.

But it was to the BBC in those wartime days that people - in countries all over the world - tuned in to find out what was happening. Clara Milburn, who lived in a village not far from Coventry, recorded in her diary that

> the 6 p.m. news says that so far our landings have gone 'according to plan' and in some places we have 'penetrated several miles'. Mr Churchill has spoken to the House this afternoon. Some 31,000 airmen have been over France during the day. There was much less loss of airborne troops than was expected, though the battle is expected to increase in intensity as the days go by. The air umbrella spread for 200 miles!

At nine o'clock

> His Gracious Majesty broadcast to his people, and his talk was heard in the United States as well as the Empire. He called us all to prayer on this most historic occasion. His little impediment of speech endears him to us, I think. We grow anxious for him if he falters and rejoice when he overcomes his difficulty of enunciation. He went along very well tonight.

Whilst many people might well have been moved by King George VI's stammer, they were less pleased with the content of his speech. A Birmingham man finished his typing in order to tune in to hear the King, too:

> He was very bad to start with, but he improved during the middle of his talk, and fell off again towards the end. I suppose some folks get comfort from what he said, but a lot of religious stuff seems mere tripe to me. There is also a lot of inconsistency in these appeals to the Lord to look after his children. If I believed there was a Lord I should expect him to regard all the human race, including the Germans, as his children.

A London postal sorter also commented upon

> the sudden intensification of 'religious bilge' which is now being pushed out hourly over the radio. A good deal of it seems to be directed at children through the medium of 'Children's Hour'. I personally feel very sick at the sanctimonious attitude on religion adopted by the BBC at this time...and even [a neighbour] said, 'I do wish they would leave God out of it.'

But if they were less than happy about the religious propaganda on the BBC most listeners seemed to have been overwhelmingly in favour of the introduction of eyewitness reports modelled somewhat on Ed Murrow's hugely popular 'London Calling', broadcast nightly to the US by NBC. 'Howard Marshall went with the troops,' recalled Mrs Milburn,

> and landed and now he is back again telling us what happened. He has been twice in the sea and his notes are sodden and useless, so he is just telling us - all impromptu - how his barge arrived. The Germans had prepared pronged obstacles with a mine on the prong, one of which blew up his barge, but the men waded out and the Bren-gun carrier went through five feet of water and on to the beach! Somehow or other he got to another barge and, after that had sunk, he got on to an M. L. and came back, having 'done his stuff' in time to get home and broadcast.

'It was a masterpiece,' agreed the Birmingham man. 'I thought the BBC gave one of the best broadcasts I have ever heard in its summing up of the day's events. It was a very clear picture, factual and objective, and refreshingly free from the blah that often spoils some of the programmes for me.'

The Atlantic time difference meant that insomniacs in New York heard about the landings at 3.32 a.m. on 6 June. 'Under the command of General Eisenhower, Allied naval forces, supported by strong air forces, began landing Allied armies this morning on the coast of France...' Then Eisenhower's message to the Allied Expeditionary Force was broadcast:

> You are about to embark on a great crusade...in the company with our brave Allies and brothers-in-arms on other fronts, you will bring about the destruction of the German war machine, elimination of the Nazi tyranny over the oppressed people of Europe, and security for ourselves in a free world...Good luck and let us beseech the blessing of almighty God upon this great and noble undertaking.

Taxi drivers who heard the news on their car radios pulled into the kerb and shouted out to passers-by; the neon signs in Times Square flashed out the message 'It's on!'

Americans woke that morning to read the headlines in their morning papers. The *Los Angeles Times* published a map of the landing areas 'west of the Somme,' the *Chicago Tribune* a cartoon under the headline 'Sprung' showed a warlike GI bayonetting into Europe like a jack-in-the-box; a huge gathering of prayer and thanksgiving was held in Madison Square Gardens in New York to echo similar events in St Paul's Cathedral and Westminster Abbey; and at 10 a.m. President Roosevelt broadcast to the nation with a prayer that he had specially composed for the occasion: 'Almighty God - our sons, pride of our nation, this day have set out on a mighty endeavour, a struggle to preserve our civilization and set free a struggling humanity.' To preserve the fiction of the FORTITUDE deception plan, he spoke of successes attained 'thus far.'

News of the invasion brought hope, too, to those whose home was in an occupied country. Marie Thomas was a young girl in June 1944, visiting relations in Dumfries; also there were some Free French parachutists who had fought on for four years without news of their families. They were 'specially trained in sabotage and guerrilla warfare and soon to be dropped behind enemy lines.' But on 6 June, as the news of the invasion came through,

> we had a celebration picnic, cooked over a fire of twigs and eaten from mess tins. With wild herbs they transformed their army rations, fish from a mountain loch and game they had poached, into a gourmet meal. Everyone sang and danced and we drank a toast to Scotland and France - the Auld Alliance. As night fell I was taken home, warmly wrapped in their captain's tunic. The war was far from over, and many of those soldiers did not live to see their loved ones again, but for the rest of my life I shall remember them and that glorious day.

Another French woman, in hospital in Bideford in Devon with both her feet in plaster, hobbled to the piano when she heard the news, and all day sat there thumping away and singing *La Marseillaise* as the news came in that the liberation of France had begun.

In Rome, liberated only the day before, 'the massed pipes of several Highland Regiments, kilts swinging, heads held high with regimental pride' were marching and counter-marching in front of the Coliseum. During the display, which was watched by thousands of Italian spectators, a British officer marched into the arena and signalled to the bands to stop playing. A hush fell over the crowd as he put his hand up and calmly announced: 'The Allied troops landed in France early this morning.' Bedlam as hats flew into the air and Italians and British hugged and kissed each other in the street in sheer intoxication at the dramatic announcement. 'Surely the Coliseum even in its former days of glory had seen nothing like it,' thought a piper of the Gordon Highlanders.

In Jersey, one of the German-occupied Channel Islands, Charles Le Cornu and his wife both put on headphones to listen to the radio and 'were greeted with "This is London. Our forces have landed on several points of the Normandy coast and are forming a spearhead into occupied France".' Le Cornu 'waited no more: I dropped my headphones and dashed out of the door to tell my neighbour the good news, believing that I was the only person who possessed a radio, but to my astonishment as I rushed out of my front door I looked down the road, and saw six other chaps bent on the same mission.'

Another Jersey resident, Mr G. W. Rabet, had heard the rumbling of bombers and gunfire coming from the Cherbourg peninsula, but had given it little thought. On his way to work as a gardener he saw German soldiers rushing about everywhere, looking anxious and bewildered. When he arrived he made straight for the garden shed where

> I and my workmates had hidden a radio for many years and soon discovered the reason. We had a large map pinned to the inside of the door on which we had stuck coloured flags showing the progress of the Italian front, and that of the Russians in the east. The first flag of the D-Day campaign went on Omaha Beach…the strangest sight over the next few days was to see scores of little Union Jacks displayed everywhere and the Germans did not know what to do about it.

In Paris a young woman was walking home when she saw the concierge of the flats where she lived hurrying towards her. 'They have landed. Tell your father to listen to the BBC news and tell us what is happening,' she whispered urgently.

Mme Desenne hurried home and rushed into the bedroom where her British father had been in hiding ever since the German occupation of France began. '"They are coming, listen to the news." As he turned it on, we heard, "Français, Françaises, at this very moment…"' With tears of joy they hugged each other as the father kept repeating, "Had I not said so? That they did not need a port, that they would come where there was none."

An English woman married to a Dutch man and living in Occupied Holland was hiding two American airmen (concealed when necessary under the bathroom floorboards) and a Jewish woman and her daughter in her flat in the Hague. They were all very cold, weak and hungry, but when Gladys de Carpentier heard on her radio the news of the D-Day landings and Winston Churchill's voice promising 'Wherever you are, we will not fail you.' It 'gave me hope to go on.'

Only a few people in occupied Holland had a radio on which they could receive BBC transmissions. It was prohibited to listen and the punishment was deportation to a concentration camp. But, as Hans van Rooy remembers, people risked it, and it was from them that the members of the Dutch Resistance learned about D-Day. 'We had all seen pictures of the Atlantic Wall. How could soldiers coming out of the sea storm it and survive? An old Dutch captain predicted, "By God they will have a hell of a job". Hans's mother said, "Let us pray for those who will die and also for those who will survive"- so we did.' And they pinned little flags on a new spot on the map they kept illegally in a cupboard showing the Allies' progress: Normandy.

In a POW camp in Weinsberg, Germany, the British prisoner who was acting as Camp Entertainments Officer and producer of an all-male production of Gilbert and Sullivan's *The Mikado* had gone to discuss the possibility of borrowing some costumes from the Stuttgart Opera House with a German officer. The 'normally jolly Rittmeister Knapp' greeted the Britisher with a grim face that morning and the serious news that the British Allied forces had landed in Normandy. 'This will be a disaster for your country. Your soldiers will be swept back into the sea as at Dunkirk. The only consolation will be that the war will be over that much sooner and you will go home. Convey my sorrow to your colleagues on this disaster.' Newling Ward found it 'hard to conceal from him my obvious delight at this news which was conveyed to a thousand happy officers within minutes.'

Pointing the way. Invasion fears over, road signs removed to confuse the enemy are replaced.

Fred Howell was a POW of the Japanese on Blakani Mati, a small island off Singapore, in June 1944. He was one of a working party of five. Nearby was a hut with a radio in it. The men were eager for news, so it was decided that one of them would try to get New Delhi on the radio. They drew lots. Mick Harrison, an Australian, drew the short straw. Two others, including Howell, agreed to attempt to keep the guards occupied and the other two were posted as look-outs. The warning for the Japanese approaching was to be a rendition of 'Land of Hope and Glory'. For fifteen agonizing minutes the men maintained a conversation, part English, part Japanese, with the guards. At last Harrison returned, giving the 'thumbs up' sign. Howell managed to get him aside from the captors. 'It's happened. They've landed.' It was 11.20 a.m. on 6 June 1944.

In Burma a Sussex man lay on a 'mattress' of bamboo slats covered by an old torn rice sack. He was in an advanced stage of malaria with paralysis and blindness threatening. It was 6 June 1944, a day after his twenty-sixth birthday. Struggling, he managed to make out the words spoken by the Australian Medical Sergeant 'We have invaded Europe. Come on, Snowy, we're on our way back. Don't get left behind.' 'For me, and countless others,' he wrote, 'that was a ray of hope in our desolation. We were on the way to Victory!'

A Midland man's diary for 6 June 1944 reads:

> Nagasaki, Japan. Almost certain that we've landed in France. A Jap kept drawing ships and soldiers on a boiler and saying 'Franso, Franso'. Other chaps had the same message from other sources. Looks pretty good…Guards very touchy. Flogged before a crowd of Jap workers…didn't collapse…but can't sit as a result…Rat hunt after our meal. Caught six this time, best haul yet…Salt-making successful at last: white and tasty, not muddy and revolting. Rice tastes better with salt: something to bargain with now on the black market…Guards crashed in, breaking up noisy discussion of landings in France. Grabbed two of our lads. Beat them up terribly. Something has upset the bastards - perhaps the rumour of landing is actually true. God! How much longer!

The men who went to France on 6 June 1944 were the first wave of the invasion. Reinforcements would pour across the Channel - and after the capture of Cherbourg on 25 June, began, slowly to come from across the Atlantic too.

But as Roosevelt had told the press at his D-Day briefing 'The war is by no means over yet.' It was 'up to schedule, [which strictly speaking it wasn't] but you don't just walk to Berlin. The sooner everyone realizes this the better.' It was not over in a matter of weeks or even days as some had predicted; from D-Day to VE Day took eleven more months of war save a single day.

In military planning terms the casualties of D-Day had been 'lighter than expected.' But the 'real meaning of D-Day' was the meaning of war. It was brought home to a young Gosport woman who 'did not have much time during the morning to listen to the news of the landing, having my four children to attend to.' During the afternoon she was crossing Portsmouth harbour in a ferry boat when she saw two landing craft being towed into the dockyard. They were full of soldiers 'blood-stained, bullet-ridden, silent witnesses of the Armageddon they had left behind on the shores of France. We had indeed invaded Hitler's stronghold, but at what a cost!'

BIBLIOGRAPHY

Ambrose, Stephen E., *The Supreme Commander: The War Years of General Dwight D. Eisenhower* (New York: Doubleday, 1970); *Pegasus Bridge* (London: Allen & Unwin, 1984).

Arbib, Robert S. Jnr., *Here We Are Together* (London: Longman, Green & Co., 1946).0

Babington Smith, Constance, *Evidence in Camera* (London: Chatto and Windus, 1958).

Balfour, Michael, *Propaganda in War, 1939-45* (London: Routledge, Kegan Paul, 1979).

Beardmore, George, *Civilians at War: Journals, 1938-46* (London: John Murray, 1984).

Bedell Smith, General Walter, *Eisenhower's Six Great Decisions* (New York: Longman, Green & Co., 1956).

Bradley, General Omar N., *A Soldier's Story* (London: Eyre & Spottiswood, 1952); *A General's Life* (London: Sidgwick and Jackson, 1982).

Briggs, Susan, *Keep Smiling Through: The Home Front 1939-45* (London: Weidenfeld & Nicolson, 1975).

Brittain, Vera, *Wartime Chronicles* (London: Gollancz, 1989)

Brown, John Hope Mason, *Many a Watchful Night* (London: Hamish Hamilton, 1944).

Burgett, Donald, *Curahee!* (Boston: Houghton Mifflin, 1967).

Butcher, Captain Harry C. USNR, *Three Years with Eisenhower* (London: William Heinemann, 1946).

Bryher, *The Days of Mars: A Memoir, 1940-1946* (London: Calder & Boyars, 1972).

Calder, Angus, *The People's War* (London: Jonathan Cape, 1969).

Capa, Robert, *Slightly Out of Focus* (New York: Henry Holt, 1947).

Cawthon, Charles R., *Other Clay: A Remembrance of the World War II Infantry* (Colorado: University of Colorado Press, 1990).

Churchill, Rt. Hon. Winston S., *The Second World War* (6 vols., London: Cassell, 1948-54); *The War Speeches of the Rt. Hon. Winston S. Churchill* (compiled by Charles Eade in three volumes. London: Cassell, 1952).

Clifton-James, M. E., *I Was Monty's Double* (London: Rider, 1954).

Collier, Richard, *The Warcos* (London: Weidenfeld & Nicolson, 1989); *D-Day* (London: Cassell, 1992).

Craven, Wesley F. and Cate, James I., *The Army Air Force in World War Two: Europe - Torch to Point Blank* (Chicago: University of Chicago Press, 1949).

D-Day: the Normandy Invasion in Retrospect (Kansas: Eisenhower Foundation, University of Kansas Press, 1971).

Dank, Milton, *The Glider Gang* (London: Cassell, 1978).

Davis, Kenneth S., *The American Experience of War* (London: Secker & Warburg, 1967).

D'Este, Carlos, *Decision in Normandy* (London: William Collins, 1983).

Durnford-Slater, John, *Commando* (London: William Kimber, 1953).

Ehrman, John, *Grand Strategy* Volume V (London: HMSO, 1956).

Eisenhower, David, *Eisenhower at War 1943-1945* (London: Collins:1986).

Eisenhower, Dwight D., *Crusade in Europe* (London: William Heinemann, 1948).

Ellis, Major L. F., *Victory in the West* Volume I (London: HMSO, 1962).

Fergusson, Sir Bernard, *The Watery Maze* (London: William Collins, 1961).

Fletcher, Eugene, *The Lucky Bastard Club: A B-17 Pilot in Training and Combat, 1943-45* (Washington DC: University of Washington Press, 1993).

Frankland, Noble, *The Bombing Offensive Against Germany* (London: Faber & Faber, 1965).

Freeman, Roger A., *The Mighty Eighth* (London: MacDonald & Co. 1970).

Gale, General Sir Richard, *Call to Arms* (London: Hutchinson, 1968).

Gardiner, Juliet, *'Over Here': GIs in Wartime Britain* (London: Collins & Brown, 1992).

Gilchrist, Donald, *Don't Cry for Me* (London: Robert Hale, 1982).

Gilbert, Martin, *Churchill: A Life* (London: Heinemann, 1991); *Second World War* (London: Weidenfeld & Nicolson, 1989).

Giles, Henry E., *The GI Journal of Sergeant Giles* (Boston: Houghton Mifflin, 1965).

Grigg, John, *1943: The Victory that Never Was* (London: Methuen 1980).

Hale, Edwin R. W. and Turner, John Frayn, *The Yanks are Coming* (Tunbridge Wells: Midas Books,1983).

Hamilton, Nigel, *Monty: Master of the Battlefield, 1942-1944* (London: Hamish Hamilton, 1983).

Hammond, Ralph, *My GI Aching Back* (New York: The Hobson Book Press, 1946).

Harrison, Gordon A., *Cross-Channel Attack* (Washington DC: Office of the Chief of Military History, Department of the Army, 1951).

Harrison, Michael, *Mulberry: The Return in Triumph* (London: W.H. Allen, 1965).

Hastings, Max, *Overlord* (London: Michael Joseph, 1984).

Hawkins, Desmond (with Donald Boyd) (ed.), *BBC War Report* (London: Oxford University Press, 1946).

Herbert, A. P., *Siren Song* (London: Methuen, 1940); *Bring Back the Bells* (London: Methuen, 1943).

Hinsley, Professor F. H. and others, *British Intelligence in the Second World War*. Volume II (London: HMSO, 1981).

Hollis, Lieutenant-General Sir Leslie (with James Leasor), *War on the Top* (London: Michael Joseph, 1959).

Hope, Bob, *I Never Left Home* (New York: Simon & Schuster, 1944).

Horrocks, Sir Brian, *A Full Life* (London: William Collins, 1960).

Howard, Michael, *British Intelligence in the Second World War* Volume V (London: HMSO, 1990).

Hoyt, Edwin P., *The Invasion Before Normandy* (London: Robert Hale, 1987); *The GI's War* (New York: McGraw Hill Book Company, 1988).

Ingersoll, Ralph, *Top Secret* (New York: Harcourt Brace, 1946).

Jones, Professor R. V., *Most Secret War* (London: Hamish Hamilton, 1978).

Kaplan, Philip (with Rex Oliver Smith), *One Last Look* (New York: Abbeville Press, 1983).

Keegan, John, *Six Armies in Normandy* (London: Jonathan Cape, 1982).

Kieffer, Cdt. Philippe, *Beret Vert* (Paris: Editions France-Empire, 1962).

Kluger, Steve (ed.), *Yank: The Army Weekly: World War II from the Guys Who Brought You Victory* (London: Arms & Armour, 1991).

Lewis, Peter, *A People's War* (London: Methuen, 1986).

Liddell Hart, B. H. (ed.), *Rommel Paper* (London: William Collins, 1953).

Longmate, Norman, *How We Lived Then* (London: Hutchinson, 1971); (ed.) *The Home Front* (London: Chatto & Windus, 1981).

McBryde, Brenda, *A Nurse's War* (London: Chatto & Windus, 1979).

Maiskey, Ivan, *Memoirs of a Soviet Ambassador, 1939-43* (London: Hutchinson, 1967).

Martin, Ralph G., *The GI War, 1941-1945* (Boston: Little, Brown, 1967).

Mrs Milburn's Diaries: An Englishwoman's Day-to-Day Reflections, 1939-45 (London: Harrap, 1979).

Miller, Russell, *Nothing Less than Victory* (London: Michael Joseph, 1993).

Minns, Rayne, *Bombers and Mash* (London: Virago, 1981).

Montgomery, Field-Marshal The Viscount, *The Memoirs of Field Marshal Montgomery of Alamein* (London: William Collins, 1958).

Morgan, Lieutenant-General Sir Frederick, *Overture to Overlord* (London: Hodder & Stoughton, 1950).

Murch, Muriel and David and Fairweather, Len, *The American Forces at Salcombe and Slapton During the Second World War* (privately published, 1984).

Nalty, B. (ed.), *D-Day: Operation Overlord* (London: Salamander Books, 1993).

Neillands, Robin and de Norman, Roderick, *D-Day, 1944: Voices from Normandy* (London: Weidenfeld & Nicolson, 1993).

Nicolson, Harold, *The War Years 1939-1945* (ed. Nigel Nicolson) (London: William Collins, 1967).

Panter-Downes, Mollie, *London War Notes 1939-1945* (London: Longman, 1972).

Perrault, G., *The Secrets of D-Day* (London: Arthur Barker, 1965).

Pogue, Forrest C., *The Supreme Command* (Washington DC: Office of the Chief of Military History, Department of the Army, 1946).

Pyle, Ernie, *Brave Men* (New York: Henry Holt, 1944).

Ridgway, General Matthew B., *Soldier: The Memoirs of Matthew B. Ridgway* (New York: Harper & Bros. 1956).

Ruge, Rear Admiral Friedrich, *Rommel in Normandy* (London: MacDonald, 1979).

Rupenthal, Major Roland G., *Utah to Cherbourg* (Washington DC: Office of the Chief of Military History, Department of the Army, 1946).

Ryan, Cornelius, *The Longest Day* (London: Victor Gollancz, 1960).

Saunders, Hilary St George, *The Green Beret* (London: Michael Joseph, 1949); *The Red Beret* (London: Michael Joseph, 1960).

Stagg, James M., *Forecast for Overlord* (New York: W. W. Norton, 1972).

Storey, Joyce, *Joyce's War, 1939-1945* (London: Virago, 1992).

Taylor, General Maxwell D., *Swords and Ploughshares* (New York: W. W. Norton, 1972)

Tedder, Marshal of the RAF Lord, *With Prejudice* (London: Cassell, 1966).

Terkel, Studs, *The Good War* (London: Hamish Hamilton, 1984).

Tute, Warren (with John Costelloe and Terry Hughes), *D-Day* (London: Sidgwick & Jackson, 1974).

Vian, Admiral Sir Philip, *Action This Day* (London: Frederick Muller, 1970).

Wyndham, Joan, *Love is Blue* (London: William Heinemann, 1986).

Young, Peter, *Storm from the Sea* (London: William Kimber, 1956).

INDEX

INDEX

INDEX

ACKNOWLEDGEMENTS

I am grateful to Charles Cawthon and the University Press of Colorado for permission to quote from *Other Clay: A Remembrance of the World War II Infantry*; to Penguin Books for permission to quote from Mollie Panter-Downes' *London War Notes 1939-1945*; to Weidenfeld and Nicolson for permission to quote from *March Past: A Memoir* by Lord Lovat; to the Department of Documents, Imperial War Museum for access to the letters of entrants to the *Sunday Express* D-Day memories in the May 1974 competition.The Mass Observation extracts were reproduced with the permission of the Trustees of the Mass Observation Archive, University of Sussex. Every attempt has been made to trace copyright holders of material and the author apologises for any omissions.The author is also most grateful to Gabrielle Townsend and to Colin Ziegler and Claire Graham of Collins and Brown.

ILLUSTRATION ACKNOWLEDGEMENTS

Chicago Tribune: 141. *The Children's Invasion Book*, (Faber, 1944): 105. The Cornish Studies Library: front cover, 25, 28, 29, 45, 49, 55, 183. Giles cartoons (permission *Daily Express* newspapers): 75, 133. The Hulton Deutsch Collection: 11, 13, 20, 32, 35, 39 bottom, 63, 71, 83, 87 top and bottom, 94, 101, 121, 127, 131, 145, 149, 151, 153, 159. The Robert Hunt Picture Library: 17, 39 top, 41, 124, 179. The Imperial War Museum: front and back cover background, 59, 69, 89, 93, 97, 104, 109, 110, 114, 137 top and bottom, 157, 161, 162, 165, 166, 167, 177. Lancaster cartoon (permission *Daily Express* newspapers): 65. *Punch*: 14, 23, 46, 56, 77, 81, 91, 113, 115, 173. Smithsonian Institution: 51.
  The author is grateful to Harriet Orr and Leon Meyer from the Hulton Deutsch Collection.